"Take a handful of culinary masters, toss in stories of utter humiliation or heartache, and you wind up with a spicy little essay collection . . . Lots of fun for foodies both ardent and casual." —*Kirkus Reviews*

"A reminder that—in real life as in the kitchen—guts are as important as genius." —*People* ****

"A dishy collection of stories . . . lively additions to the *Kitchen Confidential* genre." —Julie Powell, *Food & Wine*

"Surely, you think, real chefs aren't bedeviled by these problems. Think again. You can't even imagine the hidden kitchen terrors recounted by professionals in *Don't Try This At Home*." —*Washington Post Book World*

"Happily reminds us that even big shots have off days." —*Publishers Weekly*

"A sometimes comical and always unique glimpse behind the scenes of restaurant kitchens [and] a fantastic collection of personal stories that depict these great chefs as real people." —*Library Journal*

"As in every other profession, chefs love their war stories. Finally someone had the good sense to collect some of the best." —*Los Angeles Times*

"Witherspoon and Friedman have gathered memorable stories from some of the best chefs in the world, and it's just plain satisfying to read about their flubs." —*New York Sun*

"You'll love *Don't Try This at Home* . . . It's proof that celeb chefs climb into their checked trousers one leg at a time just like the rest of us." —*Oregonian*

"For those considering a life in the kitchen, these are cautionary tales, since they suggest that a career in a place replete with sharp tools, open flames and stressed-out lunatics may be fraught with peril. But for true foodies, these comic tales are a delight." —*Winston Salem-Journal*

"An inspiration for anyone who has been discouraged or shy to return to the kitchen after burning a soup or adding sugar instead of salt to a recipe." —*San Antonio Express-News*

"What a wonderful idea for a bedside table book . . . these comic tales are a delight." —*Virginian-Pilot*

"There's often humor in disaster, especially at the hands and in the kitchens of some of the world's top chefs . . . You'll smile and remember your own kitchen disasters." —*Kansas City Star*

D0092089

A NOTE ON THE EDITORS

Kimberly Witherspoon is a founding partner of Inkwell Management, a literary agency based in Manhattan. She is also the coeditor of the collection *How I Learned to Cook* and is very proud to represent seven of the chefs in this anthology: Anthony Bourdain, Tamasin Day-Lewis, Gabrielle Hamilton, Fergus Henderson, Pino Luongo, Marcus Samuelsson, and Norman Van Aken. She and her family live in North Salem, New York.

Andrew Friedman has coauthored more than fifteen cookbooks with some of the most successful chefs in the country, including Pino Luongo, Alfred Portale, Jimmy Bradley, and former White House chef Walter Scheib. He is also the coauthor of *Breaking Back*, the autobiography of American tennis star James Blake. He lives in New York City with his family.

DON'T TRY
THIS AT HOME

*Culinary Catastrophes from
the World's Greatest Chefs*

Edited by Kimberly Witherspoon
and Andrew Friedman

BLOOMSBURY

To Summer and Paul

—K.W.

As always, to Caitlin, and for the first time,
to Declan and Taylor, two great kids

—A.F.

Copyright © 2005 by Inkwell Management

All rights reserved. No part of this book may be used or
reproduced in any manner whatsoever without written permission
from the publisher except in the case of brief quotations embodied
in critical articles or reviews. For information address
Bloomsbury USA, 175 Fifth Avenue, New York, NY 10010.

Published by Bloomsbury USA, New York
Distributed to the trade by Holtzbrinck Publishers

All papers used by Bloomsbury USA are natural,
recyclable products made from wood grown in well-managed
forests. The manufacturing processes conform to the
environmental regulations of the country of origin.

THE LIBRARY OF CONGRESS HAS CATALOGED THE HARDCOVER EDITION AS FOLLOWS:

Don't try this at home : culinary catastrophes from the world's
greatest chefs / edited by Kimberly Witherspoon and
Andrew Friedman.
p. cm.
ISBN-13 978-1-59691-070-6 (hardcover)
ISBN-10 1-59691-070-4 (hardcover)
1. Cooks—Anecdotes. 2. Cookery—Anecdotes. I. Witherspoon, Kimberly. II. Friedman,
Andrew, 1967–

TX649.A1D66 2005
641.5—dc22
2005017992

Excerpt from "Brick House": Words and music by Lionel Richie, Ronald LaPread, Walter
Orange, Milan Williams, Thomas McClary, and William King. © 1977 Jobete Music Co.,
Inc., Libren Music, Cambrae Music, Walter Orange Music, Old Fashion Publishing,
Macawrite Music, and Hanna Music. All rights controlled and administered by EMI April
Music Inc. All rights reserved. International copyright secured. Used by permission.

First published in the United States by Bloomsbury in 2005
This paperback edition published in 2007

Paperback ISBN-10 1-59691-157-3
ISBN-13 978-1-59691-157-4

1 3 5 7 9 10 8 6 4 2

Typeset by Hewer Text UK Ltd, Edinburgh
Printed in the United States of America by Quebecor World Fairfield

CONTENTS

CONTENTS

Introduction

NEARLY TWO HUNDRED years ago, the legendary French gastronome Jean Anthelme Brillat-Savarin observed that "the truly dedicated chef or the true lover of food is a person who has learned to go beyond mere catastrophe and to salvage at least one golden moment from every meal."

In these pages, a selection of the world's finest chefs share, in refreshingly frank detail, the stories of their biggest mishaps, missteps, misfortunes, and misadventures. To our delight, much of what they salvage goes beyond the strictly culinary.

For their honesty, we thank the chefs themselves, who may surprise you as they discuss moments they'd rather forget, bringing their stories to life with revelations of humility, self-doubt, and even shame. Disasters, especially those involving food, are funny to look back on, but can be ego-deflating when they occur—it's a credit to these chefs that they are able to be simultaneously profound and laugh-provoking.

As we consider the stories, a number of themes emerge: The fish-out-of-water syndrome that greets young cooks working and traveling abroad proves itself a fertile breeding ground for near-farcical scenarios. The constant struggle to find and keep good employees is another popular motif, leading to tales of everything from a blind line cook to a culinary faith healing. Restaurants make for strange bedfellows, a truth examined in these pages via the tension between cooks and chefs and chefs and owners. Finally, the chaos that ensues when a chef leaves his or her kitchen and takes the show on the road can lead to countless unforeseen catastrophes.

For all of us, both cooks and noncooks, this book offers its own form of hope—evidence that even those who are the very best in their chosen field, famous for exhibiting perfection on a nightly basis, can make a mistake, maybe even a disastrous one, and then laugh at it, and at themselves.

Even more reassuring is how often, and how well, these storytellers improvise a way out, finding inspiration when they need it most, and emerging victorious, even if it means sometimes telling a white lie.

"In my business, failure is not an option," writes one chef in his story. It's one thing to say that and quite another to live it. These professionals live it on a daily basis, and we're grateful that they took time out to rummage through their memories and pick out the worst—by which we mean the "best"—ones to share.

KIMBERLY WITHERSPOON
ANDREW FRIEDMAN

Horror in Gerona
FERRÁN ADRIÀ

Ferrán Adrià began his famed culinary career washing dishes at a French restaurant in the town of Castelldefels, Spain. He has since worked at various restaurants, served in the Spanish military at the naval base of Cartagena, and in 1984, at the age of twenty-two, he joined the kitchen staff of El Bulli. Only eighteen months later, he became head chef of the restaurant—which went on to receive its third Michelin star in 1997. Adrià's gift for combining unexpected contrasts of flavor, temperature, and texture has won him global acclaim as one of the most creative and inventive culinary geniuses in the world; Gourmet magazine has hailed him as "the Salvador Dalí of the kitchen."

"THE LOBSTERS ARE off," said the voice on the other end of the telephone.

This was *not* good news: *Off* is the word we in the culinary business use to express succinctly that something has spoiled, or gone bad in some way. Usually, when something is off, it's so far gone that you can detect it by smell alone. Indeed, tasting something that's off is often a very bad idea.

That the lobsters were off on this particular day was worse news than it would normally be. Normally, you could remove them from your menu for one night, or secure enough replacement lobsters to remedy the situation before your first customers arrived, and nobody would be the wiser.

But on the day in question, the lobsters were to be the main course of a private function we were catering: an international medical congress in Gerona, a beautiful city in northern Catalonia, near the French border. Dinner was to consist of four courses, what we called our Fall Menu: a chestnut cream and egg white starter, hot pickled monkfish with spring onions and mushrooms, and a dessert of wild berries with vanilla cream. The pièce de résistance was a lobster dish garnished with a cepes carpaccio and a salad with Parmigiano and a pine nut vinaigrette.

And there was another detail that made the lobster news particularly alarming.

The dinner was to serve thirty-two hundred people.

When chefs have nightmares, it's moments such as these that play out in our heads. Unfortunately, I was wide awake and the situation was very, very real.

A banquet for thirty-two hundred people was not something I did every day. Never in my twenty-five years as a chef had I catered for anywhere close to such numbers. Our routine at El Bulli is fifty people a night. Admittedly, we serve fifteen hundred dishes at each sitting, but still, going from fifty to thirty-two hundred is like jumping out of a warm, familiar bath into an icy hurricane sea.

Naturally, our kitchen at El Bulli wasn't up to the task. So, to ensure ample space, we commandeered three production centers: two vast kitchens nearby in Gerona and one in Barcelona. In addition, we hired plenty of extra help; more than a hundred people were on the job. But even if we'd had a thousand people on board, that wouldn't have prevented the lobsters from going bad.

I received the lobster call at 8:00 a.m. on November 18, 1995—a date forever imprinted in my memory—and was instantly plunged into a state of fear, uncertainty, and panic the likes of which I have never experienced in my professional life, and hope never to experience again. The call came from the Barcelona kitchen, ironically situated in the city aquarium, right on the waterfront.

It wasn't just some of the lobster that was off; practically our entire stock had fermented overnight: 80 percent of our lobster haul was unusable, inedible, unfit for human consumption— never mind in any state to grace a dish prepared by the chefs of what was then a two-star Michelin restaurant.

How could this have happened?

To maximize efficiency, we had shared out different tasks among the three production centers. The chief task of the aquarium team was to clean, boil, and cut the lobster, before dispatching it to Gerona by road for assembly on the plate alongside the carpaccio and the salad. They had already done the cleaning and boiling and cutting—three pieces of lobster per dish—the night before, and the idea was that we'd simply load it all onto a van the next morning and off we'd go. Consequently, the lobster, all cut up and ready, had been placed inside white polystyrene containers until morning. We'd never done such a thing on such a scale and we supposed this was the right thing to do. The thermal containers insulated the lobster from the out-side temperature, which seemed like a perfectly good idea; indeed it *was* a good idea—at least for the hot road trip north to Gerona. When it came to the refrigerator, however, the night before, it was an absolute calamity. Inside the containers, the lobster pieces were also insulated from the cold of the refrigerator. And so, while we had carefully refrigerated the lobster, none of the cold could actually get through the polystyrene to reach the lobster—which consequently remained at room temperature all night. Room temperature, for that length of time, was the lobsters' ruin.

So, as you can see, it was the end of the world, the end of civilization as we know it. My first reaction—which I imagine is the first reaction of anyone, in any context, on receiving catastrophic news—was, "It's not possible. I cannot believe it. It cannot be true. Tell me, please tell me it's a bad joke." Once I had digested the indigestible and acknowledged that it was, indeed, true, that I was awake and so it was actually a lot worse than a nightmare, I proceeded to descend into despair. As second by mortifying second passed, the implications of what had happened sank in deeper: thirty-two hundred mouths to feed in thirteen hours' time and the chief raw material of our main dish missing! I kept asking myself, "What are we going to do? What the hell are we going to do? How in God's name are we going to manage now?"

But then, with my heart still hammering at a hundred kilometers an hour, I thought, Okay, calm down. This is probably an absolutely hopeless case . . . but maybe there is something we can do, maybe we'll get lucky. Maybe there will be a miracle. So I started to think and think, trying to come up with ways to get around this. Though the one thing I knew for sure was that, whatever finally happened, ahead of me lay the most excruciatingly stressful day of my life.

The first and foremost question, of course, was how were we going to find the one thousand lobsters we needed—yes, a thousand—in time to get them cleaned, cooked, delivered to

Gerona (more than two hours away), and ready for consumption by nine o'clock that same night. So, amid the utter chaos of it all, I gave the order, "Let's hunt down every last lobster in this city! Let's get them all until not one is left!" We got on the phone and called everyone and anyone who could possibly have a stock of fresh lobster ready to go. "How many have you got? You've got fifteen? Great! Hold them, we'll go and collect them now . . . How many have you got? Twenty-five! Fantastic! Can you bring them over? Perfect." After a frantic rush of phone calls, we assembled a team of ten people in the aquarium kitchen—most of them having imagined that their work had been over the day before—to clean, boil, and cut up the lobsters as they arrived.

By late morning, we realized that five hundred lobsters was the maximum that we were going to get. So what to do? Simple. Here was the solution: reduce the contents of each dish by one piece of lobster, from three to two. That allowed us to stretch the utility of the 20 percent that had not gone off overnight and to fill the quota we needed, especially as the happy news filtered down from Gerona around lunchtime—this did help bring the temperature down a bit, at last—that a few hundred participants of the medical congress would be going home early, and the total number of dishes required had fallen below the three thousand mark.

By 11:00 a.m. we had our first batch ready, a hundred or so lobsters' worth. Off went the first vanload to Gerona. There was some slight relief at its departure, but it was mostly overshadowed by the suspense, the worry that the van might break down or crash or God knows what. In those days, we didn't have mobile phones. You couldn't keep track of the van's progress the way you could now. So what happened was that the van driver, under strict orders to reassure us, would phone us at intervals—the team in Barcelona *and* the two kitchens in

Gerona—from a highway café or gas station to let us know that he was making progress, that he was edging his way up to his destination. "It's okay. All's well. I'm on my way. Relax, guys!" We would all cheer with relief. But between calls, it was hell. After what had happened, we were preconditioned for disaster. If anything could go wrong, we imagined, it would.

And yet, miraculously, it didn't. Five vanloads of chopped lobster successfully made it from the Barcelona aquarium to Gerona—each time inspiring the same drama of anxiety and reassuring phone calls—and finally, at about six in the evening, we looked at the dish, reduced to two pieces of lobster but beefed up with an extra helping of cepes carpaccio, and knew that, barring the habitual worries that always loom for a chef at this time of night, the immediate crisis was over. We had survived.

And, in the end, I learned some lessons from all this. First, never store things that need to be cold inside a fridge in closed polystyrene containers. Second, keep a closer eye on things, especially when you have so much to do in so little time, when your available reaction time, in case things go wrong, is drastically reduced. When you're feeding up to two hundred people there's a certain amount of flexibility built in, some room to maneuver. More than two hundred and you're in a totally new space. The logistical dimension of the exercise becomes so much more unwieldy.

The final and most valuable lesson I learned is that every day you start fresh. I know it sounds trite, maybe even foolish, but it's true. Every day is a new challenge, a new adventure, and you must never be complacent; you must be constantly on your toes, ready to deal with the unexpected, ready to respond—with as cool a head as you can—to whatever surprise comes.

(Translated from the Spanish and co-written with John Carlin)

All by Myself
JOSÉ ANDRÉS

José Andrés was born in Asturias, Spain, and attended Escola de Restauracio i Hostalatge de Barcelona, apprenticing at restaurant El Bulli under celebrated master chef and mentor Ferrán Adrià. In 1990, Andrés moved to New York City to work for the Barcelona-based restaurant El Dorado Petit. In 1993, he moved to Washington, D.C., to become a chef and partner of Jaleo Spanish restaurant. He has since opened two more Jaleo locations, and serves as executive chef-partner of Café Atlantico and Zaytinya, as well as the much-lauded six-seat minibar within Café Atlantico. In 2004, he opened Oyamel, a Mexican small-dishes restaurant. In 2003, the James Beard Foundation named Andrés Best Chef/Mid-Atlantic Region. His first cookbook, Tapas: A Taste of Spain in America, *debuts fall 2005.*

WHEN I WAS fifteen years old, I spent the summer working in a small restaurant in Roses, north of Barcelona, called L'Antull, that's no longer there. It was a traditional Spanish fish restaurant, and in the middle of the dining room was a tank in which we kept wild striped bass and live lobsters from the Bay of Roses.

Striped bass need room to swim, and this fish tank certainly gave it to them. It was enormous, and in comparison to the tiny dining room—we had only about forty seats—the tank seemed even bigger than it actually was, totally dominating the space. All day the bass would swim laps in the water, propelling themselves from one end of the tank to the other, gracefully turning, and swimming back, while the lobsters rested on the floor beneath them—an exciting, mesmerizing display.

In addition to the many fish dishes we prepared, we also made traditional Catalan dishes, like *canelones*, our version of the Italian *cannellóni*. L'Antull's *canelones* were so popular that a lot of people who never ate in the restaurant would order them to go, especially for large parties.

To prepare the *canelones*, we would arrange the boiled pasta shells on a big tray, top them with grated Parmesan and béchamel, and finish them under the salamander, a big, open-sided broiler, to melt the cheese and cook the cream.

One Sunday, a customer came in and placed a take-out order of *canelones* for twenty-four people. On Sunday mornings, it was just me and the chef, Pere. Because I had been cooking all my life, I was already very capable at all the things we had to do—shop, clean fish, cook paellas and other traditional dishes—so Pere tended to leave me on my own. Unconcerned, he told me to make the large order and pack it up for the customer, and then he went off to finish something else.

We had an incredibly long, thin stainless-steel tray in the kitchen, and I decided to use it to bake the *canelones* in one shot. I arranged about seventy-five little pasta cylinders on the $1\frac{1}{2}$-meter-long tray, then topped them evenly with cheese and the creamy white béchamel. Beautiful!

The tray was so long that you had to put it under the salamander in three stages—broiling one end, then pushing the tray through so the middle was under the heat, and then finally doing the other side—cooking the *canelones* in thirds.

For a little kid, this was hard work. I started off on one side of the machine, and had to quickly run around it to hold the tray by the hot end while the final third was cooking.

Once the entire tray had been broiled, my next task was to pack up the *canelones* for our customer. I lifted the steaming hot tray, balanced it on a kitchen towel atop my open left palm, and steadied it with my right hand, also protected by a towel.

Now, remember, I'm just fifteen years old, so the tray was disproportionately big on me. As I struggled to keep my balance in the kitchen, the tray wobbled dangerously on my shoulder. I looked like a tightrope walker staggering on the line.

Pere noticed this and asked, "José, you want me to help you?"

What fifteen-year-old boy would admit defeat?

"No, no. I'm fine," I said.

"You're sure?"

"I'm fine, I'm fine," I insisted, as I continued to wrestle with the tray. Pere shook his head skeptically. You didn't have to be a wise man to know that trouble was on the horizon.

Finally, I got the tray steadied and started to leave the kitchen. I gently kicked the swinging doors open with one foot and stepped hastily through them and out into the dining room, the doors swinging shut safely behind me.

As a waiter passed in front of me, however, I stepped back to avoid a collision, and the doors, still swinging slightly, struck the edge of the tray, propelling it forward.

Things started to happen very quickly: I ran along under the length of the tray to keep up with it. But I got too far ahead of it and it started to tip backward, so I backed up. *Then* it tipped to the side . . .

I couldn't win. No matter which way I turned, I was either moving too far or not far enough. And the tray was lurching ever-forward, toward the center of the dining room, where the aquarium stood right in my path.

Finally, I just couldn't control it anymore. The tray tipped forward and off of my hands and slid right into the fish tank. A cloud of steam hissed up out of the water as hot met cold, and the water turned a milky white as the cheese and béchamel dissolved. Inside, the striped bass began voraciously attacking the sinking *canelones*, having a real feast.

I began to laugh at the sight of it, until Pere started screaming at me, telling me what an idiot I was for not letting him help. He apologized to the customer and sent him home, telling him that we would deliver the food to his house.

But it ended up being not such a terrible thing. I made another batch, and this time the *canelones* made it out of the restaurant and to their destination without incident. And I learned one of the great lessons of the kitchen: What you can do by yourself you should do by yourself. But it's just as important to recognize when you need help and to ask for it.

Meet David Bouley
DAN BARBER

A native of Manhattan, Dan Barber worked in California and several restaurants in Paris and the South of France before returning to New York City, where he cooked at the original Bouley restaurant until it closed in 1996. In May 2000, Barber opened Blue Hill restaurant in New York City. The restaurant was nominated as Best New Restaurant by the James Beard Foundation in 2001, was named one of America's best restaurants by Gourmet *magazine, and in 2002, Barber was named one of* Food & Wine Magazine's *Best New Chefs. In May 2004, he opened Blue Hill at Stone Barns in Pocatino Hills, New York, as well as Stone Barns Center for Food and Agriculture, the mission of which is to help create a consciousness about the effect of everyday food choices. Blue Hill at Stone Barns received three stars from the* New York Times *and was nominated as Best New Restaurant by the James Beard Foundation in 2005, the same year Barber himself received a nomination as Best Chef/ New York City.*

"**Y**OU'RE NOT TALKING to your fish," moans the chef. I hear the moan from the other side of the kitchen.

There is mayhem all around. A nonstop circus of people appears and disappears through swinging doors. The expediter yells, "Ordering: two hamachi, three skate, a bass, and a halibut à la carte. Ordering: one crab salad—make that two—*two* crab salads, two sardines, and a finnan haddie *on the fly* . . ."

Cooks are everywhere, spinning, dodging, and impossibly stretching their way across vast distances to reach plates, spoons, garnishes. Chef's whites suddenly blur into a mountain of vanilla ice cream. I'm rushing now, fumbling for pans. I refuse to be licked.

But the expediter will not stop: "Waiters, pick up table seven. Hello? Waiters. Here we go, waiters!" he screams in a tattoo of insistence that cuts through the kitchen's screech and hurry. "One snapper, two veal, three is a duck—I'm holdin' a duck. I need a duck, please. Where the fuck's my duck? Where's my goddamn fuckin' duck, *please*?"

I am witness to an unfolding madness: a night in the famed kitchen of David Bouley. It is my first time cooking here, but I have heard stories of the intensity and the confusion, of the six-course tasting menus ordered by two hundred or so customers every night—twelve hundred plates of food flowing out of the kitchen in a matter of hours.

The sweat trickles from behind my kneecaps, down my legs. I am working on the fish line, and the chef has a hand in nearly every plate. Few chefs believe this is possible. Bouley, though, has made a career of confounding expectations. Years ago, no one in the culinary establishment believed that a self-proclaimed country hick from Connecticut, a mercurial drea-mer, would be able to survive in the best (and toughest) kitchens of the world, as Bouley had done, some of them so abusive and demanding that Bouley himself can only describe them as "numbing."

"I said you're not speaking to your mackerel," repeats the chef, now incensed. I look dumbly at the stove. Could he possibly be talking to me? He's all the way across the kitchen. I've spread a dozen small saucepots on the searing heat of the flat top. Sauté pans align themselves like train cars. I season furiously, dropping and flipping fish, basting, and seasoning again.

The expediter bellows orders from the pass, the window through which dishes travel from the kitchen to the dining room. Around him there is an orbit of madness. Are there twenty-eight cooks or have I counted the bread warmer twice? Here a cook lunges to sauce a naked scallop, as another picks sprigs of lemon thyme from one of the twelve herb plants standing at attention by the door; here a dishwasher waltzes through a sea of cooks, plates stacked so high as to obstruct his face.

Why all this confusion, I wonder. "Forget confusion," a cook tells me at the end of service. "Chaos. He wants the chaos. He *needs* it."

Another cook tells me about one evening's service when the orders were coming in slowly. Chef was unhappy with how relaxed all the cooks were during the first seating. "Changed the menu," the cook tells me, his eyes widening in shock and awe at the memory as though it were unfolding before him all over again. "Never said shit, neither. All of a sudden the second seating arrives, tickets come in, and the dishes ordered no one had prepped for. Totally nuts, man. He's four goddamn stars one night and Dirty Harry the next. Taught me a big lesson," he says, still wide-eyed, though he doesn't explain what the lesson was.

Steve, the philosopher-cook of the brigade, sums it up: "The qualities that mark Chef as a lunatic-genius are his absolute fearlessness, and his profound, unabashed enjoyment of his own strangeness. That's the sort of dementia these cooks respect, and perhaps even share."

The lunatic-genius's gaze intensifies in my direction, and cooks are beginning to look my way as well. I am scared, and losing control. I realize I'm the only one cooking mackerel, and that the chef, who was at the Fulton Fish Market after last evening's service until 4 a.m., who went home to "nap and shave" and return by 8 a.m., and cook straight through the day, a day so utterly exhausting that by the end of it you will often find him holding his left hand to the left side of his face—holding up his collapsed cheek so cooks can make out what he's mumbling—is, from a hundred feet away, in the midst of a crush of crazed cooks, talking to me about not talking to my mackerel.

Chef appears to be garnishing a plate of raw tuna from across the kitchen, but his eyes are somehow also locked on me. I have read that David Bouley's shyness is his most striking quality, that he relies on observation, rather than inquiry, to understand things.

This moment—our first "meeting"—confirms that assessment. He seems to be soaking up nuances and details. It isn't a hostile gaze, but it isn't exactly empathetic. He can have a big smile, an actor's guffaw at even the slightest quip, and act like he knows you well. And he's studied you so closely that you are sure he *does* know you well. The awkward thing is that you hardly know him, if you know him at all.

"Get that mackerel out of the pan," says the chef, mingling directive and threat. The kitchen falls suddenly silent as he appears next to me and pulls me close. Just as quickly, the noise roars back up. Everyone around us has resumed the whirling, except for Chef and me. We are in our own world. I hear the expediter: "Chef: table six—old man—he's fading. He won't last—he needs his food, he needs it now."

"Be cool," says the cool chef, with one hand pulling the fated mackerel from the flame, the other pulling me close to him. "You're not talking to your fish." He pauses for effect, bracing my neck against his forearm. We stand together and gaze at the mackerel. I'm about to introduce myself when he interrupts the thought. "I *always* talk to my fish," he says, staring at the sizzling mackerel.

"How else would I know when she's done?" In the observation of great Hollywood scriptwriters, the best endings must be surprising and yet inevitable; and the best of Bouley's pronouncements take this same shape.

"How else?" he asks again.

The expediter yells—there are twenty tickets on the board. I tense, trying to push free. Chef squeezes my neck with his bicep. Sweat is pouring from my face, and I find myself quickly, almost imperceptibly, rubbing my wet temple into his crisply starched chef's jacket.

"I'm going to tell you a story," he says.

"I need some tables, people. I need tables," yells the expediter.

"No time for stories," I mumble halfheartedly.

"Two bulls," Chef says, ignoring me, tightening the grip. We're still standing side by side, Chef's arm tightly wound around my neck as the kitchen blazes before us. I wonder if I might faint.

"Two bulls standing on a small hill, an older and a younger bull, overlooking a field of beautiful lady cows," he says to me.

"Oh, man," yells the expediter. "I need table six. I need that table."

The chef's lips are now only inches from my ear. "The

younger bull looks up to the older bull: 'Hey, hey, you know what I'm gonna' do? I'm gonna' run as fast as I can right now, as fast as my legs will take me, as fast as I can run down this hill, and I'm gonna get me one of those lady cows and make her my own.'" He pauses now, as if to let me marinate in the genius. "Do you know what the older bull said back to the younger bull?"

As I shook my head no, that I did not know what the older bull said to the younger bull, I lifted my eyes from his arm and peeked around. Chaos of the sort I had never seen. Cooks were yelling at busboys who yelled at dishwashers who yelled at each other.

"I don't know, Chef," I muttered.

He put his nose in my left ear and leaned heavily on me. I felt the heat of his breath as he held me there. "Well, the older bull paused for a moment," and here too the chef paused. "'Son,' said the older bull, 'I'm going to slowly walk down this hill, and I'm going to make them *all* my own.'

"Don't rush what you do here," he said, and let me go.

The Last Straw
MARIO BATALI

One of the most recognizable food personalities in New York City, Mario Batali is the chef and co-owner of a handful of restaurants that have redefined Italian dining for New Yorkers over the past decade: Babbo, Lupa, Esca, Otto Enoteca Pizzeria, and others. Before he became a chef, restaurateur, cookbook author, and television personality, Batali was reared in Seattle, attended high school in Spain, and went on to cooking school in London, the site of this formative anecdote.

AS AUTUMN FELL on London in 1984, I was a student at the local outpost of Le Cordon Bleu cooking school. For extra money, I tended bar three nights a week at a big, working-class watering hole (we sold pints mostly, with the occasional gin and tonic, no ice) on a parcel of private property in the middle of an essentially unremarkable road in Central London.

I hadn't been there long when the owners decided to convert the tavern into something much more ambitious than a tavern: a "serious" restaurant that served trendy, contemporary food, quite a sea change from the burgers and fries that were the top-selling items among our regulars. They blew out the back door of the place and performed an exhaustive renovation, transforming it—in a very efficient four weeks—into a sprawling restaurant with a garden out back.

To create and execute a menu for the new restaurant, the owners installed a young chef we'll call Richard Lewison. Propriety prevents me from sharing his real name, but trust me, you've heard of him. He's the creative force behind a number of sickeningly successful restaurants in England. But at the time he was a complete unknown, one of countless young cooks who had toiled anonymously in the shadow of a couple of Michelin-starred restaurants.

Richard fashioned a two-man kitchen in the new restaurant, and I was kept on as the second man, quite an upgrade from bartender in just four weeks' time. The kitchen was an open one, in full view of the diners, with a little station that had pendant heat lamps suspended over it where finished dishes took a moment in the spotlight before being shuttled to the appropriate table.

Richard was an amazingly fit guy, with a sinewy build that brought to mind a young pugilist. This impression was reinforced by his frequent macho demonstrations, like his morning ritual of hoisting a fifty-pound bag of spuds up over his shoulder and depositing it in another part of the kitchen. (I'm not being a smartass when I say that I think that was the highlight of his day.) He was also a very creative, thoughtful, and smart cook. Sure, he was copying the greats he had worked with, but that's a necessary rite of passage for any chef. At the same time, he was busy developing his own style, and there was much that a young pup like myself, just starting cooking school, could learn from a guy who hailed from a Michelin darling like Le Gavroche.

For example, I saw up close and personal one of the great efficiencies of a classic French kitchen: the use of "mother sauces" to create any sauce required for service. All of Richard's sauces could be fashioned by embellishing one of the two bases we made every morning. One was a classic mother sauce, hollandaise, an emulsification of egg yolks and clarified butter. The other wasn't, strictly speaking, a mother sauce, but we used it as one, and that was a beurre blanc (literally translated as "white butter"), a reduction of vinegar and shallots, to which butter was added.

I mention this because, as you're about to learn, Richard was given to the sorts of fits common to European kitchens at the time: big public outbursts that involved chewing out his staff like Lee Ermey's drill sergeant in *Full Metal Jacket*. He'd get right into your face and let you have it, with all kinds of weather spraying forth from his mouth. (He also had his human moments and graces, like when he used the term of endearment *chups*, by which he sometimes addressed me.) So, if you're wondering why I put up with it, it's because it was worth whatever it took to try to hang on, keep pace with him, and soak up as much knowledge as I could.

Or perhaps I should say, it was worth it, *up to a point*. And this, my friends, is the story of the day on which that point revealed itself.

Now, Richard liked his hollandaise whipped to an extreme froth. So every morning, I'd come in, make the yolk base, whip it for what felt like an eternity, then work in the butter. I don't know what, if anything, happened to him before he showed up for work on the evening in question, but he came in, took one look at the hollandaise, and started in on me. "What the fuck is this? What the fuck is this? There's no air in this!" I found this particularly annoying because when Richard got his back up, a French accent seeped into his voice ("*What zee fuk iz sis?*"), although, as far as I knew, he had never been to France in his life.

He then proceeded, right there in the open kitchen, with all of our customers looking on, to crack thirty-six eggs into a bowl and begin remaking the hollandaise. "This is how you make it, with the air, with the air!" he announced as he whipped the yolks, shouting and gesturing wildly so everyone in the restaurant could see and hear. When he had finished, he handed me the bowl with a satisfied grin. I glanced down at it. The hollandaise he had produced was more or less identical to the one I had made. I'll grant him that perhaps it was *a bit* airier, but it was, for all intents and purposes, the same. It was the kind of thing I was used to, however, so I shrugged it off and got back to work.

Ten minutes later came the french fries, which, like the sauces, were to be made fresh daily. Richard already had it in for the fries because he considered them beneath him; they were on the menu only because the owners insisted we have a burger and fries available for longtime customers who weren't about to order any dishes that involved a hollandaise sauce. After looking at the fries, Richard decided that I had cheated, making them the day before and stashing them in the walk-in (refrigerator). I assured him that I hadn't. In fact, I invited him to walk across the kitchen where he could see the evidence of freshness for himself: the spent potato peels, still in the garbage can.

But Richard didn't want to hear this. He so didn't want to hear it that he called me a name he had never called me before: *navvy*. To this day, I'm not sure what it means, but *I think* it's a derogatory term that the Brits use to disparage the Irish. It has something to do with someone involved in the navigation or driving of a boat, like a merchant marine—in other words, an unskilled, menial laborer, a lowlife. When he called me that, a hush fell over the restaurant staff, as though Richard had just slapped me with his gloves and I was supposed to challenge him to a duel or something.

I didn't do that, but I did let him know that I didn't appreciate his disparagement, and he went after me for my supposedly unacceptable backtalk. We never came to physical blows, but things got verbally violent. Then, as always, they subsided, and we forgot about it and got back to work.

Shortly thereafter, one of our more important customers, the owner of a nearby antiques shop, came in for dinner and ordered one of the evening's specials. Richard prepared the meat, then summoned me for my contribution: "Mario, quick, bring me the sautéed zucchini that goes with this." I brought it over. A moment later, Richard stopped what he was doing: "Chups, come look at these, these are not right."

I had no idea what he was talking about. In the pan were perfectly cut matchsticks of zucchini, glistening in oil, cooked through but with just the right amount of bite left in them.

"But Chef, this is how we've been doing the zucchini for the past two days."

"This is not the way we do them! This will never be the way we do them! This is not Michelin-star food!"

But we're not a Michelin-star restaurant, I thought, though didn't dare say it.

Richard garbaged the zucchini and I made him a fresh batch, more or less identical to the first, but somehow acceptable this time.

A little while later, another gentleman joined the antiques

shop owner at his table and ordered risotto with calf's liver. That's when things really got cooking in the kitchen.

"Mario, bring over the risotto," Richard said, summoning me again.

I obliged. Richard took one glance at the risotto and proclaimed it undercooked.

"Richard," I said, "This is al dente risotto. This is how we serve it here."

"Who's the chef here?"

"You're the chef here, Chef."

I don't know if he thought I was being sarcastic, or if maybe he detected just a smidge of had-enough-of-your-shit in my voice, but that was it. He slapped the hand in which I was holding the pan and unloaded a mess of adjectives on me, the whole drill sergeant bit again.

"Dude," I said, "this is perfect risotto."

"Perfect? This is not perfect! You'll have to cook it again!"

"Aw, for the love of fuck . . ."

Here came the French accent again: *"For zee love of fuk? For zee love of fuk?"*

And with that, he picked up the offending pan of risotto and hurled it across the five feet of space that had grown between us during the argument. The pan hit me smack in the chest before tumbling down to the ground, spilling its contents all over the newly renovated floor.

There wasn't anything else to be said. I turned my back on Richard, walked into the prep area at the rear of the kitchen, and took a fistful of salt in one hand. I paused and looked over at Richard. He had his back to me and was finishing the dish without the risotto, putting on his little show for the customers. I tossed the salt into the beurre blanc. Took another fistful and tossed it in the hollandaise. Then I took off my apron, threw it in the linen bin, and—having satisfied my appetite for knowledge and revenge at this particular place of employment—walked out the back door and into the cool London night, a *navvy* no more, whatever the hell that meant.

Two Great Tastes
That Taste Great Together

MICHELLE BERNSTEIN

A former dancer, Miami native Michelle Bernstein is executive chef of "MB" at the Aqua hotel in Cancún, Mexico. After graduating from Johnson & Wales University, Bernstein began her culinary career at Red Fish Grill and Christy's in Coral Gables, and Tantra in Miami Beach. She trained with Jean-Louis Palladin, and honed her skills at Alison on Dominick Street and Le Bernardin in New York. She then became executive chef and co-owner of the Strand, before drawing national attention as executive chef at Azul at the Mandarin Oriental hotel in Miami. For two years, she cohosted the Food Network's Melting Pot. Bernstein was nominated for the 2004 James Beard Foundation Award as Best Chef/Southeast Region.

M Y FIRST KITCHEN job was as a line cook (*commis* in the industry vernacular), at Mark's Place in North Miami Beach, Florida. One night in 1993, during my second year on the job, we were expecting two celebrity guests. The one more familiar to our customers was TV's Maude, a famous *Golden Girl* in a town of real-life Golden Girls, the actress Bea Arthur. But the guest that sent shivers through the kitchen was the late, great Jean-Louis Palladin, one of the few two- or three-Michelin-starred chefs ever to have opened a restaurant in the United States: Jean-Louis at the Watergate in Washington, D.C.

Palladin was a legendary character in the industry. Though only in his late forties, he already possessed a famously craggy face, the product of equal parts hard work and hard living, and he had the wildly unkempt hair of a mad scientist. His temper reportedly knew no equal, but he was also appreciated for his genius, was considered a true friend to his peers, and was said to have a keen eye for recognizing and appreciating talent and hard work.

Miami didn't have the number of great chefs and restaurants it does today, so this was a case of visiting royalty. Among our crew, I was the one most atwitter at the prospect of cooking for Chef Palladin, because our chef/owner Mark Millitello had arranged for me to leave my hometown of Miami and go work for Palladin in Washington in just a few months.

My role in Mark's kitchen was an unusual one. I was far from the most seasoned cook, but I was a serial perfectionist. That, combined with the fact that I was the only woman in the house, made me—I guess—a nurturing presence, as much for my fellow cooks as for Mark. On days like this one, when something special was afoot, it was typical for Mark to tell people to "run it by Michelle" before it leaves the kitchen.

Mark himself was a near nervous wreck about the visit; he spent the day in a tizzy, tasting and retasting every kitchen preparation, pulling out all the stops by embellishing the menu with extra touches. He and Jean-Louis had a passing acquaintance, as most U.S. chefs of any renown do, but they weren't intimates, and any time a chef visited from another region, you wanted to make a good impression because other chefs were sure to get a report on the meal.

The most special thing Mark did to welcome Chef Palladin was to make a foie gras terrine, one of the true labors of love in classic French gastronomy. Terrines require a deft hand and precise control throughout preparation, including careful monitoring of the temperature of the ingredients, both when you begin and when you stop cooking them.

I still remember the terrine that Mark made—featuring layers of foie gras and sauternes gelee, made from the sweet dessert wine traditionally served alongside foie gras—a truly exemplary piece of craftsmanship that beautifully filled out its huge, rectangular, stainless-steel mold.

Because of my special role in that kitchen, I was entrusted with the terrine. In order to ensure it would be as smooth as possible when the time came to slice and serve it, Mark left it out on a shelf above my station for a few hours before service.

My mission was so clear that Mark didn't have to say a word: don't screw up, especially not with my future mentor in the house.

The kitchen at Mark's Place was cramped, to say the least. There was a front kitchen and a back kitchen, separated by a wall, a most unusual configuration. I was in the back area where we made appetizers and some pastries. Accordingly, my station was crowded with both the *mise en place* (prepared ingredients) for salads and starters, and a huge bowl of warm chocolate sauce for topping various desserts.

Because of the kitchen's organization, and our enormous menu (there were more than twenty appetizers), being a cook there required quite a bit of multitasking. It wasn't unusual for me to be plating a dish with one hand and whisking a dressing with another.

The only problem is that, even though I'm an ex-ballerina, I'm also something of a klutz, prone to minor accidents, spills, and such.

When the time came to send the terrine to Palladin's table, I arranged the salad plates on which I would serve it on my work station. I was putting salad on the plates with my left hand, and reaching up for the terrine with my right.

I didn't have a very firm grip on the terrine mold, so instead of lifting it, I only succeeded in pulling it off the shelf. It eluded my slippery fingers and tumbled down past my widening eyes right into the bowl of chocolate sauce, where it bobbed for a moment, like a ship with a hull breach taking on water, and then proceeded to sink into the murky depths.

As I reached in after it, my colleagues rushed over to help me try to save it—a difficult task. Had the terrine come straight from the fridge, it would have been hard and cold, and easy to wipe off. But softened as it was, and warming even more thanks to the chocolate, it was beginning to leach out into the sauce. Tan globules were bubbling up to the surface, turning the chocolate into a mocha-colored nightmare.

I gingerly retrieved the unmolded terrine from the sauce and laid it out on my station. The other cooks and I stood over it in our chocolate-spattered whites, trying to decide how to save our patient. The first step was to halt the melting and preserve its shape, and we worked on it furiously, smoothing it over with spatulas, and our fingers.

I was panicked beyond words.

But I also couldn't help recalling, with amusement, those old television commercials for Reese's Peanut Butter Cups I used to watch as a kid. In the series of advertisements, two individuals, hurried for no apparent reason—one carrying chocolate and one peanut butter—would turn a corner and slam into each other, sending the chocolate into the peanut butter. They'd gasp in alarm, but needlessly so, because when they tasted the resulting combination, they realized that they had made the junk-food equivalent of discovering penicillin: peanut butter and chocolate, "two great tastes that taste great together."

Snobs might turn their nose up at this observation, but make no mistake about it: foie gras is the gourmet equivalent of peanut butter; insanely rich, it's best complemented by sweet or tart elements. Just as peanut butter goes with jelly, foie gras gets on famously with any number of fruit chutneys or compotes, like the sauternes gelee with which it was layered in the terrine.

Along these same lines, it turned out, as we licked our fingers, that foie gras and chocolate—just like the commercials said—were two great tastes that tasted great together. I'd be lying if I denied that we were moaning with pleasure as we licked the bittersweet chocolate and molten foie gras from our fingers, the rich concoction sticking to the roofs of our mouths like, well, like peanut butter.

Though we saved the terrine from total destruction, we weren't able to totally remove the chocolate, which had fused with the foie into a coating that could not be removed without serious risk of destroying the whole thing.

Making peace with the situation, I continued plating the terrine, racing to finish before Mark could see it. He was anxious enough that Jean-Louis was in the house; finding out about the dive the terrine had taken into the chocolate might have put him over the edge.

Finally, I sent out our new special starter: "chocolate-painted foie gras" with a lovely mâche salad.

I was too nervous to look out the kitchen to see how the

terrine went over, but it must have been fine because Jean-Louis's plates came back clean, and Mark didn't charge through the swinging kitchen doors, screaming my name.

I came away from this incident unscathed. In fact, I got three things out of it. The first was a nickname by which my old pals from that kitchen still address me: Reeses.

The second is that, years later, when I had become executive chef of Azul at the Mandarin Oriental hotel on Miami Beach, I called on this episode to fashion one of my signature dishes: Seared Foie Gras with Chocolate Mole, mole of course being the savory Mexican chocolate sauce.

If Mark reads this story, it'll be the first he ever heard of the chocolate-painted terrine incident . . . because I never quite worked up the courage to tell him. I did tell Jean-Louis, though, during one of the rare times that, while working for the great chef, I found myself sharing a quiet moment with him. This was the third thing I got from that night: when I arrived at the punch line, Jean-Louis exploded with his huge, throaty laugh—I honestly don't think I've ever heard anyone laugh harder or louder—a cherished memory that alone made the whole thing worthwhile.

Lean Times at the Fat Duck
HESTON BLUMENTHAL

One of the most celebrated culinary figures in contemporary England, self-taught chef Heston Blumenthal opened the Fat Duck in 1995 in Bray, Berkshire. The Michelin Guide *awarded the Fat Duck its first star in 1999, and upheld it in 2000 and 2001. He was awarded a second star in 2002, and a third star in 2004. Blumenthal was the first winner of the Chef of the Year award in the 2001* Good Food Guide. *His first book,* Family Food, *was published in 2001, the same year he hosted the program* Kitchen Chemistry *on Discovery Channel.*

M Y RESTAURANT, the Fat Duck, currently possesses three Michelin stars, a fact of which I am exceedingly proud. I'm all the more gratified when I look back on our formative period, about a decade ago, and recall the many incredible struggles that faced me every day. Those were pretty damn tricky times, to say the least . . .

Thanks to the physical space itself—a copper bar originally built in 1550 as part of a cottage, which had been a pub since the 1600s—the Fat Duck was challenging from the get-go. It had low ceilings, just over seven feet high, with beams that made the room seem even smaller. Though we did a refurbishing, modernizing the space and painting the walls for a stony effect, it was still a mighty old building. In fact, it was so old that the loo was located outside. I'm quite sure that we were the only restaurant with an outside bathroom to receive a Michelin star.

When we first opened, the dining room was a rather Spartan affair. There were no tablecloths. The wine list could be printed on a single piece of paper, with only twenty whites, twenty reds, and a small selection of sparkling and dessert wines. Equally minimal was the staff—a new restaurant is faced with special hiring challenges, since if you have no name and no money in the bank, it's difficult to attract the best employees. So that initial year it was just me and a pot washer in the kitchen, with three front-of-house people in the dining room.

One of the most telling details of the early days of the Fat Duck was our system of communicating with the dining room team. The kitchen was situated behind the dining room, separated by a small passageway furnished with only a bench, where a staff member could take a *very brief* respite on especially busy nights, perhaps while waiting for the final dish to complete a table's order.

Between the passageway and the kitchen was a pass-through window. When the food went up on the pass, I'd do a quick double-clap to get the attention of a waiter or the maitre d' from the dining room. It was a rapid little sound that customers didn't notice, but to which the service team's ears had become highly attuned.

In time, our business began to get more robust, and I needed more help in the kitchen. Unable to attract any cooks of note, I found myself hiring a not-insignificant number of lowlifes: ax murderers, bank robbers, and the like. (Well, not quite—at least, no *convicted* ax murderers and bank robbers.) Anyone I could lure and satisfy with my unavoidably meager wages was fair game, including one chap who had been in army prison for a time and was trying to straighten out his life. He was huge, six foot six, with humongous, gnarly hands and a coating of tattoos over his entire body. Though only twenty-one, he gave the impression of a soul who had lived a long and tortured existence.

My motley crew in the back was offset by the front-of-house employees—the ones that the customers actually saw. Thankfully, this contingent was infinitely more presentable. There was a French waiter who showed a lot of promise. And there was an English maitre d' who had worked at a two-Michelin-star restaurant in London and was very good at his job. He was thirty-five years old, balding, impeccably dressed, and very well spoken. He did have some affectations, but I found them charming. For example, like many people who had worked in French restaurants, he had developed a habit of ending his sentences with a little "unh" sound to imitate the cadence of French language, such as "More bread, unh." Or "I'm going over here, Chef, unh."

He was a true service master, fastidious almost to a fault, and would walk the dining room floor, straightening curtains, always busying himself with the betterment of the establishment.

But then something happened, and it crushed him: He had a very young girlfriend who had gone off to university. A practical person, he was quite prepared for her to meet a younger man. Instead, while she was home on holiday, she went to a party, fell in love with his best friend, also thirty-five, and ran off with him.

That he wasn't prepared for, and he lost it. I didn't realize how badly until one particular evening.

This was a Saturday and we were serving about fifty-five people, a very busy night for us. My team of criminals was working like mad. I was putting the proper finish on every dish before setting it up on the pass and doing my little double-clap, wherein a front-of-house staff member would arrive and retrieve the plates.

At one point, round about eight o'clock, I put some plates up on the pass, and did the double-clap.

Nobody came.

I did it again. *Clap-clap*. And again. *Clap-clap*.

Finally, I pounded twice on the pass itself. *BANG-BANG!* Not very quiet at all. I'm sure some customers heard that one.

But still nobody came.

For me, and for many chefs, to leave the kitchen during service is a nightmare. Not only does it slow you down, but you lose your flow and concentration—and you don't know what crisis might be waiting for you when you return. And yet I had no choice. I stalked out of the kitchen and into the dining room to see where my staff had disappeared to.

No sooner did I arrive on the service floor than I spotted my maitre d' standing over a table of three customers, laughing it up and having a good old time, completely oblivious to the operation of the restaurant.

I was positively fuming, but I had other priorities, so I made a mental note to deal with it later. Then I asked one of the waiters to come back to the kitchen and fetch the food, and got on with my evening.

When I had finished cooking for the evening, I had to run through the dining room, up the stairs to the restaurant office, and phone in orders to purveyors for the next day, before they closed.

As I made the trip, I passed a table of four—two men and two women—seated by the foot of the stairs. From their slouchy posture and uproarious laughter, it was clear that they'd had quite a bit of wine.

One of the men drunkenly grabbed my arm as I passed by.

"We have to tell you, we think your maitre d' is great," he slurred.

"Do tell," I said, trying to be every bit the charming, unruffled chef, but still crossly remembering the way the maitre d' had disappeared on me earlier.

"Well," the man went on. "He does the most amazing impression of Basil Fawlty"—this a reference to John Cleese's flamboyantly demonstrative hotelier on *Fawlty Towers*, a character infamous for his supreme lack of respect toward his clientele.

I feigned laughter, simmering under my cool countenance, and sought out more information: "How's that?"

"Well," the man said, the rest of his party already erupting in laughter at what was coming. "We were sitting here when a party of four came in the door. They asked your maitre d' if you had a table for four."

The storyteller paused here because he was too overcome with laughter to continue. "And then," he said, still struggling to compose himself. "And then," he said turning red with laughter. "And *then*," he said, finally getting on with it, "your maitre d' looks left, looks right, looks up, looks down, and says, 'No, we haven't!' "

The four of them burst into fits of laughter, banging on the table as though it were the funniest thing they had ever heard.

"*Then*," the man said, his shoulders shaking, "he walked off saying 'f—ing customers. F—ing customers.' "

They all started slamming the table harder and convulsing with laughter, barely able to breathe now.

I felt like someone had just lit a bonfire in my stomach. Out of politeness, I forced a little chuckle and headed up the stairs to do my ordering.

I had scarcely picked up the phone when the French waiter appeared. "Chef, can you come downstairs?"

"When?"

"Now please."

I scurried down the stairs, through the dining room, and into the passageway to the kitchen. Sitting there on the bench was the maitre d', with his head in his hands, rocking back and forth.

"What on earth are you doing?" I demanded, pretty well fed up with his string of odd behavior.

He removed his hands, revealing a big, red lump on his forehead.

"He hit me," he cried, indicating the tattooed behemoth in the kitchen.

Before I could gather more facts for myself, the French waiter pulled me aside and explained what had happened:

A call had come in, and in those days when the front-of-house phone was engaged, the incoming call would automatically divert to a phone on the wall outside the kitchen. It was too far from the pass for me to reach it, but this hulking figure had no problem—he had stretched out with his big, meaty arms and answered the phone in his frightening, dungeon-master's voice: "Good evening, Fat Duck."

It was a customer, seeking a reservation. The cook put the call on hold and, at that moment, the maitre d' had come into the passageway.

"I've a booking for you," said the cook, taking the phone off "hold."

"I don't want to speak to any f—ing customers," said the maitre d'. "They're all f—ing idiots."

Rightly fearful that the customer on the phone could hear this, the cook stretched out his arm, trying to put his hands over the mouth of the maitre d' and silence him. Instead, he succeeded in striking him smack on the forehead, sending him reeling back onto the bench.

Taking the waiter's word as gospel—and really, who else could I trust in this situation?—I exonerated the cook and blamed the maitre d' for the whole ugly incident.

I had no choice. The next morning, I sacked the maitre d', giving him two weeks notice.

Funny thing is, there's a lot that's changed at the Fat Duck since that night. We now have a loo inside the building. The wine list is a book—rather than a scrap of paper—reflecting the formidable cellar we've amassed. We have beautiful leather-backed chairs and three Michelin stars. We make enough money and have enough of a reputation to snare the best possible job candidates.

We've made it, as they say.

But I still would hire this chap today—and I still would have wound up having to let him go. In the restaurant business, as in life, you can only have so much control over your fate. At some point, you're at the mercy of the universe.

And of your f—ing employees.

On the Road Again
DANIEL BOULUD

A native of Lyon, France, Daniel Boulud is one of the most acclaimed chefs in New York City. His empire includes the four-star dining temple Daniel, as well as Café Boulud and DB Bistro Moderne. Trained under some of the legendary chefs of France, Boulud made his name as the executive chef of the Polo Lounge and Le Cirque in New York City, before opening his own restaurants. He is the author of several cookbooks and the designer of the Daniel Boulud Kitchen line of cookware.

W E CHEFS FREQUENTLY find ourselves practicing our craft away from our own restaurants, whether for one of the seemingly nightly benefit events carried on around New York City, at private affairs, or at smaller occasions like a television appearance or book signing.

Whenever you leave the carefully calibrated setting of your own kitchen—a facility that each chef tailors and tweaks to his own ever-changing needs and specifications—there is a risk. Away from your home base, variables abound: the setting and infrastructure, the support staff, the kitchen equipment, even the serving vessels can cause unforeseen problems.

Out-of-house disasters are funny to look back on, but only because they usually end well. I'll bet if you ask chefs for their best stories from the road, they all wrap up with the food on the table and the customers having no idea of the chaos that transpired behind the scenes. There's a very simple reason for this: *in my business, failure is not an option.* The mark of a professional is that no matter what happens, no matter how catastrophic the circumstances, you complete your job on time and to your standards and those of your guests.

To minimize the chance of a disaster, many chefs transport, even fly, their own ingredients to event sites. But sometimes this is impractical, like the time I was in Tel Aviv, Israel, to do a gala dinner for two hundred with Norman Van Aken, Thomas Keller, Nobu Matsuhisa, and Toronto's Susser Lee. Susser was going to prepare a stuffed quail, but when the quail showed up at two o'clock on the afternoon of the dinner, boneless, limp, and corroded by kosherizing salt, I saw before me a man in crisis.

It was a truly terrible situation to be stuck in. Nobu, Thomas, Norman, and I wanted to jump in and help, but Susser had to completely change gears and literally didn't have time to collaborate. He ordered the support staff to just "bring me stuff, bring me stuff," in hopes that some new ingredients would spark his imagination. And they did: by the time the dinner rolled around, he had pulled off a lovely duck dish. The happy guests had no idea that anything had gone awry.

Equipment is another fertile breeding ground for trouble. I once did a dinner at a major New York museum, in a room that had no stoves, and which was forbidden by building regulations from having any gas or electric machines brought in. One of my new cooks, looking for a way to reroast the meat dish, put fifteen to twenty cans of sterno under a sheet pan in an enclosed wooden cabinet. When we opened the cabinet door, we were greeted by a fireball; the heat was so intense—easily in excess of 700 degrees—that the sheet pan had started to melt.

But the most difficult element to control is people, especially those you didn't hire and who will only be working with you for one day. For example, one of the most heart-stopping things that ever happened to me involved the most unlikely worker: a truck driver.

The year was 1989. I was chef at Le Cirque, Sirio Maccioni's legendary restaurant. Malcolm Forbes had famously decided to throw himself a seventieth-birthday party in Morocco, and to transport his seven hundred American guests, including such legends as Henry Kissinger and Barbara Walters, he chartered two private 747s and a Concorde to fly out of Kennedy Airport.

Le Cirque was enlisted to prepare a four-star breakfast for the flights. We spared no expense, purchasing elegant little baskets and preparing individual meals of our own bread, a hard-boiled egg, sausage, Evian, orange juice, linen napkins, and so on.

To ensure the food was maintained at ultimate freshness, we hired a refrigerated truck the night before the flight. We prepped food well into the wee hours, then loaded the truck and instructed the driver to sleep in his seat and keep the truck parked outside the restaurant. We would return in the morning and head to the airport with him to present the food.

We went home at two in the morning, got a few hours' sleep, and came back at six thirty . . . only to find that the truck had disappeared.

If this story had happened today, the first thing I would have done was whip out my cell phone and called the driver on his.

But this was in 1989. Almost nobody had a cell phone—except for Sirio, who owned one roughly the size of a man's shoe.

Once we recovered from the shock of the missing truck, we decided that perhaps the driver had misunderstood and gone to the airport. We piled into a car and made for JFK, with Sirio frantically calling anyone on the planet who might be able to solve this problem.

At the airport, hundreds of Malcolm Forbes's guests, a who's who of New York society, were filing into a private hangar that had been converted into a Moroccan lounge, with decorations, live music, even a belly dancer. There was everything you could imagine.

But not a single scrap of food, and no truck in sight.

At this point, I thought Sirio might actually kill somebody. And I'll be honest: I didn't know what we were going to do.

Well, everyone is entitled to a little luck and that was the morning when I got mine. At the last possible second, the truck came barreling down the runway and we just managed to get the food served to the guests, who had by then taken their seats on board the planes. It turned out that the driver had gone home and overslept, with the most famous breakfast on Earth parked outside in his driveway.

One place you don't ever get lucky is in the kitchen. You either make the food right or you don't. Without a doubt, my biggest challenge came on a day when we *had* made the food right, but it was undone by the on-site staff.

This was in the mid-nineties. I was still operating out of the original Daniel space on East Seventy-sixth Street, and I was enlisted to be the culinary chairman of a rain forest benefit, a seated dinner for one thousand people that followed a concert by Elton John and Sting. I had complete creative control of the three courses we were to serve, except for one: they insisted that the first course be a pea soup featured on my restaurant menu at the time.

We didn't have the capacity to cook on that scale in my restaurant's kitchen, so we planned to do it at the hotel, enlisting the help of the on-site staff.

Just as it is in a home kitchen, one of the crucial concerns of making pea soup is chilling it as soon as it's been cooked, to prevent it from turning brown and to keep the vegetables from fermenting.

I love logistical challenges like this so I had already sat down with my calculator and notepad and determined how many batches we'd have to make to end up with twelve hundred servings, the one thousand for which we were contracted, plus a 20 percent contingency. I had also devised a system of keeping the soup chilled that involved storing it in batches in a number of 25-gallon stainless-steel containers set in ice water, and periodically stirring it to distribute the chilled portion within the canister and help bring down the overall temperature of the batch.

We made the soup the day before the event, then left the site, entrusting it to the hotel's kitchen staff. They were supposed to keep the canisters in the cooler, in regularly replenished ice water, and stir the soup every hour. As near as I can tell, when the shift changed in the midafternoon, the new guys didn't give a damn and just left the canisters sitting there, completely unattended.

At the end of the day, I dispatched a few guys from my kitchen to check on the status of things at the hotel. When they entered the refrigerator to inspect the soup, there was greenish-yellow-brown foam bubbling over the tops of the canisters.

Though the soup had undoubtedly fermented, this is one of those evaluations that only the chef can make, so my guys ladled a sample of the soup into a plastic container and had it shuttled up to me at Daniel. As soon as I saw it, I could tell it was gone, and a taste made this all too clear: the soup, all twelve hundred servings worth, was sour, useless garbage.

At that moment, the event—for me and my team—became more of a military operation than a culinary endeavor. I outlined a rigorous plan that began with the guys on site pouring the spoiled soup down the drain and ended with a thousand guests enjoying a perfect soup the next evening.

Okay, now here's the amazing thing about a crisis like this: the actual cooking was the *second* concern. The first concern was replenishing the supplies required to make that much soup, most notably about 400 pounds of a variety of five peas. I called every purveyor I could think of, then one of my cooks and I got in a van and personally drove around town, starting in Harlem and working our way south, buying up all the peas we could find.

As for the stock, even if we could have put our hands on enough bones to make a new one from scratch, it didn't matter, because there wasn't time for it to patiently simmer. Fortunately I know how to work with a powdered stock base if I have to.

Instead of making the entire soup hot and chilling it, we used a few kitchen tricks to save time, blanching and chilling the peas, chilling the stock separately, then combining the two. We also used a complicated series of shallow vessels set in ice water to keep it as cold as possible.

When it was time to serve the soup, one thousand little bowls came marching out of the kitchen, beautifully garnished with rosemary-infused cream and rosemary croutons, and little bowls of bacon crackling on the side for anyone who wanted it.

Just the way it was always meant to be.

New Year's Meltdown
ANTHONY BOURDAIN

Anthony Bourdain has been a chef or a cook for nearly three decades, and in 2000 he chronicled that experience in Kitchen Confidential, *which has been translated into twenty-four languages, leading Mr. Bourdain to the conclusion that "chefs are the same everywhere." He is the executive chef at Brasserie Les Halles in New York City.*

IN MY LONG and checkered career I have been witness to, party to, and even singularly responsible for any number of screwups, missteps, and overreaches. I am not Alain Ducasse. The focus of my career has not always been a relentless drive toward excellence. As a mostly journeyman chef, knocking around the restaurant business for twenty-eight years, I've witnessed some pretty ugly episodes of culinary disaster. I have seen an accidentally glass-laden breaded veal cutlet cause a customer to rise up in the middle of a crowded dining room and begin keening and screaming with pain as blood dribbled from his mouth. I've watched restaurants endure mid-dinner-rush fires, floods, and rodent infiltration—as well as the more innocuous annoyances of used Band-Aids, tufts of hair, and industrial staples showing up in the niçoise salad. Busboy stabbing busboy, customer beating up customer, waiters duking it out on the dining room floor—I've seen it all. But never have I seen such a shameful synergy of Truly Awful Things happen, and in such spectacular fashion, as on New Years Eve 1991, a date that surely deserves to live in New York restaurant infamy. It was the all-time, award-winning, jumbo-sized restaurant train wreck, a night where absolutely everything went wrong that could go wrong, where the greatest number of people got hurt, and an entire kitchen bowed its head in shame and fear—while outside the kitchen doors, waiters trembled at the slaughter-house their once hushed and elegant dining room had become.

Like Operation "Market Garden" (the ill-fated Allied invasion of the Netherlands) or Stalingrad—or the musicals of Andrew Lloyd Webber—responsibility for the disaster that followed rests, ultimately, with one man. In this case it was a talented and resourceful chef we'll call Bobby Thomas. Bobby had the idea that he could create an ambitious menu—as good as his always excellent à la carte menus—and serve it to the 350 people who would be filling the nightclub/restaurant we'll call NiteKlub. He also felt confident enough in his abilities that he could pretty much wait until the last minute to put the whole thing together: little details like telling his staff what the fuck they were going to be serving, and how. In his visionary wisdom, Bobby did not share his thinking or his plans with others. Like the strategic braniacs who thought invading Russia to be a good idea, he was undisturbed by useful details ("Mein Fuhrer? Are you aware winter is coming?"). Those who might have pointed out the obvious warning signs were not included in Bobby's conceptualizing of what could well have been a spectacular success—for a dinner party of twenty. Bobby was, after all, a kind of a genius. And it's often the geniuses who put us in a world of pain.

I arrived at NiteKlub at about a half hour before the shift, the other cooks trickling in after me. We pulled on our whites, cranked up the radio, and, as usual, stood around waiting for someone to tell us what to do. Our leader had characteristically neglected to entrust us with a prep list. So we did what cooks left unbriefed and unsupervised tend to do, which was stand around gossiping.

The lobsters arrived first. There were cases of them, so many that they reached to the ceiling, 125 of the things, skittering around under wet newspaper and heaps of crushed ice. Since I was de facto quartermaster, and the guy who signed for such things, the cooks—Frankie Five Angels, Matt, Orlando, Steven, Dougie, Adam Real Last Name Unknown, and Dog Boy—all stood there expectantly, looking at me, waiting for instructions as a puddle of water grew larger and larger from the rapidly melting ice. What do we do with them? Who knows? Bobby hadn't left a prep list. Do we blanche them? Cook them all the way? Whack 'em into wriggling chunks? Shuck them, split them, or turn the damn things into bisque? We don't know. 'Cause Bobby hasn't left a menu.

The game arrived next. Boned-out *poussin*, duck breasts, bones, a case of foie gras. We cleaned up the duck breasts nicely, put on stock with the bones (that didn't take much to surmise), and laid out the *poussins* on sheet pans and got everything in the walk-in for when Bobby showed. We wanted to start in on the case of foie gras—whole loaves of the stuff!— but were we making terrine, which would require us to open them up and start yanking out veins, or were we leaving them whole for pan-searing? We didn't know. And once you tear open a liver, you can't untear it. So we left those alone. When the meat order arrived, we cleaned up the tenderloins, but left them whole, not having any idea of portion size, whether we were making filet mignon or tournedos or chateaubriand or beef fucking Wellington for that matter.

Oysters! There was a collective moan from the team, as not even a madman would want to put oysters on a menu for over three hundred. Perhaps we could crack them open ahead of time. But should we? What if . . . what *if* Bobby had planned oysters on the half shell? In which case I'd be cracking oysters to order all night, since the customers, for the $275 per person they were paying, would prefer them moist and fresh. It was too horrible to contemplate. Out of the corner of my eye I saw Steven peel off out the back door—which meant he was probably going to score—and from the way Frankie was working his jaw muscles, half the cooks were well into the coke already and likely looking for a re-up.

When the produce order came in, it was getting toward panic time. Two cases of oranges, a case of lemons, ten cases of mache (lamb's lettuce)—which, at least, we could clean—Belgian endive, fennel, wild mushrooms, the ubiquitous baby zucchinis, yellow squashes, and pattypan squash and baby carrots that Bobby so loved. Dry goods followed, an impenetrable heap of long-haul purchases: fryer oil, salad oil, vinegar, flour, canned goods. There was no way of knowing what was for today and what was for next week.

We peeled the carrots. It was two o'clock now, cocaine and indecision grinding the heart right out of the afternoon. And still no Bobby.

Truffles arrived. Nice. Then the fish. Not so nice because it was Dover sole—a bitch to clean and an even bigger bitch to cook in large numbers. Orlando, Frankie, and I got down on the sole with rubber gloves and kitchen shears, trimming off the spines. Matt and Dougie cut chive sticks and plucked chervil tops and basil flowers and made gaufrette potatoes for garnish, because we knew—if we knew anything—that we'd be using a lot of those. Dog Boy was relegated to fiddling with the dial on the radio. A new hire, Dog Boy was a skateboarder with a recently pierced tongue and absolutely useless for anything—he could fuck up a wet dream—so it was best that he was kept safely out of the way. Adam, at least, knew we'd need bread, so he stayed reasonably busy balling dough and putting loaves in the oven—which was ironic, really, as Adam was usually the last person to know what was going on about anything, and here he was, currently the best informed person in the kitchen.

By four o'clock, with still no evidence of Bobby and no word, the mood was turning ugly. Dougie's neck and cheeks were red, which meant he'd been hitting the sauce somewhere. Frankie was retelling, for the umpteenth time, the story of how he had communicated the plot to *Cliffhanger* to Sylvester Stallone during a three-second near-telepathic encounter by the men's room of Planet Hollywood, his previous employer. He'd as good as written that movie!—despite the fact that he couldn't even pronounce it, calling it *"Clifthangah"*—and one of these days, he'd get paid for it. That's if Sly's "people" didn't "get to him first." Frankie, while high on blow, was often under the impression that various "agents of Stallone" were "watching him" as he clearly "knew too much." When we all started laughing (and how could we not?), the by now manically high, dangerously paranoid Frankie began to tweak. This was not good. As Frankie was taller and bigger and stronger than all of us (over six foot six) and a vicious hockey player sensitive to criticism, things could get really crazy.

"Fucking Bobby," muttered Dougie again. Dougie, at least, wouldn't get violent. He was more of a sulker. But he might very well just disappear if discouraged. He'd done it before—just walked out the door and disappeared for a few days.

I nervously looked at the clock and debated doing exactly that myself. Happily, when I looked back, Matt was doing his pitch-perfect Frankie Pentangeli imitation from *The Godfather II*: "Oh . . . sure, senator . . . sure . . . that Michael Corleone . . . Michael Corleone did this . . . Michael Corleone did that," which always gave Frankie the giggles. Violence, for now anyway, seemed to have been averted.

Time passed. We continued to set up as best we could. At five thirty, Bobby finally rolled in. I say rolled in because he was (not unusually) on Rollerblades, wearing a new *Blues Traveler* tour jacket he'd scored off a private client and that charming little-boy smile that had so successfully helped convince a legion of hostesses and floor staff to come into close contact with Bobby's genitals. We, however, were not so charmed.

"Uh . . . Bobby? What's the menu?" I said. "We'd really kind of like to know."

Bobby just smiled, gave us the Ronnie James Dio "devil horn" hand sign, skated back to his office, and emerged a few moments later in his whites, bearing the fatal document:

The NiteKlub New Year's Eve Menu 1992

Oysters Baked in Champagne Sauce with Beluga Caviar

or

Pan-Seared Foie Gras with Apricot Chutney,
Port Wine Sauce, and Toasted Brioche

or

Beggar's Purses of Diver Scallops and Wild Mushrooms

or

Truffle Soup

followed by
Dover Sole with Citrus Beurre
Lobster in a Shellfish Nage with Fennel
Chestnut and Truffle Stuffed *Poussin* with Foie Gras Sauce
Chateaubriand "Rossini" with Baby Vegetables
and Chive Mashed Potatoes

followed by
Harlequin Soufflé
New Year's Parfait
Lemon Tart
Profiteroles

To be honest, my memory is not perfect on the exact menu choices. I approximate. What *is* burned permanently into my brain, however, is the simple fact that this was a killer menu to do "à la minute" and seemed heavily skewed toward the sauté station. Which was not, tactically or strategically, our strongest point. The hot app station appeared overladen with dishes as well, and as Frankie Five Angels was already, at this early hour, quietly having an amusing conversation with himself, the prospects of a smooth night in that area seemed . . . unlikely. Our fearless leader, though, brimmed with insouciance that we took for confidence. My muttered concerns were dismissed— understandably, given my pessimistic nature, and my kitchen nickname of the time: "Dr. Doom."

Bobby curtly gave us our prep assignments and a brief rundown of how he expected us to prepare and present his creations. To our credit, we quickly put our stations together, set up our *mise en place*, dug in, and by seven we were loaded and ready for the first orders.

It should be pointed out that I had, basically, nothing to do but crack oysters—which I sensibly did in advance (given they were to be baked)—and help Adam plate desserts. Everything else was coming off hot appetizer (Frankie and Dougie), grill (Matt), or sauté (Steven and Orlando). Dog Boy was sent home after a less-than-grueling half day.

Half an hour later, there were still no tickets. The little printer hooked up to the waiters' computer order systems lay silent. Our two runners, Manuel and Ed, informed us that the guests were arriving, the dining room filling, and all of us hoped that they'd start getting the orders in fast, in comfortably staggered fashion, so we could set a nice pace without getting swamped all at once.

"Tell them to get those orders in," snarled Bobby. "Let's knock down some early tables! C'mon!"

But nothing happened. A half hour passed, then an hour, as our now-full house of New Year's revelers sat at their tables, admired each others' clothes, drank Veuve Clicquot, and presumably pondered their menus. It would be a long night.

The first order came in at eight thirty. *Clack clack clack . . . dit dit dit . . .* "Ordering! . . . One oysters, two foie gras . . . a scallop . . . followed by three sole . . . a lobster . . . one chateau and a *poussin!*" crowed our chef. *Clack clack clack . . . dit dit dit.* The sound of paper being torn off. "Two more oysters . . . two more foie . . . followed by three Dover sole! One lobster!" *Clack clack clack . . . dit dit dit . . .* and already I'm getting worried because they seemed to be hitting the sole hard. Each order took up a whole pan—a whole burner—meaning we could cook only four of the things at once. And sauté was also plating oysters because the lone salamander was on that station; so while I'd popped the hinges on three sheet pans of the things, the sauté guys still had to set them on rock salt, nape each oyster with sauce, brown them under the salamander, plate them, carefully top each one with an oh-so-delicate little heap of caviar (of which there was a limited amount), then garnish before putting them up in the window. The beggar's purses were inexplicably coming off that station too, with only the soup and the foie gras coming off Frankie's area.

The machine was printing full-bore now, paper spitting out end over end, and Bobby calling it all out and stuffing copies in the slide. So far we were keeping up, racing to drill out what we could before it really hit the fan.

Two big tables—a ten-top, and a twelve, one after the other—and still no main courses had been fired yet; I looked over and saw that sauté was already in the weeds, that Frankie was spazzing out on all the foie gras orders, and that the truffle soup—which was supposed to be a layup—was not cooking as quickly as anticipated. Sure, the heating-the-soup part was a breeze, but the part where Frankie stretched precut squares of puff pastry dough over the ovenproof crocks was taking a lot longer than hoped. Frankie was fumbling with the dough, which either broke because it was too cold from the refrigerator, or tore because it had been out of the refrigerator too long, or tore because Frankie was so high he was shaking—and Frankie wasn't so good at keeping a lot of orders in his head anyway, so the combination of minor frustrations and all those foie gras and the fact that the little crustless pieces of brioche that were supposed to accompany it kept burning in the toaster was taking its toll, pulling down the pace . . . already the oysters were stacking up on one end, getting cold waiting for the foie gras orders that were supposed to go with them, and Bobby (highest standards *only*, please) was sending them back for reheats and replates, which was causing some confusion as good became commingled with bad. And the printer kept clicking and the stack of orders that Bobby had yet to even call out while he waited for sauté and hot-app stations to catch up kept getting bigger and bigger (getting mixed up with the orders that he'd already called out and had yet to post in the slide), and it was clear, a half hour in, with not a single main course served—or even fired—that we were headed for collision.

Bobby's reaction to the ensuing crisis was to urge on Frankie. Forcefully. Some might say, considering Frankie's known pathologies, too forcefully: "Where's that FOIE, you idiot?! What the FUCK is up with that fucking FOIE!? What's WRONG with you, Frank? FRANK? Where's that fucking FOIE GRAS?"

Poor Frankie. He was spinning in place, trying to do ten things at once, and succeeding at none, eyes banging around in his skull, sweat pouring down his face, a dervish of confusion, the little four-burner stove full of melting foie gras and over-reducing sauce.

The runners' faces were starting to take on worried expressions as more time passed without anything coming up. A lone four-top went out—and was quickly returned as cold, causing Bobby to scream even more. Bobby tended to blame others in times of extremis. "You *idiots!*" he'd yowl at the runners when yet another order of oysters was sent back, making our already-stressed-out runners even more jumpy. And the printer, all the while still clicking and clacking and going *dit dit dit . . .*

The first of the front waiters appeared, inquiring fearfully about app orders, which made Bobby even crazier. There were easily fifty tables' worth of orders up on the board, God knows how many in Bobby's hand, and a long white strip of them curling onto the floor that Bobby had yet to even acknowledge—and nothing was coming out of the kitchen. Nothing. Bobby finally managed to slap cloches onto a few orders of oysters and foie and send them on their way; and when he finally began to take stock of what he had in his hand, and what was still coming in, and how, by now, the sauté station had come to a complete standstill, I think his brain shut down. The next waiters who came in asking about food got shrieked at.

"Just GET OUT! GET OUT OF THE FUCKING KITCH-EN!!"

The constant clicking from the computer, the background grumbling and swearing and cursing from the cooks, the back-and-forth questions necessary between line cooks working together like "Ready on Table Seven? Ready on those oysters and that scallop?" and the occasional whispered request from a runner combined was too much noise for the chef. He shouted: "SHUT UP! EVERYBODY SHUT THE FUCK UP! NOT A SINGLE FUCKING WORD! I WANT TOTAL SILENCE!"

He then issued orders for Matt to move some of the foie orders over to sauté, put Dougie in exclusive charge of the toaster, told Orlando and Steven both to get out of the way, and took over the sauté responsibilities himself, while abandoning expediting responsibility to me.

The pile of intermingled dupes I inherited was discouraging. The board itself—meaning the orders that had already been begun, or fired—was a mess, with orders already dispatched mixed up with stuff still to come. I had no idea what had been called and what had yet to be called. Fortunately, the printer had calmed down. There was silence, *real* silence, as Bobby stepped into sauté and began putting together orders, running back and forth between hot-app station and his own to per-sonally make sure tables were complete before putting them in the window.

We managed to get some apps out, and some more, and even a few more—before runners started whispering in my ear that they needed entrees, like *now*. The printer was strangely silent still, and I was thankful for it, figuring they were backed up at the terminals downstairs, or that maybe, just maybe, between all the orders in my hand and the ones that I was slowly feeding onto the board and the pile I was getting ready to call out, maybe we'd actually got the whole dining room in. I called out a few fire orders for mains but Bobby just screamed: "SHUT UP! I DON'T WANT TO HEAR IT!" He was cooking foie gras orders now, in addition to doing the oysters, and the beggar's purses, and dealing with the sole, and though a very fine line cook, he was biting off way more than he, or any cook alive, could chew. Alone in his head, out there on the edge all by himself, ignoring me, ignoring the waiters, ignoring the other cooks, he was slinging pans at high speed, just trying, as best he could, to knock down some of those hanging tickets, to get the food out. So I just kept my mouth closed and clutched my stack of dupes and held my breath.

The printer. Something was wrong with it. I knew it. It was too quiet. It had been too long. Not a click or a clack for twenty minutes, not a single fire code or dessert order. I checked the roll of paper. No jam. The machine seemed plugged in. Jumping on the intercom, I called Joe, the deejay and techie who knew about such things, and asked him discreetly to check and see if there was a problem.

Apparently there was. Suddenly the machine came alive, clacking away like nobody's business, spitting out orders in a terrifying, unending stream, one after the other after the other, faster than I could tear them off: twenty-five minutes of backed-up orders we hadn't even heard about. Worried front waiters entered the kitchen, took one look at what was going on, and retreated silently. Nothing to be done here.

It was clear to all of us by now—except maybe Bobby, who

was still in his own ninth circle of personal restaurant hell, cursing and spitting and doing his best to cook, plate, and assemble orders, elbowing us out of the way as he ran heroically back and forth between stations—that we were now involved in a complete disaster. The situation was beyond saving. We could dig out . . . eventually. At some time, yes, we might feed these people. But we would not bring honor to our clan tonight. We would not go home proud. There would be no celebratory drinks at the end of this night (if it ever ended), only shame and recriminations.

Then I looked over at the kitchen doors and saw a particularly dismaying sight: three or four waiters clustered silently in the hallway. I hurried over to confer, away from Bobby's hearing. When waiters stop complaining, it is an unnatural thing. What were they doing out there? Things were bad in the dining room, I knew, but shouldn't they be down on the floor, putting out fires? Comping champagne? Reassuring their tables with self-deprecating apologies and offers of free cognac and port?

"What's up?" I inquired of the most reasonable of the lot, an aspiring playwright with many years of table service experience.

"Dude . . . they're drunk out there," he replied. "They've been sitting out there without food for an hour and a half. Drinking champagne. They've got nothing in their bellies but alcohol—and they're getting belligerent."

Veronica, a chubby waitress with (we had heard) a rose tattoo on her ass, was red faced and shaking. "A customer choked me," she cried, eyes filling with tears. "He stood up and put his hands around my neck and fucking *choked* me, screaming 'WHERE'S MY FUCKING FOOD?!' . . . It's out of control, Tony! I'm afraid to go out there. We all are!"

I rushed back to the kitchen, where Bobby was successfully

putting out a few tables of appetizers. But orders were still coming back. There was more stuff coming back than going out, and with all the replates and refires, the caviar supply was running low.

"Bobby," I said, carefully. "I think we should 86 the oysters."

"We are *not* 86ing the fucking oysters," snarled Bobby.

The kitchen doors swung open. It was Larry the waiter with tears running down his face. Now this was about as bad a sign as you could see, as Larry only moonlighted as a waiter. His day job was as a cop in the South Bronx. What, on the floor of a restaurant, could be so bad, so frightful, so monstrous as to cause a ten-year veteran of the force, a guy who'd been shot twice in the line of duty, to become so traumatized?

"They're beating the customers," Larry wailed. "People are getting up and trying to leave—and security is beating them! They're going fucking nuts!"

"It's out of control," moaned Ed, the runner. "It's a nightmare."

NiteKlub, it should be pointed out, usually operated as exactly that once the dinner shift was over. Consequently, we employed a security staff of twenty-three heavily muscled gorillas. These folks, though quite nice when not frog-marching you out the front door or dragging you down the steps, were employed to deal with the more rigorous demands of keeping order in a busy dance club: organized posses of gate-crashers, out-of-control drunks, belligerent ex-boyfriends—many of them potentially armed. They were frequently injured, often for giving a momentary benefit of doubt, for instance, to some barely-out-of-adolescence knucklehead half their weight denied entry to the VIP area, who promptly sucker-punched them or cold-cocked them with a beer bottle. This kind of thing gave our average security guy a rather shorter fuse than most ordinary restaurant floor staff. That this was a tonier crowd was a distinction security could hardly be expected to make. Especially as the customers were drunk and outraged at having spent hundreds of dollars for nothing, and heading for the doors in droves. Though they were said to be dealing out beat-downs to middle-aged couples from the suburbs who'd only wanted a nice New Year's Eve and some swing music, they could hardly be blamed for following the same orders they had been given every other night.

"I'm not going back out there. For anything," said Larry.

We tried. We did the best we could that awful night. To his credit, Bobby cooked as hard and as fast as he could until the very end, pretty much doing everything himself, unwilling or unable to trust anyone to help him out of the hole he'd put us all in. It was probably the wisest thing to do. Between my calling and his cooking, there was a nice, direct simplicity, less chance of confusion. We served—eventually—a lot of cold baked oysters (many without caviar) and undercooked foie gras, leathery Dover sole and overcooked lobster, lukewarm birds and roasted beef.

1991 slipped into 1992 without notice or mention in the kitchen. No one dared speak. The word "Happy" in relation to anything would not have occurred to any of us. At twelve forty-five, in what was perhaps the perfect coda to the evening, a lone, bespectacled customer in a rumpled tuxedo entered the kitchen, wandered up to the sauté end (where Bobby was still doing his best to get out entrees), and, peering back at the stove, asked, in a disconcertingly bemused voice: "Pardon me . . . but is that my appetizer order?"

He'd been waiting for it since eight forty-five.

I thought he'd showed remarkable patience.

At the end of the night, as it turned out, management had to comp (meaning return money) for $7,500 worth of meals. A few overzealous security goons had (allegedly) incited a few of our guests to file lawsuits claiming varying degrees of violent assault. And the effect on the kitchen staff was palpable.

Dougie and Steven quit. Adam became a titanic discipline problem, his respect for his chef declining to the point that it would, much later, lead to fisticuffs. Morale sank to the point that cooks arrived high—rather than waiting until later. And I got the chef's job after Bobby, wisely, went elsewhere.

And I learned. Nobody likes a "learning experience"—translating as it does to "a total ass-fucking"—but I learned. When the next year's New Year's Eve event loomed, I planned. I planned that mother like Ike planned Normandy. My menu was circulated (to management, floor, and every cook), discussed, tested, and retested. Each and every menu choice was an indestructible ocean liner classic—preseared or half-cooked hours before the first guest arrived. There wasn't an oyster in sight, or on any of the many New Year's menus I've done since. Just slice and serve terrine of foie gras. Slap-and-serve salads. *My* truffle soup the next year (it had been a good idea, actually) sat prebowled and precovered in a hot bain, ready to toss in the oven. I spread dishes around evenly between stations, imagining always the worst-case scenario. As, of course, I'd lived through it. My tournedos were preseared and required only a pop in the oven, some reheated spuds, a quickly tossed medley of veg, and a ready-to-pour sauce. My lobsters took a swift pop under the salamander. I'd be proud of the fact that *my* New Year's went flawlessly, that *my* full dining room of customers went home happy and content, and that I, unlike the vastly-more-talented-but-less-organized Bobby, brought honor and profit to my masters.

But the fact is, I could have served the following year's menu with a line crew of chimps. The food was nowhere as good as it could have been. My food arrived fast. It arrived hot. It arrived at the same time as the other orders on the table. But it was no better (or worse) than what a bunch of overdressed drunks dumb enough to eat at our club expected. Having tasted total defeat the previous year, when my last entree went out at eleven thirty, leaving only the mopping-up operations (aka desserts), I was ebullient. Not a single order had come back. I jumped up on the stainless-steel table we'd used to stack assembled dishes and beat my chest and congratulated one and all. We turned up the music, peeled off our reeking whites, changed into our street clothes, and I ordered us up a few pitchers of Long Island Iced Teas and beer. We drank like champions. And felt like champions. We went home exhausted but proud.

Sometimes, you just have to make compromises to get the job done.

Ship of Fools
JIMMY BRADLEY

Jimmy Bradley co-owns and operates a number of New York City restaurants that started out as neighborhood joints and wound up as destinations for diners from across the country: the Red Cat, the Harrison, the Mermaid Inn, and (the more grandscaled) Pace. After attending the University of Rhode Island, Bradley worked in some of Philadelphia and Rhode Island's top kitchens before becoming executive chef of Savoir Fare, a progressive Martha's Vineyard bistro where he began his trademark style of straightforward, boldly flavored seasonal cooking.

T HIS STORY WOULD never happen today. It probably could only have taken place in the 1980s, when drug and alcohol abuse in the restaurant industry were at their zenith. The names of the restaurant, the chef, and the owner have been changed to protect the innocent, the not-so-innocent, and—most importantly—myself.

In 1986, I was a young cook working in a seaside resort town along the coast of Rhode Island, not unlike the kind of place you

might find along the Jersey Shore. I worked for a restaurant—
we'll call it the Harbor Cove Inn—that was one of the better
eateries in the area, one of the few places that didn't make its
money on an autopilot menu of baked scrod with Ritz cracker
crumbs, lobster Newburg, and baked stuffed shrimp.

The Harbor Cove Inn was as close to fine dining as it got in
this town, a nondescript, carpeted dining room; walls papered
with parchment; a staff of salty locals, high school students, and
college kids; and a small but serviceable kitchen in the back.

Credit for our noteworthy offerings belonged to the chef—
we'll call him Fernando—a Puerto Rican who had worked in
New York City and, through some cruel twist of fate that I
never really understood, wound up in this tiny hamlet. I liked
Fernando. He was talented, both creatively and as a kitchen
technician. And he liked me, enough that he promoted me from
line cook to sous-chef in a very short time.

The third character in this ill-fated tale is the restaurant's
owner, a Rhode Island wise guy who for our purposes will go by
the name of Frankie. You've seen men like Frankie in the
movies, or on *The Sopranos*—connected guys who have their
hands in a mix of local businesses. Frankie owned not only a
restaurant but also an auto dealership and a liquor store, and he
was on the board of just about every committee in town. Like
those movie and TV characters, Frankie had a base of operations, an office in a huge complex, where he ran his empire, his
only visible aid coming from the "girl" at the secretary station
outside his office, a sweet, maternal figure named (not really)
Delores.

Frankie was a real local character. He might not have stood
out much in New York or New Jersey, but in this little Rhode
Island town, his three-piece suits combined with his diminutive
stature and bruiser's gait made it easy to spot him from a mile

away—as did his hair, which, though he was only in his mid- to late thirties, was prematurely gray.

I had been working at the Harbor Cove Inn for eight or nine months when, one February day, a ray of sunshine broke upon my bleak New England winter. Frankie strutted into the restaurant and, apropos of nothing, pulled aside me and Fernando. "Listen," he told us, "I just saw this new space that's up for grabs. I think we could do something really nice there. You guys can have some more creative freedom, the town'll get another good restaurant, and we'll all make some more money. Everybody's gonna win."

Fernando and I couldn't have been more excited. We drove over to check out the space and discovered, to our delight, a charming little converted house with enough space between its white clapboard walls and the street to allow for outdoor seating in the spring and summer. Inside, the dining room had space enough to comfortably accommodate about a hundred people—significantly more than the Harbor Cove—and a bar from which we could already imagine the flow of white Zinfandels and Fuzzy Navels, the drinks of the moment in 1980s Rhode Island beach towns.

We headed straight back to the Harbor Cove and started making up dishes for the new place—doing our thing with lobster, filet mignon, and veal—running them as nightly specials starting that very day.

Over the next four months, we did everything in our power to ensure that when the restaurant opened in the summer, it would make a big splash—continuing to evolve those dishes, designing the kitchen, and so on.

Come summertime, Frankie planned a big opening party for the new restaurant. We had what was supposed to be our last meeting a week before the party, but on the day of the party, Frankie abruptly summoned us to another meeting. When we arrived, Fernando and I were in sky-high spirits, chattering about how much fun we were going to have that night.

And then, Frankie threw a big wet blanket over the two of us. "Listen, fellas," he said, "the rest of the investors and I talked it over and we decided that, since this is really an invite-only party, you two shouldn't be there."

It took a moment for this to sink in. After all, how could the chef and sous-chef not attend the opening of the restaurant they'd just spent four months getting ready? Did it mean we were being fired? I glanced over at Fernando, who looked equally worried.

"Shouldn't *one* of us be there?" Fernando said, taking a shot at an appeal.

Frankie shook his little gray head.

"No. You guys did a great job getting the food ready, but I really need you to stay back at the Harbor Cove Inn and make sure things run smoothly there tonight."

Heads hanging low, and wondering if our livelihoods were at stake—not to mention feeling considerably insulted—we returned to the Harbor Cove Inn and did what cooks do: our jobs, sullenly starting to prep for that evening's service. In an attempt to take my mind off the situation, I turned on the radio I kept at my station, and even started making a big vat of spaghetti sauce for the next day, stirring it with a long, paddlelike wand as it simmered away.

But Fernando was consumed with anger. For the next hour, I watched it boil up within him. He didn't say a word, but everything he did was fueled by fury. When he'd put a sauté pan to the flame, he'd bang it down like he was clubbing someone over the head. When he'd cut a cucumber, he'd bring the knife down so hard, I was sure he was picturing Frankie's neck there on his cutting board.

One thing was certain: if Fernando didn't get a grip, this was going to be a long night.

Less than an hour before service, Fernando was still stomping around, slamming refrigerator doors and flinging pans into the sink. The kitchen staff was on edge and the waiters were nervously keeping their distance. I took it upon myself to perform an intervention.

"Chef, what're we gonna do about this? We gotta find a way to chill out."

Fernando ignored me, continuing his sadistic vivisection of yet another hapless vegetable. But then, suddenly, he was gripped with inspiration. He put down his knife, turned, and looked me in the eye. "Fuck this!" he said. "You wanna know what the fuck we're gonna do? I'll tell you what the fuck we're gonna do!"

I stepped back, thinking, Oh, shit. This ain't gonna be good.

Fernando was possessed with a dark clarity that, if it weren't so scary, would have been impressive. He began barking orders to the kitchen staff: "*You*, go get me a bucket. *You*, go get me three bottles of vodka and two bottles of triple sec. *You*, go get a big mess of limes and squeeze 'em, and bring me the juice. *You*, bring me some ice."

Those of us who weren't scattered about to do Fernando's bidding stood there in rapt anticipation, watching our commander in chief, wondering where this was all headed.

"And *me*," he said, the glimmer in his eye approaching supernova status. "I'm gonna stand here and make five gallons worth of shots."

Shots? So he was going to get hammered? Big deal.

If only that were the case.

Fernando wasn't just going to get himself hammered. He had devised a new drinking game for the express entertainment of the staff of the Harbor Cove Inn. He summoned the entire crew—the waiters, the bartenders, the busboys, the dishwashers, and the cooks—and began to explain the rules. Normally, the maitre d' would've stepped in and put a stop to this, but—guess what?—he was invited to the party. The cat was away, so to speak.

"Listen up," Fernando said to us. "I've come to a decision and I feel strongly about it. This is what's going to happen tonight: if you are going to perform any duty that has anything to do with fulfilling your job, then before you do that duty, you *must* do a shot. So, bartenders, if you're going to make a drink, you do a shot. Busboys, if you're going to clear a table, you do a shot. Waiters, before you take a tray of food to a table, you do a shot. Dishwashers, before you take a rack out of the steamer, you do a shot."

We were all taken aback by this scheme, but before we could say a word in protest, Fernando cemented the deal.

"Okay. Right now. Everybody, let's do a shot. Come on!"

We obeyed our orders, even the fresh-faced kids, and knocked back a shot. Then we got into positions for the first guests.

I must admit that much of that evening is a blur to me. It was like being on a ship that was rocking to and fro; I and everybody else were doing our best just to stay on our feet, wobbling and weaving and fighting occasional bouts of nausea, yet somehow, miraculously, maintaining verticality.

As the evening wore on, Fernando got more and more aggressive with the game. Doing a shot became part of his commands: "We need some more sauté pans over here. Bring me some sauté pans *and do a shot*." "Table Twelve is ready. Pick up Table Twelve *and do a shot*."

By eight thirty, the kitchen was inundated with orders, and struggling to work through. Fernando, though drunk, had enough presence of mind to know that we were at the point of no return. He once again summoned the entire staff into the kitchen, including the front-of-the-house team.

With everyone assembled, dizzily listing to one side, or leaning on each other for balance, Fernando continued his fierce display of leadership. "Okay, guys. We're almost there. One last big push and we're through the night. I know you can all do it . . . so let's do a shot and keep on going."

As we all did yet another shot, Fernando came over to my station and turned the radio up full blast. The kitchen was flooded with the theme song of *Hawaii Five-O: Buh buh buh buh buh buh. Ba puh puh puh puh.*

Fernando took the wand out of my hand and began rowing an imaginary canoe.

. . . buh buh buh buh buh buh . . .

He did it with such gusto that I joined in, paddling in synch with the music and my fearless leader . . .

. . . bah puh puh puh puh . . .

One by one, the entire staff joined in, grabbing paddles, and when those ran out, tongs, spatulas, wooden spoons, anything that would get the idea across.

I later learned that, unbeknownst to us, at about the time Fernando was giving us his pep talk, Frankie had returned to the Harbor Cove Inn from his party. He had walked in through the front door and seen a dining room full of customers, with not one staff member in sight. No coffee was being poured, no bread was being served, no dirty plates were being cleared—just a lot of confused diners wondering what the hell was going on.

And at the moment that we were all hopping on board the incredible, invisible canoe, Frankie had come into the kitchen, witnessed the spectacle for himself, and slipped back out. Amazingly, he went unnoticed by the entire drunken lot of us.

The next day, I managed to find my way back to the Harbor Cove Inn. Fernando, professional that he was, was already there. Also on hand was the general manager, who had been at the party the night before. We didn't know why, but the manager gave us the cold shoulder all morning. "What's *his* problem," I wondered. "*He* got to go to the party."

Later that morning, we got a call from Delores, Frankie's secretary, informing us that Frankie wanted us to come to his office for a meeting.

Fernando and I smiled at each other. Surely, we thought, we were being summoned over for a belated apology for the party slight.

We drove to the complex that housed Frankie's office and took the elevator up to his suite. As always, Delores was sitting at the desk outside.

"Hi ya, boys, how ya doin'?"

"Great, Delores. You?"

"Okay, I guess."

"What's Frankie want?"

"I don't know. He wouldn't say. But go on in. He's ready for you."

Fernando and I exchanged a wry smile and I opened the door to Frankie's office, a huge, Spartan room with wraparound picture windows that offered a spectacular view of the Atlantic.

Frankie had one of those old-fashioned, high-backed leather executive chairs and when we entered the room, he was seated in it, facing the ocean. We couldn't see him at all. As we sat on the couch in front of the desk, we found ourselves staring at this monolithic wall of leather.

We waited in silence for what felt like a week. Frankie didn't make a sound, just let us sit there, wondering what was coming.

Finally, he spun around in the chair. His face was purple with anger. He stood up and leaned forward against the desk, putting the palms of his hands on the shiny black surface for support, and stared us both right in the eyes. But he didn't say a word. Instead, he picked up the newspaper and walked around to our side of the desk. Then he tossed the paper at our chests and sauntered out the door.

Fernando and I looked at each other in bewilderment, then down at the paper. Staring back at us was the "Help Wanted" section, opened to the page featuring Restaurants and Bars.

"Are we fired?" I asked Fernando.

"I don't know."

We left the office and found Delores parked at her desk.

"Hey, Delores, are we fired?"

"Yeah. I'm sorry, boys. Frankie just told me on the way out. He said to have you escorted out of the building, and to tell you that he'd like to never see either of you again."

I've been in the restaurant business for close to twenty years. That was the first time I was fired, and—since I own my own places now—probably the last.

Fernando doesn't own his own restaurants, but the two of us found work just two days later in another fine restaurant about five miles away from Frankie's joint, and Fernando's still working there to this day. So even though we haven't spoken in years, I like to think that he looks back on that night with humor and some measure of pride, for giving us one hell of an evening to look back on . . . even if we can't remember many of the details.

If You Can't Stand the Heat
SCOTT BRYAN

Scott Bryan is the executive chef of Veritas in New York City. He began his career working for his mentor, Bob Kinkead of the Harvest restaurant in Boston (currently the chef-owner of Kinkead's in Washington, D.C.), whom he also worked for at 21 Federal on Nantucket. Bryan went on to learn at many of the best restaurants in New York, including Gotham Bar and Grill, Restaurant Bouley, Le Bernardin, Lespinasse, and Mondrian, as well as Square One in San Francisco. In 1994, he became executive chef of Soleil, then of Alison on Dominick Street, after which he entered into a partnership with Gino Diaferia that spawned a series of restaurants including Luma, Indigo, and ultimately Veritas. In 1996, Bryan was named one of the Best New Chefs in the United States by Food & Wine Magazine.

T HIS IS A story about practicality, or rather about the highs and lows that impracticality can visit upon you.

When I was a cook, I worked for a number of great chefs, more than most guys have. I took from each of them what I could.

Alfred Portale was the best *garde manger* I'd ever seen; he did beautiful, graceful things with herbs and greens, dressing and seasoning them better than anyone I had worked with before, or have since. David Bouley was the most artistic; he could pull stuff out of his hat that nobody else would have thought of—*and* make it work. He also taught me how to plate food from the center out, a valuable technique that has stayed with me to this day.

But, in many ways, the man who had the biggest influence on me was one of the least famous chefs who ever hired me, Robert Kinkead, whom I worked for at a restaurant called the Harvest way back when I was just getting started.

I think of Kinkead as my mentor because he taught me about *both* parts of being a chef: technique and management. While less recognized, the second is just as important, because if you can't manage a kitchen, you can't get the food done the way you want it and you *will* fail.

Don't get me wrong, I didn't respect Kinkead only for his ability to marshal the troops. He was a great chef. I include him in my personal pantheon of masters because he was the best *saucier* I ever worked with.

But of the many impressive things I learned from Kinkead, perhaps the most invaluable was to let your staff express an idea. If you had a thought for a new dish, or even a way to improve an existing one, he'd listen. If he didn't like it, he would tell you why. But if he *did*, he'd implement it.

You can call it being modest, or humble, or just open-minded. Whatever it is, it's practical. If you see a better way, why *wouldn't* you go with it?

Unfortunately, it isn't like that in every kitchen. I remember trying to offer my two cents on a dish at Square One restaurant in San Francisco, and being quietly reprimanded with the house catchphrase: "We don't do that here."

Kinkead's lack of pretension and ego, his reverence for the practical, stuck with me so much that it would become the reason I left one of the most famous kitchens in the United States after just six months.

But it's amazing that it took that long.

I did things in the opposite order of a lot of guys. I had worked for a bunch of American chefs before I ever spent time in a French kitchen. My impression was that I had probably learned to do everything fast and half-assed, and I always wondered what it would be like to cook in a more formal kitchen organized after the French model.

This impulse reached critical mass the night I had an extraordinary dinner at Bouley in 1987. Restaurant Bouley was one of the few four-star restaurants in New York, and I came away from the meal having finally made up my mind to go for it and see how I fared in a place like that.

I spent the next few years working in some of the best restaurants in town, including Bouley itself, as well as Mondrian and Le Bernardin. But, without a doubt, the most memorable time I spent in a four-star kitchen, for mostly the wrong reasons, was at Lespinasse.

Lespinasse, if you don't know, was situated in the St. Regis Hotel, which had just undergone a renovation that cost something like $100 million. The new dining room was the most opulent one in town, so extravagant and old fashioned that you could have worn a powdered wig and Restoration-era costume in to dinner and looked right at home.

Gray Kunz, who now presides over Café Gray in the Time Warner Center, had made a name for himself at the Peninsula Hotel. Gray is a soft-spoken Swiss guy, a true gentleman, who was raised partially in Singapore and had worked under the legendary Fredy Girardet. He had also cooked in Hong Kong for years, so he brought all kinds of Asian ingredients to his menu, which was far less common in those days.

Lespinasse was supposed to be the Next Big Thing, and it was widely expected that it would receive four stars, which it did. After a series of interviews with Gray, I was hired as one of two *poissonniers* (fish cooks), starting work just two weeks after the restaurant opened.

There were two kitchens at Lespinasse: one for the restaurant, and another kitchen around a corner that handled room service for the hotel, which we had nothing to do with. As you might expect, the restaurant kitchen was an intense and serious place. Each cook kept his head down and was focused on the job at hand. When I started, I jumped right in, preparing the dishes that had been described to me in the morning, and cooking them for lunch service that day.

After only a few hours, however, I began to notice problems that seemed odd, especially for such a well-funded enterprise. The kitchen was big and roomy, with state-of-the-art equipment, but it was oppressively hot. The extreme heat was only aggravated by the fact that Gray, a classicist, insisted we wear hats and neckerchiefs at all times. (Eventually, I stopped wearing underwear to lower my body temperature a few degrees, but it didn't help much.)

Additionally, at the end of my first night, I discovered another, even more bizarre oddity: there wasn't enough staff. There were plenty of cooks, sure, but there weren't any porters, not a single one, and no cleaning crew, either. Which meant that after putting in a full day in a sweltering hot kitchen, you had to clean all your utensils, lay them out according to Gray's precise instructions on your prep table, and then mop the floor at your station.

Since we all started our day at about seven thirty in the morning, these late nights, which typically ran to one thirty or two a.m., cost the restaurant a small fortune, as we were each paid time-and-a-half after our first eight hours.

Impractical? To say the least.

But impracticality can also create some memorable by-products, and Lespinasse's food was stunningly, gloriously impractical. I'll tell you right now that I will never again see anything like the food we did there.

Most restaurants at the level of a Lespinasse strive to keep their food costs (the ratio of expense to menu price) anywhere from 30 to 40 percent. Ours, however, easily ran to 60. For example, one item on the tasting menu was a sweetbread dish that featured a perfectly turned, cooked artichoke bottom topped with a spoonful of wild-mushroom risotto and a nugget of sautéed sweetbread, all surrounded by a shallow moat of black truffle sauce. It easily cost thirty-five dollars to make, and it was just one of the *five* tasting menu dishes—a meal that sold for the whopping grand total of eighty-five dollars.

Chefs dream about those kinds of dishes, and it was something to behold so many of them under one roof.

I'll say it one more time: I'll never see that kind of thing again.

Every day at Lespinasse was crazed. We were all working ridiculous hours, eighteen to twenty per day, with just thirty minutes off after lunch service, and sometimes seven days a week. During my busiest week, I logged 126 hours.

Within a couple months, the nonstop hours and the pressure began to take their toll. Cooks were still able to perform their work, but they were often in a semiconscious state. Guys would get careless, cut their fingers, be too tired or distracted to keep the wound clean, and end up out for a week with an infection.

One guy let an ingrown toenail go for so long that he had to take a leave of absence. I started to understand how soldiers did desperate things, like shooting themselves in the foot, to get discharged and sent home.

One Saturday morning, I was informed by the manager that Cristophe, the French cook who was the other *poissonnier*, had called in sick. I was going to have to run the station on my own.

"Did he give any details?" I asked.

The manager shook his head. "Just sick."

That's weird, I thought, because Cristophe had gone home the night before—which in that kitchen meant just a few hours earlier—looking fine. And Cristophe was a seasoned professional, with great credentials, having worked at such restaurants as Taillevent, one of the best places in Paris.

The next day, Cristophe called in sick again. And the next. In fact, he continued to make a morning phone call every day for the rest of the week, all of them with the same message: I'm sick and I won't be coming in.

The following Saturday, Cristophe returned to the kitchen, looking fresh and pink cheeked. I pulled him into the walk-in and confronted him.

"What the fuck? You don't seem sick. You sure as hell weren't sick when you went home last Friday night. What happened?"

Cristophe looked off into the distance, which in the walk-in meant up into a plastic bin full of arugula on the highest rack.

"Man," he said, in his thick French accent, the word full of wistful weariness. "I went home last Friday night and went to bed. I woke up Saturday. I was so depressed. So I call in sick. I woke up Sunday, I was still depressed. I went out to lunch. It was so great to go to lunch. So I don't come in Monday . . ."

*   *   *

I stayed at Lespinasse for six months. I might have stayed longer, but something happened that had nothing to do with how crazy the kitchen was, and everything to do with how impractical it was—and also with the lasting impression that Kinkead made on me.

At my station, there were two salamanders, long broiling machines that are open on both sides with a heating element under the lid. They were both to be kept on at all times.

But one quiet Sunday night, with few customers in the restaurant, I turned off one of the salamanders. We used them for only a single dish, a braised snapper that was flashed under the heat for a quick second before being served. I could get four servings in one salamander at a time, or eight if I turned the plates in a certain direction. And we *never*, not even on our busiest night, got hit with four orders simultaneously.

One of the sous-chefs, a guy about my age, came up to me and informed me that Gray wanted both salamanders on at all times.

"Yeah, I know, but it's wicked hot in here and we never get more than four orders at once."

"Sorry, Scott, that's the way Gray wants it."

"That's ridiculous. Tell him I'll take responsibility. If there's a fuckup, you can fire me."

"Scott . . ."

Give me a break!, I thought. Sweat was soaking through my uniform and they wanted me to sit there in my own little private tanning salon? I pointed up in the general direction of the office, one flight up from the kitchen: "Go tell Gray I'm not doing it."

The sous-chef walked off toward Gray's office. A few minutes later, he returned and told me Gray wanted to see me upstairs.

I climbed the stairs to Gray's office. He was sitting behind a large desk, dressed immaculately. He waved me in and, dispensing with the formalities, politely laid down the law.

"You have to have two salamanders on at all times. You can't say no to the chef."

"Gray, you and I both know it's not that busy, and it's not gonna get that busy. I can fit eight dishes in that thing."

He remained cool, utterly impassive: "Scott, you can't say no to the chef."

Fuck that, I thought, this isn't Hong Kong, where you can exploit your workers. This is America.

"You have to do it," he said. "Or leave."

We looked at each other for a long moment, neither one of us speaking. Gray crossed his arms, waiting. And I'll tell you truthfully, even if it hadn't been such a strange and exhausting six months, I would have done what I did next.

"Okay. Then I guess I'm giving you my two-week notice."

Gray shook his head. "No. If you're not going to obey the chef, you have to leave now."

"Then I'll get my stuff."

We shook hands, I collected my things, and left.

And that was how my time at Lespinasse came to a close.

Neither Gray nor I hold a grudge about the day I quit. Gray even sends me some foie gras and kugel (noodle pudding) every Christmas. We don't hold a grudge because it's a small world in our business, and we're both good guys at the end of the day. And on top of all that, it just wouldn't be practical.

White Lie

DAVID BURKE

The chef/owner of davidburke&donatella, David Burke first rose to prominence at New York's River Cafe. He then went on to become executive chef of Park Avenue Cafe and vice president of Culinary Development for the Smith & Wollensky Restaurant Group. Burke trained at the Culinary Institute of America and alongside legends such as Pierre Troisgros, Georges Blanc, and Gaston Lenôtre. He has been a part of several American Culinary Gold Cup Competitions, was voted Chef of the Year by his peers in America in 1991, and was the first non-Frenchman to win the Meilleurs Ouvriers de France Association medal and diploma, France's highest cooking honor. He is the creator of several gourmet packaged goods and the author of Cooking with David Burke.

S EVERAL YEARS BACK, one of my customers, a real nice lady, told me that she wanted me to cater a fiftieth-birthday party for her husband. They were an artistic pair, with friends in the arts and entertainment field, and she flattered me right into it: "We love your food. It's unique and different, and I know you'll do something that'll make him happy. Please, won't you do it?"

How can you say no to that?

The details were manageable: Two hundred people. A huge, rented event hall with a decent kitchen. A couple of hors d'oeuvres, two main courses to choose from, dessert. The usual.

I said I'd be happy to. Hell, it'd be my honor.

And *then* she tells me that there's a hook. The birthday boy loves surprises, and is a soufflé fanatic, and she wants to combine these passions, blowing him away with a giant floating island—the classic French dessert that features clouds of meringue adrift in a sea of custard—his favorite thing in the world. She envisioned an island big enough to serve two hundred rolling into the room as the climax of the celebration, the pièce de résistance.

I didn't know how in the world I was going to make such a thing, so as we shook on it, I said what any good chef would say.

"No problem."

I had to be out of town for a few days leading right up to the day of the party, so my team and I had a planning meeting before I left. We went over the canapés, the meal, and then came up with a pretty straightforward strategy for the dessert. The pastry chef would make twenty enormous meringue clouds and bake them. Then we would press them together and, simply because of the tacky nature of meringue, they would stick to one another. Finally, we'd transfer them into the biggest bowl we could find, surround the island with crème anglaise, shower it with mint and powdered sugar, and float candles in the crème.

We weren't going to serve this thing, mind you. No, no, no.

We were going to wheel it into the hall on a cart—like a wedding cake, if you will—let everyone sing "Happy Birthday," then wheel it out. Behind the scenes, we'd have already made two hundred individual servings, ready to be presented in their ramekins. Everyone would think that the giant island had been divvied up; in reality it would just be thrown away.

On the day of the party, I was about to board an airplane back to New York, when one of the guys called me on my cell to tell me there was a problem with the meringue.

"Don't worry about it. We'll deal with it when I'm on the ground," I said, and hung up. How bad could it be?

Arriving at the banquet hall that afternoon, I was impressed. My customer had spared no expense, turning it into an elegant dining space, with white linens, exotic floral centerpieces, and a very sexy lighting design.

But when I left this little paradise and pushed through the door into the dark kitchen, I saw that the meringues had all collapsed when baked. They were flat and big as manhole covers, and totally useless.

I turned to my pastry chef. "*And*," he said with the grin of one who thrives on adversity, "there ain't no more egg whites to be had."

He knew what he was talking about. It was a Sunday, and a few of the cooks had made a trip to all the markets in the immediate vicinity, only to discover that they had been mercilessly picked over, with maybe a carton or two of eggs remaining per store.

There's some genetic thing that chefs have. A perfectionist gene, I guess. I could have done something easy to get out of this predicament. I could have piled up the two hundred finished servings in a big pyramid, lit the hell out of it with candles, and probably everyone would have been happy. It wouldn't have been a *Guinness Book*–worthy floating island, but it would have worked fine.

However, one of my customers had ordered a floating island, damn it, and I was gonna give it to them.

"We have to do something," I muttered to myself. "This is the pièce de résistance. We have to do something . . ."

I stood there, eyes closed. Thinking. Thinking. All the while feeling the gaze of my team upon me . . .

"Okay, I got it!" I said, and my crew's eyes lit up. Here was the quick thinking they expected from their leader.

But what I said next was definitely *not* what they had planned on: "Everybody, bring me your dirty laundry. Aprons, towels, chef coats, whatever." I paused, then clarified: "As long as it's white."

I went over to our supply table and found the big white garbage bags we used to clean up after ourselves at events like this. I walked around, holding the bag open wide with both hands, like somebody taking a collection, and the guys threw all their linens inside.

We loaded the bag into the enormous bowl that was supposed to have the meringue in it, teased the plastic to create little meringuelike wisps, and poured the crème anglaise around it. Then we dusted it with powdered sugar and mint leaves, and lit the floating votives that were standing in for birthday candles, setting them afloat in the custard.

It looked just like it was supposed to—a giant floating island—even though it was really a miniature garbage barge.

Right before we wheeled this decoy out into the banquet hall, I instructed my guys to stand around it and sing "Happy Birthday" along with the other guests. Their mission was twofold: one, to provide a security detail for the barge, making sure nobody touched it; and, two, to sing at a really fast clip, so the song would be over and the island was out of sight as quickly as possible.

We walked out into the room singing "Happy Birthday" and the entire place stood up and cheered, oohing and ahhing at the sight of the beautiful floating island. As soon as the last speedy note had been sung, my guys helped the guest of honor blow out his candles. He maybe blew one out himself.

Then we ran the cart out of the room and into the kitchen. We dismantled it immediately, just in case someone came back looking to take a picture or something.

The desserts were served and nobody was the wiser. It was a triumph of on-your-feet thinking, if I do say so myself.

I'm still pretty friendly with that woman, and her husband. I never did tell them about the secret of the floating island, though if they see this, the jig is up.

Well, she *did* say that he loved surprises as much as he loved meringue.

Surprise!

A Simple Request
SAMUEL CLARK

Samuel Clark is partners with his wife, Samantha Clark, and the couple are known to the British food lovers simply as Sam and Sam Clark. They met working at the Eagle gastropub, and then worked together at London's famed River Cafe. They spent their honeymoon touring Morocco and Spain, then opened Moro in the Clerkenwell district of London in 1997, with their associates Mark Sainsbury and Jake Hodges. The restaurant won both the Time Out *and* BBC Good Food *awards for Best New Restaurant. Sam and Sam Clark are authors of* The Moro Cookbook *and* Casa Moro: The Second Cookbook.

I N THE LATE 1980s, when I was a young cook just out of cooking college, not yet employed in a restaurant, the famous British art dealer Adrian Ward-Jackson, a friend of my mother, informed me that he was having Princess Margaret round to dinner.

"Perhaps you'd like to cook for us," he suggested very sweetly, downplaying the enormity of the suggestion.

How could I resist? It was a thrilling proposition.

"Great. Sure," I said, attempting to contain my excitement.

When the day of the dinner arrived, I shopped for the freshest and finest of ingredients, as befitted a royal affair such as this, and then made my way to Adrian's flat in Mayfair. It was a beautiful home, modest in scope but very richly and ornately decorated. Adrian also dealt in antiques, so the sitting room was crowded with paintings, sculptures, and various objets d'art. And the overall design of the home was the equal of the collection it housed; every fabric was textured; every surface, polished to the perfect finish. Despite the lavish decorations, it was also remarkably cozy, and had the effect of putting one quite at ease, rather than causing any undue intimidation.

The kitchen, too, was delightful, done up in wonderful découpage. For instance, the refrigerator was made to look like a bookcase loaded with clothbound classics; but when you pulled on the door, it of course opened and inside were the bright, fully functioning shelves of a refrigerator.

In preparation for the evening, I had made a number of careful decisions, all of them intended to eliminate any element of risk. I hadn't yet worked in restaurants or developed my own personal style, so for the menu, I turned to the same dishes most cooking students would make: I prepared a soup (though I can't for the life of me remember what kind), and a rack of lamb with potatoes Dauphinoise, and for dessert a rhubarb fool, a mousse made by folding rhubarb compote into whipped cream.

My goal was to prepare a meal that could be described as unadventurous but delicious, if only ultimately of very average quality. Put another way: my mission was not to embarrass myself.

To remove any lofty expectations, I even downplayed my culinary education, dressing for the occasion in a beautiful shirt and apron, in no way indicative of any professional training.

My attire and the meal selection were also intended to make me as comfortable as possible. I had been cooking in a home setting since I was a child, so I created the environment to which I was accustomed.

By all accounts, as the dinner hour approached, my plan seemed to be working. I spent the better part of the afternoon making the meal at a relaxed pace, feeling quite at ease. Adrian left me to go about my business, though I could hear him moving about, talking on the telephone, and so on.

Finally, I heard the princess arrive and felt a tingle of excitement. A member of the royal family was going to be enjoying a meal prepared by my hand! I was confident that she would enjoy it because most of the dishes were nearly finished: the lamb was attaining a lovely burnished golden brown exterior in the oven; the soup was done and kept nicely warm under a pot lid, even the rhubarb fool had been set to cool in the traditional serving vessels, long-stemmed, glass wine goblets that show off its brilliant ruby-red color.

Adrian's home was designed so that one passed by the kitchen on the way in from the front door to the dining room. As Adrian and the princess neared, I again felt a twinge of giddiness. No sooner had they completed their pass than Adrian reappeared, stuck his head in the door, and casually whispered, "Oh, by the way, I'd like to have some biscuits with dessert," before disappearing again, following after the princess.

What's that? I thought. Did he just say "biscuits"? How odd, because we never discussed biscuits.

Panic set in quickly. Christ, I thought. Biscuits! What am I going to do?

I hadn't planned on biscuits, hadn't brought along the ingredients necessary to make biscuits, and—if I'm to be honest—

didn't really know *how* to make biscuits, not being a pastry cook and not having any recipe books with me.

I can't very well march out there and tell them that I don't know how to make bloody biscuits, now, can I?

Adrian had employed a waiter for the evening and I sent the first course, the soup, out with him. As Adrian and Princess Margaret began their meal, I rooted hurriedly through the cupboards to see what ingredients I had at my disposal to pull off this last-minute request. The decoupage didn't seem quite so charming as all of a sudden my carefully laid plans were turning to rubbish.

In one of the cupboards, I found a box of inexpensive gingersnap cookies, known to all in England as a supermarket staple of completely unremarkable quality.

I studied the box in my hand, thinking: Okay, how can I make these taste different, better than they are?

On the counter, I espied a bottle of brandy and snapped my fingers.

I've got it!

I laid the cookies out in a glass baking dish and drizzled enough brandy over them to submerge them. Then I set them aside to let them soak.

When the waiter returned a little while later, I sent him out with the lamb and potatoes, and concentrated on finishing the dessert. As I began to lift a cookie from the dish, however, I discovered that it had become hopelessly limp, tearing in half like a soggy sheet of newspaper.

Hurriedly, I turned on the oven, still hot from the lamb, delicately transferred the cookies to a baking sheet with the aid of a spatula, and slid them inside.

It was a torturous situation: I had no time to lose, and yet I had to keep the heat relatively low, for fear of burning the cookies—or perhaps even igniting the alcohol. That would've been a truly fine mess, if I had started a fire in Adrian's miniature museum.

Time was ticking away and I stood shaking my head impatiently and looking into the oven, whispering to the cookies, "Dry, you bastards. Dry."

Finally, I couldn't delay the dessert any longer. I took the biscuits out of the oven, only to discover that they were still limp and soggy. As the waiter looked on in bemusement, I fanned them with my hand, trying to get them to dry just a little bit more, but it was hopeless.

I plated the biscuits, which were slightly hard around the edges and mushy in the center, with an alcoholic aroma emanating from them—and sent them out along with the glasses full of rhubarb fool.

To take my mind off of what must be transpiring in the dining room, I began cleaning up the kitchen, scrubbing the pots and pans, and returning the ingredients, including that box of gingersnaps, to their proper homes.

A few minutes later, a figure appeared in the kitchen door, but this time it wasn't the waiter; it was Adrian himself—holding the empty biscuits plate in his hands. With a twinkle in his eye, Adrian informed me that "Her Majesty would love some more biscuits." Then he disappeared back into the dining room.

It was an unbelievable turn of events. I could scarcely fathom how the appalling biscuits had been so well received. Not that it mattered much at that point. My astonishment was instantly overwhelmed by the realization that . . . *Christ! I have to go through all of that again*!

Hastily, I dug the box of gingersnaps out from the cupboard, sprinkled the bloody things with brandy, shoved them in the oven, took them out, fanned them like an idiot, and plated them, noisily bumping around the kitchen as if I were in some sort of vaudeville routine.

To this day, I don't know if Adrian and his royal guest were having a bit of fun at my expense. Perhaps, as I've sometimes imagined, they flushed the biscuits down the toilet and were only asking for a second serving as a sort of private, though good-natured joke.

When Adrian brought the princess round on her way out the door, she stopped by the kitchen to say, "Thank you for a lovely meal."

I wanted to ask if she really had liked the biscuits, but there simply wasn't any appropriate way of doing so.

"You're quite welcome, Your Majesty," I said. "I'm glad you enjoyed it."

I suppose I could have asked Adrian about the true reception the cookies had received but I decided to leave it alone. It was awfully nice of him to give me such an opportunity, and if they were having a laugh at my expense, then it was richly deserved, the least I could do to say thank you.

The Traveling Chef
TOM COLICCHIO

*Tom Colicchio, originally from Elizabeth, New Jersey, is the chef/
co-owner of New York's celebrated Gramercy Tavern, ranked
New Yorker's #1 favorite restaurant in the 2005 Zagat Survey, as
well as chef/owner of Craft, the 2002 James Beard Best New
Restaurant in America. In 2002 Colicchio opened Craftbar, a
casual adjunct to Craft, and CraftSteak in Las Vegas' MGM
Grand Hotel. In 2003 he followed up with 'wichcraft, next door
to Craftbar in New York's Flatiron District, bringing Craft's ethic
of simplicity and great ingredients to the ever-popular sandwich.
His first book,* Think Like a Chef, *won the James Beard Best
General Cookbook in 2001, and was followed by* Craft of
Cooking: Notes and Recipes from a Restaurant Kitchen *in
2003. He is married to filmmaker Lori Silverbush, and is the
father of Dante, who is a big fan of his father's scrambled eggs.*

O NE OF THE great benefits of being a chef is that you get
to travel. Cooking around the world has helped me learn
about different cuisines, people, and customs. Traveling widely

as a chef has also taught me a few valuable lessons about my own craft.

My first chance to see the world as a cook was at the age of twenty; I was on my way from Elizabeth, New Jersey, to the Gascony region in the Southwest of France, for a *stage* at a famed two-star inn and hotel. This was to be my first time away from home, and my family threw me a big going-away party. I left a couple weeks before my *stage* began, figuring it would allow me plenty of time to get to Gascony from Brussels, where my $99 People's Express flight would touch down. On the flight over I found myself seated near a friend, a waiter at a restaurant where I had worked in New Jersey. He was on his way to Brussels to work as a model. He invited me to join him for a week, as he was crashing in the apartment of two gorgeous Belgian girls—sisters. I quickly agreed, figuring that this, too, would be an important learning experience. The girls welcomed me enthusiastically. An actual American chef! They treated me like a rock star. The apartment was so small, it had only one bed. This was great! Let the education begin!

As I recall, I later found out that one of the sisters had a boyfriend. The other one was . . . uninterested, to say the least. I learned that striking out overseas felt exactly as it did at home— it sucked.

But life went on, and I had a great experience in France. My career steadily grew when I returned to the States, and many years later I found myself bombarded with invitations to travel the world over. I've cooked alone and with teams of chefs, on cruise ships in the Baltics, in the great hotel kitchens of Tokyo, for Olympic athletes in Athens, and for food enthusiasts in private homes around the world. It's always a thrill, but coordinating a meal (or numerous meals) in a faraway place is never without its hazards. As I travel from place to place with my cooks, trying to raise awareness for important causes or just to show people a good time, I've learned two things.

1. The folks inviting me will promise the world: a first-class kitchen loaded with the best equipment, an eager and skilled prep staff hungering for a chance to learn alongside a "celebrity chef," extraordinary local ingredients . . . wild game, organic vegetables . . . etc., etc.

2. I must never rely on this. Ever.

Plenty of events have found me and my loyal crew cooking in a shoebox kitchen with two working burners. We've learned that local staff often don't show up, or don't show up with knife skills; and as for those amazing, local ingredients . . . let's just say I've determined exactly how many frozen squab I can fit into my fishing bag. If I don't bring it, you don't eat it.

You may think I'm joking, but I'm dead serious. On one trip to the Bahamas, where I was asked to teach a cooking class, I packed a couple dozen squab into my fishing bag. All went well until I hit Customs in Nassau. The Bahamian customs agent didn't give a damn about my cooking class, but once I palmed him $50, he was happy to wave me through. From this I learned to always have some ready cash at hand—literally.

For bigger events, my cooks and I have the travel thing down to a science, but even so, things sometimes go awry. Once we were invited to cook an important dinner for Condé Nast's worldwide ad sales team, in a country club just outside Detroit. The event was a sit-down five-course dinner for 250 people. In other words . . . 1,250 portions, i.e., a *lot* of food. Experience dictated that I pack every last morsel and bring it all along with me on the plane. This might seem anal, but my relationships with farmers and growers have accustomed me to great ingredients, and my style of cooking wholly depends on this. So my cooks and I packed it all up—short ribs sealed in their Cryovac casing, shelled lobster claws and tails nestled into giant plastic bins, tubs of veal demi-glace and bundles of fresh herbs—crammed everything into large, insulated cartons and hauled it along with us to the airport. At the terminal, the gate agents informed us that the cartons each weighed too much to go on the plane. We offered to pay the extra fare—and were politely declined. As the minutes ticked by and boarding began, we offered to ship everything freight, but were told that the cartons exceeded FAA weight regulations. So I got on the phone to D'Artagnan, the legendary specialty foods company, whose warehouses were nearby in Newark, and asked them to rush over more insulated cartons, which they did. We missed our flight while my cooks and I opened each of the boxes in the middle of the terminal, and under the wide-eyed gaze of vacationing families, repacked the food into many more boxes, each weighing under the freight regulation 50 pounds. We were able to rebook onto a later flight, which would still get us into Detroit in time to prep for the dinner. The new cartons were wheeled off on hand trucks to wherever freight goes.

In Detroit we deplaned and awaited our boxes. They didn't arrive. The airline insisted that the crates would be on the next plane, due in two hours. My cooks snuck nervous glances at me and at their watches, and we settled into those plastic bucket seats in the Northwest terminal to wait. In the meantime, I chatted with the driver who had been sent to meet us.

"You know," I told him, "we have a lot of boxes coming. Dozens, in fact. And they're quite large."

The driver laughed it off. "I have a truck," he answered. "I drive entire hockey teams in that thing. You ever see a hockey team—those bags of theirs?"

I suggested he send for a second truck anyway. He shook his

head at my worrying. I think he chalked it up to a New York thing.

Eventually the food arrived. My able-bodied cooks and I hauled them one by one off the conveyer belt and stacked them. The driver watched as the stacks grew, then shook his head. "No way are those gonna fit in my truck."

I sprinted to Hertz and rented two Ford Expeditions. We squeezed the food into the truck and the two vans and headed to the country club where 250 people expected the meal of a lifetime in a few short hours. We got there late. We worked our asses off. We sweated. Condé Nast arrived. The food went out. And none of the guests that night knew just how close they had come to going hungry.

On another occasion, however, they did. I had donated a dinner for twelve in a private home as an auction gift to a children's charity. The day of the private dinner arrived and we packed our boxes and loaded them into my SUV to drive out to the host's house in New Jersey. The weather report said snow, so we left extra early. The snow hit, along with driving ice and sleet, and the trip to this bedroom community—ordinarily a forty-five-minute drive—took three hours. The hostess began calling my cell phone at ten-minute intervals, alternating between tears and tirades. As her guests arrived, we were trapped in a highway whiteout. I felt awful.

We showed up to a house full of guests and flew into action. This is when I know how good my cooks are. We barely need to speak as we whirl around the kitchen dicing, sautéing, stirring, and plating; our communication is wordless and complete. Suddenly, I heard: "Oh, shit!" I looked up to find that Johnny Schaefer, my right-hand man at Gramercy Tavern, had gone pale. "We forgot the lobster," he said. Our pièce de résistance that night was a favorite from the menu at Gramercy, poached lobster served in a lobster sauce gently scented with vanilla. We had the sauce, even the garnish, but somehow the lobster hadn't made it onto the truck.

A long beat while we all just stood there. Suddenly I hit on an idea. We had brought a few beautiful lobes of foie gras, originally meant to be roasted, sliced, and served on rounds of toast as hors d'ouevres, but the late hour had pushed us right into dinner. To make up for the missing lobster, we poached the foie gras and served it in the lobster sauce. The dinner was a hit. If I remember correctly, the wife got thoroughly drunk and hugged me on the way out.

There have been times when I simply can't bring food with me. Invited to cook a dinner on the *Sea Goddess*, a small high-end cruise ship set to sail through the Mediterranean, I was told I could purchase my ingredients before we set sail in the markets of Helsinki. I did just that, availing myself of the wonderful fresh produce and seafood. I loaded everything into the galley's walk-in and headed to my cabin for a quick nap as the ship pushed off. A couple hours later, when I returned to start prepping, I found that my food was gone. The cooks, prepping for lunch and other daily meals, had seen my hand-chosen ingredients, preferred them to the stuff they normally had to cook with, and had helped themselves. From that I learned to label everything that goes into another chef's kitchens as MINE— DO NOT TOUCH.

One favorite trip is my annual jaunt to the Aspen Food and Wine Festival, in June. I'm always looking for ways to spend more time with my son, so one year I decided to bring Dante, then three, along for the ride. I was invited to participate in a panel discussion with a host of other chefs, and rather than track down a babysitter, I decided to stash Dante with his Legos under the table at my feet. The long cloth kept him hidden out of sight of the audience members who'd paid a hefty price to hear me and others talk about food. About halfway through the panel, I noticed that everything we "experts" were saying was eliciting peals of delighted laughter. I mean, we were killing them. One look down and I understood why. My son had lifted the long cloth, discovered hundreds of people in the room, and had started to entertain them with funny faces. Dante was such a hit that the festival organizers brought him up to the microphone at a later panel and asked him to introduce Mary Sue Milliken and Susan Feniger of the Border Grill, aka the "Two Hot Tamales." Not one to waste the limelight, my son grabbed the mic and introduced the talented chefs as "Two Hot Poopies!" Boy, was I proud.

Another year at the Aspen Food and Wine Fest, Michael Romano and I were asked to cook a dinner for American Express Platinum Card members at the Ritz-Carlton. Again I had decided to prepare squab, one of my favorites, as the main course. The kitchen was a long trek from the dining room so I asked the hotel to set up a grill nearby. They accommodated me by placing the grill just outside the dining building, where it abutted a parking garage. Moments before the dinner, the smoke from the grill made its way to the parking structure's internal fire alarm and set it off, which in turn triggered the alarms for the entire hotel. Soon, panicked guests in their haste to get away began streaming out of the hotel's back door in various stages of undress, even knocking over our prep table, where my squab and Michael's food went spilling onto the concrete. One guy had apparently been caught in a hotel fire in Hawaii and no amount of explanation could get him to calm down. I learned there to look for hair-trigger fire alarms (and not set up my prep table in the line of traffic).

Traveling for work means performing a delicate tap dance

with my schedule—one that allows me time in the kitchens of my restaurants, face time with my staff, as well as a decent personal life. But sometimes the dance falls flat. Case in point: recently I was invited to perform with a friend's rock band at D'Artagnan's gala twenty-fifth-anniversary bash. I'm no Clapton, but I take my playing seriously enough that I'd practiced nonstop for weeks in the early mornings and late at night, driving my poor wife to distraction. This was a dream come true for me; I was set to solo on two numbers and play backup on the rest, and I had to get it right. The only problem: I was slated to attend a major food and wine festival in Knoxville. The organizers had asked me to teach a cooking course one day and to cook at a charity dinner the following night, and the concert fell smack in between. So I arranged to fly home after the class, play the gig, and then fly right back into Knoxville for the charity dinner. As fate would have it, a freak March blizzard on the night in question kept me grounded in Knoxville and the band went on without me. That was the beginning and the end of my rock star career.

This past summer, I took off with Dante, now twelve, for the summer Olympics, where I was invited to cook for guests on a ship harbored in Athens. I was asked to fax the recipes ahead of time so that the food and beverage team could shop and prep for my arrival—this was crucial since scheduling conflicts were keeping me from arriving until the morning of my big dinner. As Dante and I boarded the boat, I was immediately summoned into an emergency meeting with the food and beverage team.

"We don't have your food," they told me.

I figured it was the jet lag affecting my hearing, but sure enough, there wasn't so much as a breadstick awaiting my arrival. "Didn't you get the recipes?" I asked. They had. But they hadn't understood them, they told me. So they did nothing.

I set up Dante in the cabin with a bunch of videos and immediately went to work, teetering with exhaustion. I marshaled a team to leave the ship and shop, another to start on the stocks, and somehow we pulled it off. My son and I spent the rest of the week enjoying the games, but it was a close call. From this I learned to call ahead and double-check. To not assume I'm being understood. And then to *call again*.

The travel stories are endless, but at the end of the day I guess all of these experiences have taught me that if I'm lucky enough to get invited to see the world one kitchen at a time, than ultimately it's my job to get it right—whatever that takes. Sometimes it's hard, sometimes it's nerve-racking, but the rewards always outweigh the inconveniences and mishaps. It's a job I wouldn't trade for any other in the world. Except maybe rock star.

This Whole Place Is Slithering
SCOTT CONANT

Scott Conant opened L'Impero restaurant in Manhattan's Tudor City in fall 2002, and quickly earned three stars from the New York Times, *as well as James Beard Foundation Awards for Best New Restaurant 2003 and Best Restaurant Design 2003. In April 2004, he was named one of America's Best New Chefs by* Food & Wine Magazine. *In April 2005, Conant and his L'Impero partners opened Alto, also in New York City. Conant graduated from the Culinary Institute of America in 1989 and worked under chefs Paul Bartolotta and Theo Schoenegger at San Domenico, and under chef Cesare Casella as sous-chef of Pino Luongo's Il Toscanaccio. Conant's short tenure as opening executive chef of City Eatery garnered him a positive two-star review from the* New York Times. *Conant's first cookbook,* New Italian Cooking, *will be published in fall 2005.*

I N 1992, I was the twenty-one-year-old *saucier* at an authentic Italian restaurant in New York City. In the small, 30-by-30 kitchen, I was the only American, and along with two

Dominican guys, one of only three non-Italians on the fifteen-man team.

Working in that kitchen was like going to my own private Little Italy every day. In addition to the overall mood conjured by the owner, the chefs, and the other cooks, one of the things that made the experience so thoroughly Italian was the ingredients. Everything was imported, from the prosciutto to the olive oil to the pasta to the cheeses. Italians are insanely partial about a lot of things, and none more than food: if it don't come from the Old Country, then it ain't the real thing.

One of the most impressive items we imported to that kitchen was eels. And when we did, it was a sight to see: two or three times a year, we received a delivery of live eels, 400 or 500 pounds of the little suckers, all packed up in plastic bags, which were in turn crammed into big Styrofoam crates that would arrive from overseas with all kinds of customs stamps and labels pasted onto the sides.

We purchased eels in such huge bulk quantities because, at that time, live eels were hard to come by, so the owner wanted to deal with the headache of acquiring them as infrequently as possible.

Eels range in size from 1 pound to 50 pounds. The ones we bought were 1 to 1½ pounds each, so the 400 or 500 pounds comprised several hundred eels.

On those few and far-between occasions when we received the delivery, a porter would stack the Styrofoam crates in a corner of the kitchen, until the butcher—one of the two Dominicans—had time to go through a one-man production ritual that involved killing, cleaning, breaking down (filleting), and freezing them.

First, he'd hoist the bags up out of the Styrofoam; the still-live eels would be squirming for all they were worth, causing the bag to swing in the air like a pendulum. They'd continue to squirm as he'd break the bags open over industrial Lexan containers—think of them as giant Tupperware—dust them liberally with sea salt, and douse them with vinegar, which would cause the eels to thrash more violently than ever, and to gasp pathetically, as the salt dehydrated and killed them.

Then the butcher would snap on the lid, locking them in. He'd stack the Lexan containers, one on top of the other, in a corner of the kitchen and place heavy weights such as food-service-size cans of tomatoes on top of the uppermost container to keep the lid from popping off.

He wouldn't remove the eels from their plastic tombs until the next day, when he'd have to pull them out of a soupy ooze made up of their liquid, salt, and vinegar, hose them off, break them down, pack them up in clean plastic bags, and freeze them. Then we would thaw and use them as needed for dishes, such as a house specialty of eel wrapped in grape leaves and grilled.

One day, just before lunch service, one of those shipments arrived. The butcher got to work—loading box after box with the eels, topping them off with the salt-and-vinegar mixture, and stacking the boxes off to one side of the kitchen, weighing down the uppermost box with the huge cans of tomatoes.

Then the butcher went to take care of some other business, filleting lamb and breaking down chickens for the dinner shift. At one point, while crossing the small kitchen, he accidentally brushed up against the boxes of eels, which teetered precariously for a moment . . . and then collapsed.

All in a rush, the lids popped off of each box, and the eels slid out and across the floor, replacing the tiles beneath our feet with a sea of slithering black sea creatures, twitching in pain and sucking for air. To make matters worse, the extracted liquid and salt washed into any gaps between the eels, filling the room with an odor usually associated with high-school science classes.

It was a horrific disaster, but the rest of us couldn't be bothered; lunch was in full swing by then and we were concerned only with getting dishes out of the kitchen. The only problem for us was that we wore clogs—a popular footwear in Italian kitchens—and no socks, so every time you had to cross the kitchen, you would dance over the writhing, struggling eels, feeling their sickeningly slimy skin against your ankles as the juice splashed up against you. Disgusting.

The butcher, meanwhile, was absolutely shell-shocked by the sight of all those eels. He stood there dumbfounded, unsure of how to even begin reining in the mess. Before long, word spread through the entire restaurant and waiters and busboys were scurrying back to get a look at the spectacle, and briefly laugh at the paralyzed butcher, before hurrying back to work.

After about ten minutes of this, the owner of the restaurant, an Italian businessman right out of Central Casting, with a beautiful silk suit, striped tie, and chiseled-looking coiffed hair, appeared in the doorway of the kitchen. Placing great emphasis on each word, he screamed:

"Pick. Up. The. Fucking. Eels."

The butcher looked at him blankly.

So the restaurateur repeated himself:

"Pick. Up. The. Fucking. Eels."

Still nothing from the butcher, who could only shrug in bewilderment.

"Come on," barked the owner, clapping his hands twice. "The eels. Pick 'em up. Whatsa matter with you?"

Finally, the butcher figured it out. He ran off, returning a moment later with a snow shovel borrowed from the building's super, and began scooping up eels by the dozen. After depositing them all in the Lexan containers, he had to rinse and drain them, reapply the salt, and pack them up again until they died their sorry little death.

He did all of this by the time lunch was done, and we got on with our shift like nothing had ever happened.

But it was an unforgettable moment. To this day, whenever I see an eel, am served an eel dish, or even just hear the word *eel*, I remember the sensation of that slime against my ankle, the poor butcher being laughed at by all the Italians, and the owner standing there screaming, "Pick up the fucking eels," and I can't help but laugh all over again, as though I were still standing there with them slithering between my bare feet.

Euphoria
TAMASIN DAY-LEWIS

For the last five years Tamasin Day-Lewis has written an avidly followed column for Saturday's Daily Telegraph. *Tamasin's cookbooks have covered a range of comforting rural recipes, from the preparation of seasonal dishes and picnics to the art of pie-baking and "proper" slow cooking. She is the author of* West of Ireland Summers *and* Last Letters Home *and is a regular contributor to* American Vogue, Vanity Fair, *and* Country Homes & Interiors. *She has directed many television documentaries.*

THE COLLEGE BUTLER had been detailed to find fine wines and sherry and to repair to my "set" to serve them. Cambridge University has a language all its own, and when I became an undergraduate there at King's College, I learned pretty quickly that you didn't have bedrooms or studies in your third year, you had sets comprising a sitting room complete with fireplace for toasting crumpets and teacakes from High Street's most-prized patisserie, Fitzbillies, and a bedroom—the two kept self-contained behind a stout pair of double doors. The outside door was traditionally left ajar if you were open to callers, but closed if you were up to no good or trying to write an essay, in which case you were said to be "sporting your oak." There were eight similar sets on "U" Staircase, looking out over the River Cam, where, as all picture postcards show, students spend their summers punting, picnicking, and eschewing their studies.

We had a tiny "gyp" room where we could cook, though its resemblance to a kitchen was not immediately apparent. I had fought hard to secure my room, U4, when booking the staircase with my posse of foodie friends; after all, if people were to ask, "Where's Tamasin?" the reply could only be "in Euphoria!" As luck would have it, my rooms were also closest to the kitchen.

So, the butler had appeared with white-starched linen tablecloth and napkins that would have stood as frostily to attention as anything at Le Cirque or one of the great temples to cuisine; the bottles were on their way, presently being chambreed in the bowels of the college kitchen; all I had to do was prepare a dinner the likes of which no student had prepared in the collective living memories of the dons about to attend it. A Roman feast. Would I have attempted this Everest of a task if I had known that disaster was about to strike? That I cannot say, but I can tell you that this picture of order and organization, of tradition and good taste, was about to be blown apart by my combination of ignorance and ambition.

What had I let myself in for? The confidence of youth, the not knowing what you don't know, the desire to show off and not be like the other students eating pigswill in hall every night or stirring packet soup into chipped mugs in their rooms; spooning cold rice pudding from the tin, surviving on toasted sandwiches from a tiny café opposite the austerely beautiful world-famous façade of Cambridge's best known college, founded by Henry VI, who also founded Eton.

Having been accepted as one of the first women at King's when they decided to go coeducational after centuries as an all-male domain, here I was trying to introduce a more female take on its world of entertaining, away from the world of the "top table" that the dons dined ceremoniously at every night in their gowns, sweeping in like great flapping birds for Latin grace, to plunder the college's world-class wine cellar, and partake of its grim, institutional apology for good food.

Here I was, about to preside over a lavish dinner party despite the exigencies of my student grant, with a burgeoning sense that the women in the college should be responsible for transforming this previously all-male bastion into a more homely, civilized place where fine dining and good wines could coexist, and even become de rigueur.

The rampant, politically correct feminist student lobby would have been horrified had they known of my belief in the civilizing effects of a good dinner or the fact that I was prepared to cook for as many boys and girls on my staircase as wanted to dine every night. The feminists were busy trying to get a condom machine installed in the girl's cloakroom on the grounds that it was sexist if there was one only in the boy's. Meanwhile I was learning about budgeting; how to buy cheap cuts of scrag of lamb or choose between the end-of-the-day's fruit and vegetables in the market at a discount, and making sure there was some sort of equal distribution of labor when I cooked; that the boys brought the wine, washed up, even went shopping from time to time.

Hell, I didn't want to pander to the well-known sobriquet of being a "blue stocking," the barely veiled insult that still exists to describe the confirmed spinster in academics whose eccentricity, unworldliness, and unforgivingly plain looks only the rarefied and obscure sanctuary of an Oxford or Cambridge college could absorb.

At this point, I should probably explain my suitability for the task ahead. When I left home for university, I could cook an omelet. And that is just about it. It was, however, a very good omelet; my mother had taught me that it took precisely fifty-five seconds to cook THE PERFECT OMELET, exactly how long it took to recite a Shakespeare sonnet. Not so odd a comparison given that my father, C. Day Lewis, was the poet laureate; I have no doubt that my mother probably recited the bard's canon of sonnets by memory as she worried the buttery eggs in the pan with her palette knife and flipped them out with the desired *baveuse centres* and perfectly pale primrose undersides.

My limited repertoire at this stage was understandable. My mother dominated her tiny kitchen and it was not a place where there could ever be room for two cooks. My experiments were confined to pressing the extra bits of pastry remaining from one of her tarts firmly into small patty tins until they were so overworked and greasy and thick that they came out of the oven half raw, the burnt, bubbling jam—no child ever learns less is more—erupting Vesuvially and stickily and breaching the pastry walls and then eaten so hot by me and my brother that it welded itself to the roofs of our mouths, or else scraping the last bits of cake mixture raw from the bowl when she'd made one of her weekly teatime treats and eating it straight from the wooden spoon.

Though I had been brought up in a house with a tradition of good food, I never really wanted to learn to cook. As a child, it didn't occur to me that it might be an interesting or exciting thing to do. Eating was always the pleasure. My grandparents, unusually for the time, kept a marvelous, traditional English table, and their cook, the redoubtable Rhoda Fisher, was still busy turning out three meals if not four a day well into her seventies. My grandmother did what ladies in her position did, which was to know all about good food, to order exactly what she wanted when the cook went into my grandfather's dressing room every morning to discuss the day's menu, to even know the ingredients of every dish she ordered, but to have never actually cooked anything herself.

There was an apocryphal story about her first dinner party when she married my grandfather. She was all of seventeen and had no idea how to address the cook or what to order, but felt she'd better not let on. There were going to be ten people at the party that evening. Quick as a flash, when asked what should be bought for dinner, my grandmother replied "ten pounds of fillet steak."

By the time I was born, she'd had nearly three decades of practice and as long to cultivate the other imperative qualification, greed, a must-have for any serious cook or bon vivant and one which hasn't bypassed anyone in at least four generations of my family, including my own three children.

And so it was that one dinnertime when I had been allowed to stay up, although it was not given to me to actually dine with my grandparents, my grandfather ate his bloodily rare grouse served *à l'ancienne* with fresh peppery watercress, game chips, bread sauce, fried bread crumbs, and gravy and then asked me if I'd like to try it. I was given the carcass and remember only the thrill, the indefinable thrill of a new taste so transporting and beyond the realms of any expectation that for a minute you wonder that something can defy even your imagination. I picked every tiddly bone clean as though it were the last supper and have continued to do so with game birds and bones of any sort throughout my life. That night was like a shaft of light into a secret world, a grown-up world of taste whose discovery was going to alter the way I thought about food from thereon in. Somewhere the thought lodged in my brain that good food was all about good ingredients and good cooking. Perhaps I ought to find out how to cook.

I began the next term at school not even realizing that recipes were there for a purpose, that weighing and measuring were a means to a delicious end, that only the best and most experienced of cooks could cook without paying attention to such trifling little details. I purchased a bottle of Ribena, a stickily sweet blackcurrant cordial that we used to drink with hot water before lights out. I managed to get to the local tuck shop and buy cream, icing sugar, and a lemon. I stuck my head through the school kitchen window and begged Chef for an ice tray, promising to return it and cajoling him into helping me in my mission. Blackcurrant juice, cream, and lemon were stirred into a putrid pink mixture as thick as paint and poured into the ice tray. I carried it gingerly back to Chef, who promised to freeze it for me. That night I collected the frozen pink ice cream and took it proudly back to my dormitory to tempt my dorm mates with. It was toothachingly sweet and sickly with cream, but the funny thing was I didn't see it as a complete disaster; it was an experiment, and that meant critical faculties had to be employed, as did that thing I was unaware existed at that stage, let alone that I might have it, the palate. Next time I would use more lemon, less sugar, and less cream. I might even read a recipe book and find out how to make *real* blackcurrant ice cream.

My mother, unlike my grandmother, did not have a cook; indeed, she had had a rude awakening on marrying my father coming from this world of cooks and housekeepers, governesses and maids. My father insisted on having a pudding every night.

My mother had to rise to the challenge, and on the first night presented my father with pancakes. Child's play, you might think. No one had told her that you didn't use self-rising flour to make pancake batter, so the slim pancakes she'd aspired to flipping and folding and spritzing with lemon juice and sugar were not quite as she'd imagined them to be. My father looked at the sorry, gray leather effigies on his plate and hurled one against the wall, where it stuck, proclaiming that it looked exactly like the poet Keats's death mask.

Perhaps these stories from two generations of women in my family were the things that spurred me on, made me realize that failure, kitchen disaster, was not only an option, it was a given. It didn't mean you should give up, that you were a bad cook; at worst you could dine out on the stories and tell them to your children and grandchildren; at best you would improve as a result.

My only real memory of cooking for my father, who died when I was eighteen, so had no idea that I had any talent at the stove, let alone that I would end up becoming a food writer and cookbook author, was an occasion more disastrous than my mother's first. It was something of a warm-up act and wake-up call for me to finally get down to learning the basics, understanding the importance of technique and how to read a recipe.

My mother had gone away and asked me to cook for my father and I, presuming that there was really no great skill or knowledge required, and oblivious to timing and technique, pronounced I would fry some aubergines to go with the lamb chops that I assumed just needed a little cremating under the grill.

I cut the spongy purple grenades into fat wedges and plunged them into a pan of oil, oil not even hot enough to begin the frying process. It wasn't long before the oily bath seemed to have disappeared and things began to smoke. I poured a further libation of oil into the hot pan. This time the aubergines seemed to be turning dusky brown rather too quickly. I thought I'd better drain them and remove them before it was too late. My father cut into the resistant brown discs. They managed to be as tough and hard as to almost appear raw at the same time as to be leaking oil like a tanker that had struck rock. They were so oily that even with copious amounts of kitchen paper they were inedible; but my father never breathed a word and, like a fellow conspirator, never even let on to me that my burnt offering was unacceptable.

Other than the school cookery lessons that were supposed to teach us the rudiments of good baking and where I excelled only in the greed department, shaking sap green and ink blue coloring into my sponges and meringues to make sure my dorm mates wouldn't want to help me eat them, I had had little experience of proper cooking when I left the fold for the portals of King's. My three strongest suits were my greed, my childhood exposure to really good home cooking—although it was many years before I realized just how good and unusual that was—and my sudden desire to cook, prompted by the fact that this was the first time in my life that the only way of eating good food was if I cooked it myself.

In between *Sir Gawain and the Green Knight*, Greek tragedy, the metaphysical poets, Milton, and Chaucer, I read Elizabeth David and Jane Grigson, the two seminal food writers of the time: Mrs. David for her prose and her discovery of the great regional, provincial cooking of France and Italy and the Mediterranean, and Mrs. Grigson, the scholar cook, for her more detailed instruction and the inspiration of recipes that always worked whatever your level of knowledge. And I had a boyfriend at King's who was as interested in good food as I was. He showed serious skill and a rather more sophisticated knowledge of food that didn't just amount to having good taste, a good palate, like me, and could conjure up things like the perfect crème caramel with no apparent effort. His caramel would be syrupy and burnt to just the right degree, his tremblingly set crème as silken and eggy as could be, speckled with real vanilla seeds, the whole great burnished moon of a dish turned out and served cool but not too chilled. There was an understanding of the small print, of attention to detail. I would have to raise the stakes.

I'd cooked nightly for a couple of terms for my fellow students from as many Jane Grigson and Elizabeth David recipes as I could afford to buy the ingredients for and as were simple enough for someone at my level. I felt I had worked my way up to being ready to go for the big one: a serious, grown-up dinner party of the kind my mother and grandmother appeared to give effortlessly. It hadn't occurred to me that this was a whole new thing insofar as the timing and textures and courses and sheer ambition of it were concerned, that there was far more scope for failure and disaster than there ever could be from my usual stew-and-mashed-potato suppers. The reason for holding this, my first proper dinner party, was simple. When I'd arrived at King's, several of the dons had invited a few undergraduates to their homes for drinks. Oceans of sherry were sunk at these bashes, and, not drinking the stuff in those days, particularly served almost warm—unlike the stunning chilled Palo Cortado or Finos one drinks in Jerez—I found these parties a serious ordeal. There had been one exception, however, the avuncular and kindly figure of the senior librarian at King's, Tim Munby, or A.N.L. Munby as he was more formally referred to.

Tim had invited me and a couple of friends to dinner, which his wife, Sheila, had cooked, and we had been entertained as though we were serious grown-ups, not just starved, troublesome students. During the course of dinner, Tim mentioned that in all his years at King's of giving similar dinners to a few select freshmen, and he could have been talking about a tenure of over a quarter of a century for all I knew, not one student had ever returned the invitation. Here was a challenge I could take up.

I decided to meet it with a couple of the friends who had also been so generously entertained. I sent out invitations and decided that if we put the booze on the college bill, at least I wouldn't have to pay for it until the following term. The next thing was the menu. We could hardly serve the sausage and mash, belly of pork and beans, pig's liver with root vegetables, or Irish stew that were our U Staircase staples. A stroke of luck happened the weekend before the dinner.

An old friend who was a good shot had descended on King's with a brace of pheasants for me to roast. This was not only free food, it was the kind of food befitting the kind of banquet I intended giving. I had never cooked game before, let alone plucked it or gutted it, but I can't remember, thinking back, that I was unduly fazed by the prospect. I was planning on the traditional English ritual that accompanies a brace of roast pheasants: bread sauce, roast potatoes and parsnips, carrots Vichy, dark onion gravy made with the giblets and a slug of red wine. My boyfriend could make the crème caramel, one of the cheapest puddings in the book; I would buy some cheese in the market, and the King's cellar would do the rest. It was, and still is, a marvelous tradition at King's that any undergraduate can order wine from the college butler, and the buying of good wine and laying it down over the years is reason alone to become a Kingsman, not that I would have known that when I applied for a place at the college.

My friend had arrived with the brace of birds, and, having not been brought up as au fait as he to the world of hunting, shooting, and fishing, I didn't even ask him what to do with them. I was wholly unaware of the extent of my ignorance. At least I wasn't squeamish like many of my friends about livers and gizzards and paunching and gutting. I hung the beautiful brace from the gyp-room ceiling and believed that was all there was to it.

So there I was, transforming my study into a dining room with a borrowed table and the stiffest college linen. The kitchens had agreed to lend me a few serving dishes and I was going to beg, borrow, or steal the cutlery and plates from the pantry. I went downstairs to the gyp room to get started. I switched on the tiny Baby Belling stove that would just about contain the roasting pan with the pheasants and vegetables. Other than that, there was an electric ring on top of the stove and a gas ring on the worktop. The small fridge the eight of us shared was frequently raided at night by teams of stoned, marauding students who probably knew well that if anyone was likely to have rashers and eggs and scrumptious leftovers it would be U Staircase. The vegetables were still there. I peeled and prepared them all and put them in my battered, secondhand pans. Time to get to work on the birds.

I remember opening a large black bin bag and pulling the pheasants' feathers in clumps down into it. As I got closer to skin and flesh, it all seemed rather peculiar. The normal pink goosebumpy look of the skin wasn't quite as it should be. In fact it was a rather livid shade of green. The worst horror was yet to come. The side of one of the birds was actually moving. Moving as in covered with maggots. Alive!

It is one of those bad jokes told in English aristocratic circles that a pheasant isn't hung enough until you can scrape the maggots from the flesh. Here it was for real. How come I hadn't

realized that, cold as the gyp room was, the ambient temperature was not at preservation level? I remember dropping the
hideous brace of birds into the bin and shrieking. The game was
up. I mean, the game was off. We had nothing for dinner. What
to do? The guests were arriving in a couple of hours and this was
before the days of late-night or all-night shopping; Cambridge
shut down firmly at 5:30 p.m., the market even earlier.

As is the way with selective memory, I have no recollection as
to where we found a chicken to roast (although I know we
didn't wring its neck or pluck it ourselves). It seemed like the
only thing to do; after all, the trimmings that you make for a
pheasant, right down to the bread sauce, are the same as you
make for roast chicken. Roast chicken, that culinary first, that
nursery slope of cuisine that it is, is for many of us the first thing
we attempt after the early struggles with baking cakes and
biscuits when we decide to leave the sweet world of childhood
for the savory world of adulthood.

And can you feast, indeed banquet, on the everyday common
or garden bird? Of course you can and of course we did. The
bird's interior succulence offset by its startlingly crisped, salted,
bronzed skin, the bread sauce creamy with its scent of clove and
nutmeg, the sweet parsnips caramelized in the bird's juices, the
potatoes as crunchy as you could wish for. The disaster was all
mine. The guests need never have been made aware of it, but
that would have been cheating.

The story of the pheasant dinner has gone down in the annals,
in the pages of one's memory where one coped with the
unexpected, most gruesome disaster and dined out on it afterward. The more experienced one becomes in the kitchen, the less
one is inclined to show off, anyway. I would as soon invite
people to eat a plain risotto or bowl of pasta as I would a roast
woodcock or wild salmon en croute. Simple food cooked well

with good ingredients cannot diminish the occasion of bringing friends to the table, good wine, good conversation, and the fact that you have gone to all that effort in the first place. Besides, I never learned anything from the successes except that I would still always wonder afterward, couldn't I have crisped that skin a bit more, taken that tart out two minutes sooner, upped the spicing, gone easier on the lemon juice or the cream?

Such is the nature of the passionate cook, even at the fledgling stage. And, as Samuel Beckett so succinctly put it, forbidding us to dwell on our disasters or give up, "Try again, fail again, fail again better."

Hope for Snow
TOM DOUGLAS

Tom Douglas, along with his wife and business partner, Jackie Cross, owns four of Seattle's most exciting restaurants: Dahlia Lounge, Etta's Seafood, Palace Kitchen, and Lola. For more than twenty-five years, Tom's creativity with local ingredients and his respect for Seattle's ethnic traditions have helped define the Northwest Style. Tom's love of food continues to evolve beyond the restaurant scene. He is the author of two cookbooks, Tom Douglas' Seattle Kitchen, *which won a James Beard award, and* Tom's Big Dinners. *In addition, Tom runs a specialty food line of spice rubs and barbecue and teriyaki sauces and he hosts his own weekly talk radio show.*

THIS IS NOT a story about a recipe disaster, but a story about a disastrous night where a recipe was invented and a business was eventually turned around. It's a story about a lesson learned the hard way.

I can't count how many times I've been asked: "What's your

secret? What do you do that others don't? Everything you do turns to gold! You must be rich! You can't lose!"

What a bunch of crap! Not that I don't appreciate everyone's good thoughts and well wishes. I truly, truly do. But behind any "great success" there is usually a huge collection of difficulties, mistakes, and unexpected challenges; nothing is easy—or fool-proof—even if it looks like it is.

Twenty-five years ago, I was hired as the chef and eventually the general manager of Café Sport in downtown Seattle. Of course I had been cooking for a while, but Café Sport was the first time I got to pull the strings, so to speak. Café Sport was a big operation, bigger than it seemed from the outside: open seven days a week, for breakfast, lunch, and dinner, with a satellite café in the athletic club next door, and a full-scale on-and-off-site catering arm. It was also blessed with one of the busiest and grandest locations in Seattle—the venerable Pike Place Market. But the truly unique thing, for me, was being both the GM and the chef; it's a combo that I routinely tell young chefs is essential to one day running your own place.

Our first year in business, I will politely call lumpy: fits and starts, ruts and bumps, tears and a few cheers. Despite the slow start, Café Sport was a big hit, and after a couple of years it was humming along on all cylinders. I'd even become a minor celebrity in town. At the time, regional chefs around the country were being asked to step out of the kitchen for a few minutes and be guest experts on local TV and radio shows. I was also teaching classes to curious home cooks in gleaming kitchen-supply stores, and presenting my thoughts on Northwest cuisine to throngs of foodies belonging to foodie clubs like AIWF and IACP. Hell, I was getting famous!

It was time for my wife, Jackie, and me to reap the rewards and open our own joint. The owners of Café Sport were fabulous employers and paid me extremely well, but my feet were itchy and after seven years I was ready to walk the talk of owning my own business.

First stop, the banks. Whoops! Bad idea. Every one of them turned us down for a business loan. They didn't seem very interested in my carefully scripted business plan, my immaculate letters of recommendation from business associates, or the inch-thick scrapbook of Café Sport reviews carefully cut from the esteemed pages of the *New York Times, Washington Post, Los Angeles Times, Food and Wine Magazine*, blah, blah, blah. . . . No, they wanted collateral, and that, unfortunately, was the thinnest part of my portfolio. Zero, to be exact.

I was stumped. I had worked for seven years at what many called the best restaurant in the city—and I couldn't get a loan from anyone except Jackie's uncle, Clarence Cross. So, with no recourse, and contradicting my "no family money" policy, we borrowed $100,000 from Clarence to open Dahlia. Neither Jackie nor I had been employed for months by now, and we had a staggering pile of debts. (Jackie somehow became pregnant . . . hmmm . . . unemployment equals pregnancy. Another life lesson.) Before we even signed papers to buy the business, our 100K was melting away.

To save money, Jackie and I did much of the design and some of the construction ourselves, anything to squeak by. We demo'd and cleaned up. We traded with the drywall people: their labor in exchange for us catering their staff Christmas party. We sold the glass blocks that had decorated the previous restaurant for any cash we could get. The small restaurant staff we had hired came in and cleaned and painted the kitchen. To paint the soaring 25-foot-high walls of the dining room, however, we were forced to hire professionals. After watching them spray the walls and ceiling of the whole restaurant fire engine red, we looked around and, to our horror, felt as if we were in a *National Geographic* special on what it's like to be a baby in the womb. The painters laughed and asked if we were sure we didn't want them to come back and repaint. We held our breaths while tearing away clumps of plastic masking—the painters were costing us a fortune—but it worked. When the place was finished, the color was gorgeous.

Jackie and I opened the doors November 15, 1989. Having spent all of our money and then some, we were already $150,000 in debt. No problem. I had a great reputation and many of the fabulous people that made Café Sport the highest-rated restaurant in Seattle were by my side. We'll get through this, I reasoned, and then start putting money away to pay for the new baby and the home remodel that we sorely needed. What did Kevin Costner say in *Field of Dreams*? "If you build it, they will come."

After six weeks, we were left wondering where the diners were. Reviews had been fair, location turned out to be terrible, parking nonexistent, and the economy was in the tank.

Our friends tried to help us out. Harry Yoshimura of Mutual Fish kindly supplied us a fish order worth hundreds of dollars every week, and never sent me a bill for four months. I was too busy and stressed to even realize it at the time. (My friend and co-worker Steven Steinbock joked that we would have to rename the restaurant Harry's Dahlia Lounge.) My good friend Kenny Raider, who had opened his own restaurant, Al Bocca-lino, an Italian joint, just a few months before us, let me borrow enough money to make payroll every two weeks. Brian, at Fairway Plumbing, was kind enough to let our debt slide for many months. All our suppliers were holding paper on us, but not pressing.

We had plenty of time on our hands to think up the reasons

why we weren't busy. When a restaurant is slow, it's amazing the excuses you can come up with. Blame it on the weather. It's either too hot or too cold. We're slow because it's raining. On a beautiful sunny day, the deck restaurants are taking all the business. We're dead because there's a football game today. But, if it snowed—that was the worst of all—complete and utter disaster! So we fretted over the numbers and became a bit more frantic every week.

If you don't live in Seattle, it's probably hard to imagine how just a few inches of snow can cause mass panic and shut down the city. But Seattle is a city built on hills; the city owns only a couple of snowplows and few people have snow tires or experience driving in the snow. If there's even the hint of a flake, the ratings-hungry TV and radio announcers go crazy, chanting: "Stay home, stay home, don't drive," and killing everyone's business in downtown Seattle.

So as we approached our first New Year's Eve, preparing for a blow-out, elegant, celebration, I started restlessly fretting about the weather. Every few hours I checked the weather report, living in terror of snow. I should mention that Jackie is a snow bunny who always prays for snow. This does not contribute to a harmonious family atmosphere when our business is teetering on every night's receipts. (Jackie was six months pregnant with our daughter, Loretta. She couldn't go skiing. What good was snow for her? I think she was just torturing me.)

New Year's Eve is a big night for restaurants, and we needed a big night more than anything. To be fair, our numbers weren't as atrocious as it sounds. Friday and Saturday nights were great. Lunch was decent. But weeknights were just that—weak. The numbers were far below my projections, and being undercapitalized, every seating counted. New Year's, luckily, did not disappoint. (If you can't sell out New Year's Eve, you might as well get out of the business.) We had been booked solid since Christmas, and my mouth—or my wallet—was watering.

From the start, Dahlia's concept was "comfort food"; we liked to play around with retro dishes like shrimp Newburg, macaroni and cheese, and slow-roasted pork (an homage to my friend Peter Cipra's incredible roast pork with caraway onion gravy from his unforgettable Czech-inspired restaurant Labuznik). As a consequence, we decided that the centerpiece of this important, special dinner would be lobster thermidor, similar to a dish I had cooked at Hotel Dupont in Delaware. Lobster thermidor is a classic retro dish of lobster with a bubbling creamy sauce and buttered bread crumbs passed under the broiler. Because this is Dungeness crab country, lobster is a special treat in Seattle—we have to fly in our lobster from the East Coast. Jackie and I went a little deeper into debt to order $500 worth of lobsters for the big night. Of course we had plenty of other expensive foods packed into our walk-in: sevruga caviar, dozens of silky Kumomoto oysters, and cases of tender butter lettuce for the Waldorf salads. One of my chefs, Shelley Lance, had spent several days making tray after tray of puff pastry pear tarts, crème caramels, and coconut cream pies. Meanwhile, the reefer shelves were stacked with short-lived, i.e. *perishable*, goods.

As if on cue, to satisfy the nay-saying bankers and the I've-never-been-right-before weathermen, around noon on December 31, it started to snow. It snowed and snowed and then snowed some more. Soon, the phone started to ring: "Sorry, can't come." "Sorry, no snow tires on my car." Sorry, sorry, sorry. Our very own "Big Night," with 250 reservations, started dropping faster than the stock market in '29. Before the night had even started, it was clear that it was already over. Extra staff. Extra fancy food. Extra disaster! To make things worse, we'd be closed for business the next day, New Year's Day. What would we do with all this food?

We food-banked what we could: house bread, pear tarts, anything that wouldn't last past the holiday. But my lobsters—what was I going to do with all those lively, briny, "orphaned" lobsters?

After the anger toward my pregnant wife subsided for "making it snow," I had a lemons-into-lemonade moment. Saigon Restaurant in the Pike Place Market, one of my favorite little holes in the wall, makes a delicious bowl of pork wonton soup. That must have been my inspiration, because somewhere during the first hour of service it occurred to me to make a lobster sausage with raw lobster meat and to fill wonton wrappers—which we happened to have a case of in the refrigerator. Instead of the 250 covers we had on the books, we did forty-five dinners that night. Idle cooks got busy shucking the fifty extra lobsters.

I worked on an aromatic mixture of roasted shiitakes, shredded carrots, toasted sesame seeds, and a little spicy hit of "rooster sauce," or fresh chile paste, to blend with the coarsely ground lobster meat. A couple of sprigs of fresh cilantro finished off what, if I do say so myself, was a damn tasty filling for the thin, wheat-flour wonton skins. Here we were on the busiest restaurant night of the year, standing around filling and sealing hundreds of lobster potstickers.

We played with the folds and taught ourselves how to shape them nicely. Then we boiled one—delicious! We debated how to serve them: In a ginger sauce? Sautéed with garlic oil? Our favorite was panfried in peanut oil with a sake dipping sauce. Adding sake to a dipping sauce of soy, chile, and garlic made it a little lighter; it went with the delicate flavor of the lobster better. With our fifty lobsters we made 450 potstickers, or 150 orders. We trayed them up on sheet pans and popped them in the freezer; most important of all, they froze beautifully. At least I had saved my lobster investment from this disastrous night.

The snow had melted by our next business day, and I was optimistic that we could sell all of those delicious potstickers in a couple of weeks. To my surprise, we sold out in three days! *And* we had to order more lobsters to satisfy the customer demand. The lobster potstickers instantly became the most popular appetizer on our menu. A week later, Dahlia was reviewed in the local paper and the reviewer's favorite dish, of course, was the lobster potstickers.

"What an innovation! Simply delicious!" he raved.

What do you know? A four-star review!

Customers started filling up my restaurant and, gradually, we worked ourselves out of debt. Over the years, we played around with the potstickers, trying them as wontons floating in a lobster broth made from the shells, in lobster wonton stir-fries, and as steamed dumplings in chive and red chile oil. But we always went back to our panfried lobster potstickers with sake sauce.

Every time I eat these potstickers (which are still on our menu and still selling like crazy), I think about how they saved my ass on that first snowy New Year's Eve. I haven't quite forgiven my wife for wishing for snow, but sometimes a near disaster is good for coming up with a great idea. For all those moments when you fear things are teetering on the brink, keep your chin up and hope for snow, because Jackie and I now have ten businesses, a beautiful fifteen-year-old daughter, and a twenty-two-year marriage. So, when life hands you lemons, make potstickers!

Beastmaster
WYLIE DUFRESNE

A native of Providence, Rhode Island, Wylie Dufresne studied philosophy at Colby College before enrolling at the French Culinary Institute in New York City. Following graduation, he spent several years working for Jean-Georges Vongerichten, first at JoJo, then at the four-star Jean-Georges, and finally as chef de cuisine of Vongerichten's Prime in Las Vegas. In 1999, he was opening chef at 71 Clinton Fresh Food, where his father was a partner, on New York's Lower East Side, the same neighborhood that plays home to his first restaurant, wd-50. Dufresne was nominated for the James Beard Foundation award for Rising Star Chef in 2000, and in 2001 he was named one of Food & Wine Magazine's Best New Chefs *in the country.*

I'M A MEMBER of perhaps the last generation of American chefs who considered it essential to spend at least a few weeks cooking in France early in their careers. While many of today's kitchen hopefuls feel they can learn all they need to know here at home in the United States, it was different for me and my contemporaries. Whereas liberal arts students might have taken a postgraduate month to backpack around Europe, *culinary* school grads went to Europe to cook, usually for little or no money, and to see how things were done in the birthplace of Western cuisine.

I didn't make it to France right out of cooking school. I hadn't even made it there by the time I was twenty-six.

I had my reasons. I had spent the past few years working at JoJo for Jean-Georges Vongerichten, one of the most talented, respected, and influential chefs in the country. Today, Jean-Georges operates restaurants all over the U.S. and the world. But in the mid-90s, he had a mere two, JoJo and Vong, so working at one of them meant working alongside this master. It was an exciting, wonderful, glorious place for a young cook to be, and I made the most of it, spending time at every station in the kitchen.

In 1996, my mentor was putting the finishing touches on what would become his four-star masterpiece, the self-titled Restaurant Jean-Georges, situated in the Trump International Hotel on Columbus Circle in New York City. Though he wasn't fond of moving employees from one place to another, I felt like I had gotten all I was going to get out of JoJo, and asked him if he might consider transferring me to Jean-Georges when it opened. He agreed, offering me the job of *saucier*.

I then made another request: I wanted to take the month of November, between leaving my position at JoJo and the opening of Jean-Georges, and finally fulfill my long-delayed rite of passage by traveling to France and working in a three-star Michelin kitchen, a learning period of temporary employment commonly referred to as a *stage*.

Jean-Georges's response blew me away. Not only could I have the time off, but he would arrange for me to work at Alain

Passard's Michelin three-star Arpege, his favorite restaurant of the moment. Passard was renowned for minimalist dishes that had just three or four elements on the plate and *nothing* else. What an amazing place it would be to hone my technique. And to go there with Jean-Georges's seal of approval was just too much. It was going to be the best experience of my life!

At least that's what I, at the time, naively, happily imagined. I never did discover the joys of Arpege because in all the hubbub of running JoJo, on the jam-packed heels of its *second* three-star review no less, and readying Restaurant Jean-Georges, acting as my overseas agent somehow fell off of Jean-Georges's monumental agenda. At the time I was crestfallen, but now that I'm a chef myself, I must say that I can completely understand how it happened.

Two days before my departure, the team at Jean-Georges scrambled to line up a job for me at Mark Meneau, the eponymous Michelin three-star restaurant of a member of the old guard of French gastronomy, a master chef who had never attained the celebrity of his peers like Paul Bocuse or the Troisgros brothers, but who was very well respected. In his fifties at the time, Meneau was a true scholar of classic French cuisine, who would often refer his cooks to recipes in *L'Escoffier*, an early bible of the culinary arts, providing the page number to them from his frighteningly accurate memory.

So, rather than staying in Paris when I got off the plane, I boarded a train at Gare du Nord and traveled deep into the heart of Burgundy. A taxi took me even farther into the region, shuttling me through the pretty French countryside toward the town of Saint-Père-sous-Vézelay, where I was delivered, at last, to the door of Mark Meneau.

It was everything that I expected it would be: a small restaurant on one side of the narrow road and a large banquet hall—that seemed to have a capacity double the size of the town's modest population—on the other.

Though a bit disheartened that I wasn't in Paris, I was excited to have a crack at the three-star experience. I was also determined to represent myself and Jean-Georges as well as possible. I resolved to be on time every day, and to do my level best to keep pace with what I expected to be my competition: fifteen-year-old French punks who had cooking in their blood and could do everything twice as well and twice as fast as a lowly American like myself.

I needn't have worried about receiving a chilly reception, however. I was warmly taken in by the kitchen staff, who assigned me, not surprisingly, to the *garde manger foie* (salads and cold appetizers) station, a frequent destination for newcomers to a kitchen because it involves no actual cooking, other than maybe blanching and shocking vegetables, though I was—as feared—working alongside three French teenagers who were also performing a *stage*.

The kitchen was magnificent, reason enough to have made the long trip. After working in JoJo's functional but necessarily submarinelike quarters in a converted townhouse, it was revelatory to see what a chef would design when space simply wasn't an issue. Meneau's kitchen afforded everyone ease of movement from any point to any other point. There were separate walk-ins (refrigerators) for dairy, meats, and so on. And there was meat hanging everywhere, being dried or aged to just the right effect. It was a model of French efficiency that I meticulously sketched before my two weeks were up. The dining room, too, was attractive and welcoming in a classic, country, Relais & Châteaux kind of way.

The restaurant managers were gracious enough to set me up in a little guesthouse about 100 yards down the road from the restaurant. The closer you got to the house, the more wooded and shadowy the road became. My room was at the end of a short, dark hallway on the second floor, which you reached by a spiral staircase with an old-fashioned banister. The house served as spillover accommodations for guests in the peak season, but it was nearly deserted in November, so much so that I was the only tenant on my floor.

It was at the end of that dark road, at the end of that empty hall, in a little room not much larger than a closet that I turned out the light and went to bed that first night, with urgent thoughts of punctuality occupying my last moment of consciousness. Tossing beneath the scratchy sheets, fighting off sleep, I ran through my morning routine one more time: wake up at eight fifty, leap into the bathroom, shower, towel off, dress, grab my knives and my Carhartt jacket, and make the five-minute walk to the restaurant, arriving at nine o'clock sharp and doing Jean-Georges and my nation proud.

The first couple days went well. I was on time each morning, kept my head down and focused intently on cleaning and slicing every vegetable that crossed my cutting board with the precision of a jeweler.

While I mostly kept to myself I did, however, strike up an acquaintanceship with the restaurant's baker. Or, rather, *he* struck up an acquaintanceship with me, simply by directing an occasional smile my way or giving me a friendly pat on the back. Though an accomplished baker, he was a bit of an odd duck. He sat alone at lunch, and was the only member of the kitchen staff to drink a glass of wine with the meal. And in stark contrast to the other cooks in the kitchen, who wore immaculate, starched whites, he rolled his pants up as if he were expecting a flood— his sleeves rolled up in similar country-bumpkin fashion.

So passed my first two days at Mark Meneau—not terribly

social, but efficient and capable. I was meeting my goals and settling in nicely.

On my third morning, I awoke, showered, dressed, grabbed my knives and my Carhartt, and opened the door to leave.

From out of the darkness of the corridor, a shadowy figure emerged, blindingly fast, and whooshed past me into my room.

"What the fuck was that?" I said aloud, and spun around, following its trajectory.

Sitting there on my bed, eyes blinking as it surveyed my room, was an owl.

I'm a New York City kid, so I've seen my share of mice, pigeons, rats, and other creatures that are indigenous to the island of Manhattan. I imagine there are owls in Central Park, but the only place I had ever seen one was on television, swooping down from the sky to grab some poor fish in its talons on the *National Geographic* show. I had never met one up close and personal.

Let me tell you something: owls are *huge*. And they seem even larger when they're parked on your bed in a dorm-room-sized hotel room.

I lost some time adjusting to the situation, but once I recovered, I remembered my vow to never be late to work. While my heart pounded furiously and sweat began pouring down my face, a glance at my watch revealed that I had about three minutes to make the trek.

Not knowing what else to do, I threw open the bedroom window and began gesturing at the owl, waving for it to avail itself of the exit.

Its blinking continued unabated.

I removed my Carhartt and took it in my hands like a bullfighter's cape. With a shooing motion, I tried to guide the owl toward the window, coming up around it from the side.

As I approached, it spread its wings wide like Dracula; in the heat of the moment, they appeared to fill the room. I backed off.

"Shoo," I whispered meekly, then pleaded: "C'mon, shoo."

I'm not sure, but I think the owl yawned. Forget about my wishes; he seemed oblivious to my very existence.

Another glance at my watch: I had two minutes to get to work.

I left the window open, threw on my jacket, flew down the stairs, and sprinted the 100 yards to the restaurant, arriving in the nick of time, panting, my chest sore from sucking in the cold November air.

I worked all morning, preparing vegetables for lunch service. I also performed one of my favorite tasks, taking to the woods and foraging for perfect oak leaves that were laid out on plates at the restaurant, providing a rustically elegant surface on which cheeses were arranged.

After lunch service each day, we had a ninety-minute break. As soon as we were dismissed, I snuck off from the restaurant and made my way back to my little hotel room. I opened the door and was relieved to find that the owl was gone.

Or was he? He was nowhere in sight, but I needed proof. I checked the bathroom and behind the armchair. No owl. Then, more as a nod to what I had seen in the movies than to any real concern, I got on my knees and looked under the bed.

Sure enough, the owl was standing under the bed, blinking away.

This is madness, I thought, as I left the room. I went back to the restaurant and sought out my lone acquaintance, the baker. I found him seated at a table, eating his lunch and drinking his customary glass of wine. He greeted me with a nod.

I spoke to him using the dregs of my high-school French. I was able to communicate rather adroitly about cooking, but I had long forgotten the words and syntax that would enable me to explain the nature show that was going on in my bedroom—if I had ever learned them in the first place.

In French, I said, "*I need you. To come. With me. To my room. My room. I need you to come to my room.*"

He cocked his head like a dog who knew you were giving him a command, but didn't know what it meant.

I began lurching my torso in the general direction of the guesthouse, to help make my point.

"*My room. I need you to come to my room. Come with me. With me.*"

I grabbed his arm, respectfully, to give him a sense of urgency. "*Come with me to my room!*"

He shrugged, put down his wineglass, and stood up, indicating for me to lead the way.

We made the five-minute walk to the guesthouse in silence. I had no conversational French in my repertoire, and I don't think he was in a talking mood anyway.

Then it was up the stairs, down the dark corridor, and into my room. I gestured to the bed, talking in English now because I had no idea how to explain in French what needed doing.

"My bed. Look under my bed. Under the bed."

He gave me a blank look.

Again, I resorted to physical contact, pulling him toward the bed. From the scowl on his face, I'm pretty sure that he thought I was trying to maneuver him *onto* the bed for the purposes of a between-meals tryst. But I managed to push him down close enough to the floor that when he looked *under* the bed, he saw the owl.

The baker stood back up. I threw my hands in the air, as if to say, "How the hell do you deal with a situation like this?"

He gave me a piteous look, took one of the head posts of the bed in each hand, lifted one end of it off the floor, and the owl—as if this were a routine he and the baker did all the time—alighted and flew right out the window.

The baker let the bed fall with a thud, turned on his heel, and left the room, closing the door behind him.

He wasn't quite as friendly to me during my remaining week and a half at Mark Meneau. I did all right, though: in my second week, I was promoted to the hot line to fill in for a vacationing cook, leaving those young French kids in the dust. Then I took two weeks to explore Paris, before heading back home to New York and my new job in what remains one of the best restaurants in the city.

The French word for *owl*, by the way, is *chouette*, which also means "cool" or "brilliant."

Yeah, right.

The Curious Case of Tommy Flynn
JONATHAN EISMANN

Jonathan Eismann is the chef-owner of South Beach, Florida's perennially hot Pacific Time restaurant, which has been at the center of the Lincoln Road scene since the restaurant was launched in 1993. A graduate of the Culinary Institute of America, Eismann began working professionally with Pan Asian flavors in New York City in the 1980s as chef of the Acute Café on West Broadway, and then at such restaurants as Batons, Fandango, Mondial, and China Grill. In 1994, he became one of the first chefs to receive the Robert Mondavi Award for Culinary Excellence.

THERE ARE MANY differences between a chef and a cook. A chef, in a competitive big-city environment anyway, needs to have vision, create his own dishes, and manage a crew of peripatetic soldiers for hire. He needs to be able to stay calm under pressure, navigate any number of thorny political situations, and be able to recognize and coddle the media.

A cook doesn't have to do all that. A cook has to do one

thing: execute, execute, execute—the same dishes, over and over, all day, every day, for months if not years at a time. Some cooks want to be chefs one day, and that's fine. But ambition isn't a job requirement, at least not in my kitchen. I'm looking for guys who can cook well and consistently and are willing to work their butts off.

I've always put a premium on hard work. Back before I owned my own place, you could find me right alongside the contractors, painting, tiling, and woodworking. Even *in* my own place, I'm happy to come in on, say, Christmas Day, and refinish the floors.

I respond to this work ethic when I encounter it in others. I'm not making any judgments about people who don't have it, but when I see it, I'm drawn to it.

Which is how I came to hire a young line cook named—for this story, anyway—Tommy Flynn.

This was in 1989. I had been the chef at restaurants such as Mondial and Fandango, and most recently China Grill. I was planning to open my own restaurant down in Miami—Pacific Time on Miami Beach—which I eventually did, and from where I'm writing this story. To bide my time, and make a living, I took a low-profile gig as the chef of a ninety-seat Victorian-style café way up in nosebleed land in the East Nineties on Madison Avenue.

The restaurant was really a glorified bar typical of the Upper East Side. If you've been to or read about Jim McMullen's or J. G. Mellon's, then you know the kind of place I mean. The menu was perfunctory, but I created and executed it with pride. In fact, we were once written up in *Gourmet* magazine for our burgers.

Across the street from this restaurant was a small epicurean shop fashioned as a mini-Balducci's: dark wood paneling, fresh fruits and vegetables piled artfully in crates, and lots of imported condiments and delicacies. They also had a sandwich counter from which I often bought my lunch.

This is where I met Tommy, a short, scraggly, pimply, red-headed, working-class Irish kid from Queens. He was about twenty-five years old and an intense worker, especially compared to the preppy but lethargic neighborhood kids alongside whom he worked.

Tommy had great New York sandwich-counter style. He'd slap your sandwich together in record time, always making it exactly the same way—with just the right proportion of meat to cheese to salad to bread—then snap open a paper bag with one hand—I still remember the quick "pop" it made as the air was forced into it—and pack it up for you.

I didn't know Tommy that well. Because of the counter that was always between us, I had actually never seen him from the chest down or even shaken his hand. But I admired his work ethic.

You're constantly losing employees in a restaurant kitchen, so one day I decided to stroll across the street and casually poach young Tommy. Having watched him work for months, I had no doubt that I could teach him what he'd need to know to be a cook in my five-man kitchen.

In return, I thought, I'd earn his loyalty and have a guy on board who wasn't always on the lookout for the next job.

We spoke. He took the job. We set a start date. And I stopped going to that shop for my sandwiches, a small price to pay if my plan held true to form.

When Tommy showed up in my kitchen a few days later, he pretty much looked like what I'd expected him to when he left the confines of his counter.

Except for one thing. On his left arm was a device: a tan-colored cuff of sorts around his wrist, with opaque plastic appendages that stretched under and around his knuckles. On his forearm was a lever; whenever he wanted to open or close his fist, he had to crank the lever to manipulate his hand.

If you had a GI Joe with action grip as a kid, then you get the idea.

I took one look at that device and felt terrible. This kid had left his job for me and I was pretty sure that I had screwed him up bad. Surely, he could never work in a professional kitchen.

"Tommy, I don't know what to say. There's no way you can work here, man."

Tommy had obviously been down this road before: "Listen, boss," he said. "Don't worry about it."

He went on to explain that he had gotten trashed on beer one night and fallen asleep on his arm, cutting off the circulation for hours. As a result, he had "put my nerves to sleep."

He continued, with sunny optimism, to explain that "the doctor said I was really lucky. A few more hours and they would've had to amputate it." Twice a week he was going to a Queens clinic for therapy, but it obviously wasn't doing any good.

I subsequently learned that this injury presents itself in drunks and junkies all the time. Not that Tommy was either.

To convince me of his physical dexterity, he began grabbing, lifting, then putting down a series of pans and utensils. Even though he had to crank the lever each time he picked something up and again to release it when he put it down, he had such a rhythm about it that he was, it seemed to me, faster and quicker than most guys in my kitchen.

Okay, I thought, let's give the kid a shot.

It turned out that Tommy was exactly what I had hoped he would be: a great executor. All you had to do was show him how to make a dish—explain what the signs of doneness were, what to look and sniff for, and how to plate it—and he was good to go.

And he had great instincts. For example, many young cooks who aren't blessed with natural finesse miss the center of the plate, by which I mean they will put down the protein, the starch, and the vegetable, and when all is said and done, there'll be a big white portion of plate showing through in the middle. Tommy didn't have that problem; he naturally filled out the center, making it that much easier to train him.

Over the next few months, he worked the sauté station, then the fry station.

One Sunday, we were grinding our way through a typically long, grueling brunch. The kitchen was hot—so hot that we all wore shorts in the summer—and Tommy was flowing to his own unique rhythm, a series of traditional kitchen movements punctuated by his emphatic, though strangely silent cranking of the hand lever.

As if brunch weren't enough of a circus, we had to keep producing a ridiculous amount of toast to go out with the entrees. As a result, we had a line of five or six toasters lined up along the lowboy—a waist-high stainless-steel shelf—and periodically when they were all going at once, they would overload the outlet. I'd have to stop everything and run over and play around with the cables, or reset the breaker, until they came back on.

As I was making my way over for the umpteenth time, Tommy said, "Chef, if you want, I'll come over there and fix that for you."

I told him to just stay where the hell he was and do his job. What was he, crazy? How could he tackle an electrical problem with that crazy contraption on his hand?

Tommy pulled a New York City Electrical Union worker's card out of his wallet and flashed it at me.

"Chef, I'm an electrician. I can fix that."

As always, Tommy was full of surprises.

I handed him my needle-nose pliers and stood aside. He hopped up on the lowboy, his exposed knees on the steel, and went to work on the socket.

"Tommy," I said. "You're the electrician, but that thing's hot. There's two hundred twenty volts running through it."

"Don't worry, Chef, I—"

And right there, right where it's supposed to say "know what I'm doing," a deafening boom rocked the room and the kitchen went pitch black.

A few seconds later the emergency lights came on and washed the room in their B-movie glare.

All of the cooks were standing around, rattled. But Tommy had vanished.

Then I heard a noise from the ground, like the crying of a sick baby goat. I looked down and saw Tommy in a heap, a crumpled bundle with a little pile of red hair on top. He had been blasted right off the lowboy.

"Omigod, Tommy. Are you all right?"

Not a word. Just more wounded groaning.

I dispatched one of the line cooks to call EMS and knelt down beside the kid.

"Tommy! Are you okay?"

He began to nod unconvincingly.

"Are you okay?"

"Yeah. Yeah."

"What's your name?"

"Tom . . . Tom . . . Tommy."

"Let's try to get you up."

I hooked my arms under Tommy's armpits and helped lift him up off the ground. He put his arms out, one against the lowboy and one against the door to the walk-in.

Suddenly, he snapped into consciousness, his eyes locked on the door.

No, not the door.

His left hand.

It was open, and as he stood up on his own two feet, he held his hand out before him, like an infant just discovering that it was attached to his arm. He opened and closed his fist . . . without the aid of the lever.

"Chef! My hand. It's fixed. It's fixed."

He continued opening and closing his palm with delight. Laughing.

"I can't believe it! It's fixed!"

He took off the device and threw it in the garbage can, flexing his hand again and again, faster and faster.

"It's totally back to normal!"

Of course it was. Because, Tommy later told me, his biweekly therapy consisted of a technician attaching electrodes to his hand and forearm and zapping them with little bursts of electricity. If only they had turned it up to a near-lethal dose, he might've been spared all those months with a semiprosthetic hand.

His paralysis cured, Tommy got back on the line and went back to work. He was a little thrown at first—not having to crank that lever threw off the rhythm he had established over the past few months. But Tommy was a great cook, an intrepid professional, and he adjusted soon enough, pumping out dish after dish just the way I always knew he could.

The Blob
CLAUDIA FLEMING

A native of Long Island, New York, Claudia Fleming originally moved to Manhattan to become a dancer. To support herself, she worked in the dining rooms at Jams and Union Square Café, and eventually decided to pursue a career in the kitchen, studying at Peter Kump's New York Cooking School, then working at Montrachet, Tribeca Grill, and Luxe, as well as Fauchon in Paris. She rose to fame at Gramercy Tavern in 1994. Her numerous accolades include the James Beard Foundation's Hawaiian Vintage Outstanding Pastry Chef for 2000. Pastry Art & Design magazine named her one of their 10 Best Pastry Chefs in 2000 and 2001. She is the author of The Last Course: Desserts from Gramercy Tavern.

T HEY CALLED IT the Sugar Tower.

That was the name the cooks downstairs had for the pastry kitchen on the second floor of Tribeca Grill, the Drew Nieporent–Robert DeNiro partnership in what would soon become the Tribeca Film Center in Lower Manhattan.

I was the assistant pastry chef, which means I was the daytime pastry cook, the one in charge of production, who'd get all the food prepped so the nighttime pastry team, led by Pastry Chef Gerry Hayden—also the restaurant's sous-chef—would be ready to roll come the dinner hour.

This was in 1990, before Tribeca Grill began serving lunch, and long before I had anything remotely resembling a clue.

Oh, I knew the basics. I had attended Peter Kump's New York Cooking School, and worked in a kitchen or two. But I was given this job more for my spunk than my experience: I had served my culinary externship at Montrachet, one of Drew's other restaurants, and in my spare time, I'd make myself useful by polishing glass and silverware. Drew, himself a service veteran before he became one of the most successful restaurateurs in the country, took note of my work ethic and when Tribeca was set to open, he rang me up and offered me a job. Just like that.

Having had a previous career—as a dancer—I came to cooking late, and was an old lady by kitchen standards. I was thirty-three, and the prep guys and line cooks wanted nothing to do with me. I guess I didn't want anything to do with them, either.

So I spent my mornings alone in the spookily empty restaurant, up in the Sugar Tower, a small self-contained kitchen with a counter along two walls and a big mixer in the corner, not seeing much of anyone else even after they started showing up around lunchtime.

Not that I had the time to socialize. There were cakes, ice creams, sauces, and garnishes to be made, and I was so new to all of it and so overwhelmed that I was working at a manic pace, racing frantically to keep up. I didn't even have time to enjoy or take note of the buzz the restaurant was generating. I'm told that it was frequented by celebrities galore, but I never saw them. One night, Nelson Mandela had a party there, and I didn't even know it was happening.

I was so unconnected with anything else going on at Tribeca Grill that one morning, when I ventured down into the empty dining room, and I spotted an old guy who had found his way into the restaurant and was wandering around aimlessly, pushing his bicycle, I barked, "Who are you and what do you want!"

"Umbobbyere," he mumbled.

"What! Speak up."

"Is Bobby here?"

"There's no Bobby here. Bobby who?"

"Bobby DeNiro. I'm his dad."

Turns out that not only was this guy with the bicycle the father of our superstar owner, he was also the artist whose paintings graced the walls of the dining room in which we were standing.

Whoops.

That's what it was like for me in those days. And this kind of mind-set can take a toll on you. In time, the amount of things you don't know erodes your confidence in what you actually *do* know.

Case in point: when you're a relatively newly minted cook, you look for ways to cut corners and do things your own way, and so one day, I decided to save time and get ahead of schedule with my production of meringue, the whipped-egg-white-and-sugar mixture. Rather than starting with one quart of egg whites, I would begin with about eight quarts. I dumped them in the 40-quart bowl and switched on the industrial mixer.

Then I turned to some other work, heating a pan of sugar and using a pair of pliers to pull antennaelike wands from it, setting them aside to cool.

As the mixer continued to whirr away, making the meringue, I strolled downstairs to the ladies' room.

When I returned, I was shocked to see that the whites had whipped into a giant sudsy beehive, a frothy mass that was currently peaking two feet over the top of the enormous stainless-steel bowl.

I gasped—and the sound, a quick little inhalation, seemed to be more than enough to cause the ensuing egg-white avalanche. With a plop, the beehive toppled over the sides of the bowl and ran down the sides of the counter.

My hands flew to my mouth. I stood frozen, in horror, as the blob continued to grow, sliding down to the floor and then, upon making contact, beginning a slow but steady path *right for me.*

This was just meringue, mind you, but my mental faculties were so shot that I was actually terrified of it. Indeed, visions of what this blob might do next filled my head. I imagined it flowing without end, making its way out the door, bulging into the private party space, and slithering down the stairs into the kitchen, where it—and by it, I mean "I"—would become the source of jokes for years to come.

I spun around and ran for help.

"Gerry, Gerry," I cried, to anyone within earshot, all those young cooks with their baseball caps on backward who never talked to me.

They must have thought someone was injured because they responded with genuine concern.

"What's wrong?"

In my panic, I didn't think these wet-nosed kids could help

me. Only a seasoned pro like Gerry would know how to stop the dreaded meringue from continuing its march.

"Gerry. Gerry. Where's Gerry?"

"In the dining room."

I ran out into the dining room and found Gerry having an impromptu meeting with one of his cooks.

"Gerry! Gerry!"

"What?"

Breathlessly, I described the situation: "I put too many egg whites in the machine." Deep breath. "And it came up over the top." Deep breath. "And it's running down the sides and across the room." Deep breath. "And it's almost out the door and, and—"

"What?"

I was at the end of my rope. "*What do I do?*" I screamed.

He could not have been calmer or more matter of fact: "Turn off the mixer."

Oh, right. Turn off the mixer. I guess I knew all along, back in some regrettably overlooked recess of my mind—in the same vicinity where I stored the fact that egg whites left to whip without end will multiply up to eight times in volume—that if you turn off the mixer, they will stop volumizing.

Duh.

Without a word, I ran up the stairs, back to the Sugar Tower. I stepped over the blob and approached the machine. With a defiant look at the fluffy white beast, I shut off the mixer, abruptly halting its march.

A moment later, Gerry came charging into the room with two line cooks in tow, and when they saw me huffing and puffing and nearly in tears, standing over a mountain of meringue, they burst out laughing.

I joined them. At least, I had regained my senses enough to recognize that this was funny.

Years later, after we had gone our separate ways, Gerry and I reconnected at the James Beard Awards. One thing led to another, and we fell in love and got married.

We're still laughing today.

The Blind Line Cook
GABRIELLE HAMILTON

Gabrielle Hamilton is the chef-owner of Prune, which she opened in New York City's East Village in October 1999. Prune was named in Time Out New York's *2000 Top 100 and Gael Greene's "Where to Eat in the New Millennium" in New York* magazine, *and also featured in* Saveur 100 *in 2001. She has written for the* New Yorker, Saveur *magazine, and* Food & Wine *and had the eight-week Chef's Column in the* New York Times. *Her work has been anthologized in* Best Food Writing 2001, 2002, *and* 2003.

A COUPLE YEARS AGO I placed an ad for a line cook. And there was a guy who, according to his résumé, should have been right up my alley. He held a grill position in a busy seafood joint at the shore; he had studied philosophy and political science; and he had about four years of experience in the industry. I was looking forward to meeting this guy from my own home state, with whom an after-work conversation over beers might be possible, and who had just enough years in the industry to still have something to learn, but not so few that he would need to be taught everything. I called him up and we had a pleasant phone exchange. I liked his voice, his manner; he was intelligent and articulate. I invited him in for an interview the following day.

The first thing I noticed when he arrived was that he was blind. His eyes wandered around in their sockets like tropical fish in the aquarium of a cheap hotel lobby. We managed a handshake and sat at the bar. I asked him about his responsibilities as a lunch chef at the busy seafood restaurant and he answered entirely reasonably. He understood the language I used and spoke it back to me: the sort of shorthand code that people who work in kitchens speak.

I said, "How many covers for lunch?"

And he said, "Eighty-five to one ten."

I said, "What kind of *mis* is there in a fried seafood place?"

And he laughed and said, "Yeah, it's all lemon wedges and tartar sauce."

We talked a bit about his education in political philosophy: he was a Hegel fan. Finally, I showed him our menu. He held it up to his face as if to breathe in its written contents, to discover by inhaling what it said in plain print. I felt more certain than ever when I observed this that he was blind, but naturally doubted myself because obviously the guy had worked in restaurants, which—though we may joke—really can't and shouldn't be done. And in spite of the proximity of the menu to his face, I thought maybe I was making some despicable assumptions about the "sight impaired" and needed to get my politics up to date.

So I booked him for a trail.

I went right downstairs and unpinned the schedule from the cork board and penciled him into the grill station the next night.

He wrote his new phone number on the top of his résumé in large unwieldy script and even managed, more or less, to locate and cross out the old number. I looked at him as directly in the eyes as one could, thinking maybe I should ask about what seemed obvious but instead I said, "Well, you seem average in build—we have pants and jackets in the general human range so you don't need to bring your own whites. And you'll just need a chef knife, a utility, and a paring knife. No need to bring your 40-pound kit tomorrow." He nodded, without returning my gaze.

"Is there anything else you can think of?" I asked, hopefully. He said only that he'd like to keep the menu if I didn't mind so he could study it a bit before his trail. Done deal. We shook hands again, miraculously.

For the rest of the day I thought maybe he wasn't blind, and that just because his eyes rolled around didn't mean he couldn't make out shape and color. But then I thought *shape shmape* and *color schmolor*, how is this guy going to dice a white onion on a white cutting board? I thought maybe I was an ignorant asshole who didn't realize how far the blind had come. Maybe he had worked out some kind of system to compensate. I took a mental inventory of famous accomplished blind people. Could playing the piano be anything like grilling fish over open flame, in the midst of hot fryer fat, sharp knives, macho line cooks, and slippery floors? What was the preferred term for blind these days, anyway, I wondered.

By the morning of his trail, I had talked myself into the certainty that though blind, he was obviously "sighted" in some other way. I felt sure that I was behind the times for thinking just because someone was blind that they couldn't work a job as a line cook in a busy restaurant. I knew, vaguely, that when a person lost one sense, the others kicked in expertly to compensate. I assured myself that he had developed a system by which he *heard* the food, or *felt* the food, or smelled which plate was used for which entrée. I became convinced that he, in fact, had evolved into such a higher species of line cook that we would learn greatness from him. I got so "on board" with the whole blind-line-cook thing that I was plainly righteous when asked by my incredulous— and slightly unnerved—line cooks why I had booked a trail with a blind guy. I practically had indignation in my tone. "What? You think just because the guy is *'visually challenged'* that he can't cook in a restaurant?"

When he arrived for his trail, I took him around on an introductory tour of the prep area and the walk-in and the hot line. At each station, he bent over and put his forehead against everything I showed him. It was fascinating at first—and later, heartbreaking—to note the angle at which he scrutinized each item in the refrigerator.

"Over here," I said, "is where all the proteins are kept. Fish here. Meat here. Cooked above raw. Always. Okay?" And instead of holding the six-pan of pork belly close under his nose and squinting down upon it—like a very old man might do trying to read his train ticket—he instead held each item up to his forehead, above his eyebrows, and stared up imploringly into it.

We set him up in the basement prep area with a cutting board and a menial task that wouldn't matter if he screwed it up: picking parsley. This took him most of the afternoon and it was painful to watch him bent in half, killing his back in order to have his untethered eyes close to the cutting board.

The trail is simply the time to sniff out the guy, to see how he stands, how he holds his knives, how much he talks or doesn't, and what he says. Does he ravage everything with tongs or finesse with a fork and a spoon? Does he sit at the bar at the end of his trail and get hammered? Did he bring a pen and small pad of paper? Did he thank the people who trailed him? I wasn't worried that he was supposed to hold down the grill station. And I didn't give a shit about the parsley. But I understood twenty-five minutes into his trail that there was no system of compensation, he had not become hypersensate, and that he had not, emphatically, evolved into a superior cooking machine. Sadly, the guy was just plain blind. And I still had on my hands another four hours and thirty five minutes of a trail to honor.

The night started slowly with just a couple of tickets at a time. I buckled myself into a seat at the back of the bus, so to speak, right behind the blind guy in the grill station and let my sous-chef do the driving: calling out the tickets and their timing, expediting their plating and pickups. Every time an order came into our station, I quietly narrated the procedure to the trailer, and watched, slack-jawed, as he painstakingly retrieved a portion of meat from the cooler, held it to his forehead, set it on a plate, and then proceeded to carefully season the countertop with an even sprinkling of salt. When the call to "fire" an item came, I stood back and let him place the meat onto the grill—which he managed—but I had to pull him back a few inches from the flames so he wouldn't singe his bangs.

Eventually we fell into a kind of spontaneous, unfunny vaudeville routine in which I shadowed him, without him knowing, and seasoned the meat he missed, turned the fish he couldn't, moved the plate under his approaching spatula to receive the pork, like an outfielder judging a flyball in Candlestick Park. I was not worried about him slowing down the line as we never expect a trailer to actually perform a vital function. But I really started to feel sick with worry when he pulled a full, fresh, piping hot basket of shoestring fries up out of the fat with his right hand and turned them out to drain—not into the waiting stack of giant coffee filters he held in his left hand, but into the thin air directly adjacent, pouring them out onto the dirty rubber mats and his clogs.

This did not escape the notice of the other cooks. All the lightheartedness of a good night on the line went right up the exhaust hood. The banter between *garde manger* and sauté came to a screeching halt. The fun part of getting through the night—donkey noises, addressing the male line cooks as "ladies," as in "Let's go, ladies!"—was abandoned. The stern but soft-hearted barking from the bus driver down the line lost all playful bite and got tamed down to the most perfunctory, gently articulated, "Please fire apps on seven." With one basket of hot fries cascading to the ground we all saw at once that this fellow was in physical danger.

In silence, I raked the fries up off the floor, trashed them, and dropped another order on the double. I asked him, kindly, to step back to the wall and just watch a bit, explaining that the pace was about to pick up and I wanted to keep the line moving. This is—even when you have all your wits—the most humiliating part of a trail: when the chef takes you off of the line in the middle of your task. You die one thousand deaths. For a blind guy with something to prove, maybe two thousand.

To this point I had been somehow willing to participate in whatever strange exercise this guy was putting himself through. I was suspending disbelief, like we are all asked to do every time we go to see a play or watch a movie. *I know that this isn't real but I agree to believe that it is for these two hours without intermission.* But something about the realization of the danger he was flirting with in service of his project, whatever his project was, suddenly pissed me off. I took over the station and started slamming food onto the plates, narrating my actions to him in barely suppressed snide tones. "This," I practically hissed, "is the pickup on the prawns. Three in a stack, napped with anchovy butter. Wanna *write that down?*"

I exhausted myself with passive-aggressive vitriol. "On the rack of lamb, you want an internal temp of one twenty-five. Just *read the thermometer*, okay."

This got the attention of my sous-chef, who quietly came over and asked the guy if he'd like to step into *garde manger* for a while to see how things there ran. I was relieved to have the guy away from the fire and the fat and in the relatively harmless oasis of cold leafy salads and cool creamy dressings. And I was grateful to be rescued from my worst self. The guy spent the rest of his trail with his back up against the wall in all the stations, eyes rolling around in his head, pretending to apprehend how each station worked. I spent the remainder of his trail wrestling meat and unattractive feelings triggered by this insane predicament in which we had found ourselves.

I have never known what he was doing. I allowed him to finish out the whole trail, and when he had changed his clothes, I encouraged him to sit at the bar and have something to eat, which he did. And as he was leaving I said I would call him the next day, which I did. I told him that I was looking for someone with a little more power, a bit more of a heavy-hitter, but that I would keep him in mind if a position more aligned with his skills became available. This, remarkably, he seemed to see coming.

Genus Loci
FERGUS HENDERSON

Fergus Henderson trained as an architect before becoming a chef, opening the French House Dining Room in 1992 and St John in 1995, which has won numerous awards and accolades, including Best British and Best Overall London Restaurant at the 2001 Moët & Chandon Restaurant Awards. He is the author of The Whole Beast: Nose to Tail Eating, *winner of the 2000 Andre Simon Award.*

I T WAS THE middle of an evening service, orders were rattling out of the printer on the pass; there was a good flow afoot. The chefs were, each and every one, full steam ahead. Suddenly a *commis* chef of a very bouncy nature gave out a cry and became more than usually agitated. Clasping her ample chest, she shouted, "I've lost my crystal! Where's my crystal?" A matter not of the greatest urgency during the middle of a busy service, but after sending half a pot roast pig's head for two—a thing of joy—I went to enquire what the problem was. The *commis* chef explained: in her previous life she had worked with a vet in a large stable, during which time she had discovered a lump in one of her breasts. A real do-it-yourself kind of girl, she had dosed herself up on horse tranquilizer and proceeded to cut out the lump, and then sew the wound back up. To complete this surgery, she had nestled a healing crystal into the resultant indent. This, not surprisingly, took the kitchen somewhat aback. All chefs and kitchen porters stopped what they were doing to start looking for this far-from-ordinary stone.

Well, now that we are on our hands and knees scouring the kitchen floor for the crystal, it seems a good moment to ponder the peculiar nature of restaurants, this recent discovery putting one into a thoughtful frame of mind.

The kitchen—which in my experience is staffed by an extraordinarily diverse group of people who become an incredibly close team when dressed in their whites, inhabit a fairly inhospitable space, and produce delicious food on time at different times—is the heart of a restaurant. Even speaking as a chef, a restaurant is not just the food (though let's not forget how vital that is), but it is more. It is the "whole catastrophe" which comes together to create the magic that can exist in a great restaurant. *Genus loci* (the spirit of time and place) is strong in the world of restaurants.

When asked to cook a grand lunch at another establishment, could we make it very St John? We were delighted. Encapsulating spring and St John perfectly, we prepared a lunch of gull's eggs and celery salt, then a slice of jellied tripe. (I know the word *tripe* strikes fear into the stomachs of many, but we have won over the most fervent antitripists with jellied tripe.) This was followed by braised squirrel and wild garlic. Gamekeepers at this time of year are culling squirrel, as they are seen as vermin, so there is much squirrel around. It is delicious and cooks very well, rather like wild rabbit.

This recipe, rather poetically with the aid of some dried cepes and the wilted garlic greens, re-created the bosky woods the squirrels came from. I popped my head out of the kitchen to see how the lunch went down, only to be met by the rather crushing comment: "That was a very brave menu." Now, if this lunch had taken place at St John, this comment would never have been made. It must be something to do with the musk and vibrations—the spirit of time and place.

The magic is rife, the dining room full of happy eaters, you're serving food you and your chefs love and enjoy, and that pleasure gets passed through the food to the eater. Everyone is tucking in. It's fantastic. . . . Then lo and behold, we get a message that someone on table 27 says their grouse livers on toast are not grouse livers. Crash goes the magic. What's the point of cooking the rest of that person's lunch when they just said the kitchen is lying? Where's the joy in that? I'm sure people like that get indigestion. But let us not dwell on this sour occasion.

The customer's tolerance, on the whole, is extraordinary. For example, one night pepper fell onto a hot flat top stove, causing an evil stinging smoke, which the dumbwaiter sucked up and proceeded to exhale into the dining room. It traveled like mustard gas through the trenches, table after table being affected, triggering coughing and spluttering. Strangely, once fresh air was made available and the gas attack was over, everyone was remarkably jovial about the whole affair; this was all part of the theater of the restaurant.

But woe betide the chef who is late with their supper! Here is where the tolerance ends. It is the interesting thing in the whole equation: timing. However much people love the food, and whatever strange smells and punishing gases they agree to wilfully endure, they want the food *on time*. This is no dinner party at home where you can placate your guest with another round of martinis until you've put the final touches on your creation.

A waiter came into the kitchen one evening and promptly collapsed on the floor in a writhing mess, his eyes rolling back into his head. An ambulance was called, but it was evident that he needed wiser and more prudent attention than fellow waiters or chefs could administer in the short term. So we stepped out of the kitchen and yelled "IS THERE A DOCTOR IN THE HOUSE?" Fortunately there was one who could do right by the waiter until he was wheeled away strapped to a stretcher. Now the yelling and the stretcher seem to come under the theater of a restaurant, not deflecting anyone's appetite, but the fact that we had emergency ward 10 going on in our kitchen did not seem to alter the fact that they still wanted their mains on time.

Enough ruminating. It's time to get off my hands and knees; I can hear someone's found the crystal among a pile of oyster shells. With the crystal washed, dried, and safely returned to its cozy nook, service could resume, much to everyone's relief. Except for the floor staff. A waiter cannot say, "I'm afraid your dinner's been held up for ten minutes because the kitchen have all had to stop to look for a healing crystal that fell out of a hole in one of the chef's breasts, due to her self-mutilation in a horsy haze." Even though it was the truth.

Just as a last reassuring note, I met the chef some years later. She's looking very well, I'm glad to report.

(Not) Ready for My Close-up
PAUL KAHAN

Paul Kahan, winner of the 2004 James Beard Foundation's Best Chef/Midwest award, has been executive chef of Chicago's Blackbird since the restaurant opened in 1997. Prior to Blackbird, he worked at some of Chicago's best restaurants, including Metropolis Café, Metropolis 1800, Frontera Grill, and Topolobampo. Blackbird's accolades include a place on Gourmet *magazine's list of Chicago's top five restaurants and the magazine's list of the country's top fifty restaurants. In 1999,* Food & Wine Magazine *placed Kahan on its Best New Chefs list. In September 2003, Kahan, along with Chef du Cuisine Koren Grieveson and his Blackbird team opened Avec, a wine bar located next door to Blackbird.*

A LOT OF GUYS who, like me, grew up in the era of celebrity chefs, are in it for the fame and glory. But that's not what attracted me. I came to cooking relatively late in life—in my early twenties—and got into it because I love the work, not because I need to see my mug in the papers, or on television.

But public relations is important, so you do what you need to in order to get your name and the name of your restaurant out there. You provide recipes to magazines. You share tips with the local papers. You go on television when your publicist can swing it. It all helps get the word out and keeps the dining masses aware of your restaurant and what you do there.

Despite my appreciation of this fact, there's one element of the PR mix that I've never been particularly comfortable with: the live cooking demo. I'm happy to demonstrate just about anything for one of my cooks, or even for a home cook looking for a little professional advice. But cooking demos, it seems to me, are a time when people expect chefs to ham it up, to crack jokes and clown around and really make a show of it. That's just not my style. If I wanted to do all that, I'd have become an actor.

Nevertheless, about three years ago, one of the national food magazines threw a food festival in the Grand Ballroom at the end of Navy Pier, a big attraction on Lake Michigan that's about a quarter-mile long and quite wide. Once a naval docking station, Navy Pier was converted years ago into a site for festivals, antiques shows, and so on. There are shops and a Ferris wheel and a children's museum and . . . well, you get the idea. At the end of the pier is the ballroom, a gigantic, domed space that's used for conventions and other special events.

As part of this festival, a representative from one of the major cooking-equipment companies convinced me to do a demo for them. I was told that it was a simple affair: I'd prepare the same dish three times for three different audiences, then people would file out of the auditorium into a little makeshift café where they'd sample another dish from my restaurant, prepared and served by a sous-chef and some line cooks we'd bring along for the day.

This sounded like the kind of thing that would be an ordeal for me, so I was hesitant. In fact, I initially declined. Even when the event's organizing chef told me it would be no big deal, I still had my doubts. I didn't know why, but something was tingling in the back of my head, telling me there was more here than met the eye.

Nevertheless, I eventually agreed to do it. The dish would be Seared Diver Scallop with Wild Mushrooms, Sea Beans, and Meyer Lemon, a collection of slightly exotic ingredients finished with a warm Meyer lemon vinaigrette that was emulsified with butter.

On the morning of the demo, I arrived at the Navy Pier, parked out back behind the service entrance, and found my way to the little holding area that served as a backstage of sorts. I had brought my own chef coat along, with my restaurant's logo on the left breast, but before I could put it on, one of the cooking company's reps handed me a new one, with the name of the company emblazoned on the front, and my name, in smaller letters, above it.

I found that a bit odd, but it was nothing compared to the surprise I was about to receive: when I stepped into the amphitheater, I discovered that the room was set up as a gargantuan demonstration pit, with a full kitchen in the center and seats surrounding it on all sides—360 degrees of audience. Moreover, the sheer volume was astounding: there had to be *two thousand* seats.

As if that weren't daunting enough, above the kitchen hung a huge 12-foot banner with a close-up of my face on it, and above the photo, in big block letters, my name and the name of my restaurant. When I saw that, my heart sank. This was a setting fit for a heavyweight fight, not a cooking demo.

Before I could protest, the crowd began to file in, a nonstop procession of Chicago-area food enthusiasts who had purchased tickets to see me cook. They filled every last seat.

A techie appeared from out of nowhere and clipped a little microphone onto my jacket, the house lights dimmed, and there I was, expected to perform.

I began the demonstration, slowly, tentatively, not feeling my best, beginning with some basic instruction on how to shop for and properly clean a diver scallop.

And that's when my cell phone rang.

Here's the thing with the cell phone: it's my lifeline to my restaurant, and more importantly, to the love of my life, my wife, Mary. Mary and I have been together for about twelve years and we're just as in love now as we always have been.

Beyond our deep, personal connection, Mary's been a huge supportive force in my professional career. I earned two degrees in college—applied math and computer science—but I was never happy in those fields. After college, I was killing time, driving a delivery truck for my dad's smoked fish company, when Mary got me a job working for a friend of hers at a local pastry shop and cafe. That was how I first became interested in becoming a chef. So I really do owe it all to her.

Ironically, being a chef can be a relationship killer. There are weeks when we barely see each other—I come home after midnight and she often gets up and out at the crack of dawn to hit a yoga class before heading to her office.

But we've made it work, so well in fact that I often find myself coaching young cooks on how to maintain a relationship.

One of the ways Mary and I get along is by being available to each other by cell phone. If she has something to tell me, even if it's during dinner service, I'll pick up the phone and talk to her. At first, she would detect urgency in my voice, which understandably irked her. So I worked hard at, and soon mastered, the art of sounding like I have all the time in the world, no matter what kind of chaos might be transpiring around me.

Being available in this way is important to me. Not only does it make my wife happy, but God forbid I wasn't there in a time of crisis because I was searing a piece of halibut.

Or doing a demo . . .

So when my cell phone rang that day, echoing through the hall thanks to my clip-on microphone, I glanced down and saw the name "Mary" in the caller ID window. I looked up at the two thousand people in attendance and said, "Sorry, folks, this is my wife, you'll have to excuse me."

This provoked a few chuckles. Maybe they thought I was kidding. But I went ahead and answered the phone and proceeded to have a five-minute conversation with Mary, using my Zen-like ability to hide any sense of distraction in my voice. It didn't matter that I was on stage, with burners turned on and two thousand people waiting to learn how to properly sear a scallop.

Finally, after about five minutes, there was a pause in the conversation and I told Mary where I was and what I was doing. She howled with laughter.

"Okay," she said. "Talk to you later. I love you."

I *always* reply in kind, even when I'm in the midst of twelve hardened line cooks—or two thousand strangers: "I love you too, honey."

When they heard that, every woman in the place let out a huge, sweet, "Awwwww." I laughed. They laughed. And I felt instantly at ease.

That ended up being one of the best demos I've ever done, once the ice was broken and I could stop trying to play the part of the "star" chef and just be, as I was on the phone, myself.

Just Add Water
HUBERT KELLER

Hubert Keller joined Fleur de Lys as a co-owner in 1986, where he was credited with breathing new life into the San Francisco institution. Born in France, he has been the recipient of many awards, including Best Chef: California from the James Beard Foundation. The New York Times has described Fleur de Lys as being "arguably the best French restaurant in San Francisco." Fleur de Lys Las Vegas opened at the Mandalay Bay Resort and Casino in September of 2004. Burger Bar opened at Mandalay Place in February of 2004.

NOW I HAVE to warn you: this story may discourage future generations of caterers from ever entering the business. And I'll admit, it might raise an eyebrow or two. If it weren't for the fact that I was caught smack dab in the middle of this debacle, I might not even believe the tale myself. . . .

With all of that said, picture a young bride from Carmel, her well-to-do father and mother, and enough money to make anyone's dream wedding a reality. In theory, this would seem like that perfect party to host, the perfect party to attend and, like most fairy tales, it would end with the bride and groom riding off into the sunset—while the parents handed over the family fortune to me and my staff for services rendered. But Nature had a different plan that day, and as you will soon find out, no amount of planning could have prepared me for the disastrous results.

The bride's parents lived on a beautiful piece of property that overlooked the Pacific Ocean. Their house resembled a Hollywood home on the Malibu coastline, where the gated entrance and driveway started at street level and descended down the side of a hill. They had spared no expense to plan a lavish wedding on site for 250 of their closest friends and relatives. The main event would feature a five-course menu by yours truly, and a $30,000 cake flown in from New York, a cake so huge and extravagant that it took four hired hands to deplane.

The day before the event, while tents were being erected and flowers being delivered by the truckloads, I overheard the bride's father frantically asking where the three-hundred-year-old oak tree on the property had disappeared to. The bride's mother casually replied, "I had that old thing removed this morning, dear. How else was I supposed to fit the tent?" To conclude her point, she turned to me and said, "Hubert, nothing is impossible here. If you need it done, we'll make it happen." The father looked flushed, and I really couldn't blame him. I'm not particularly superstitious, but it didn't seem like anything good could come from such a frivolous act.

I left the parents of the bride and returned to the kitchen. To accommodate my cooking needs, the bride's mother had essentially created an extension of her kitchen, including additional ovens, gas stoves, etc.—an indispensable addition considering the elaborate degree of preparation involved. There were floor plans, seating charts, endless checklists, and a wedding-day itinerary that was to be followed to the tee: one hour of cocktails and passed canapés, first course to follow immediately afterward. And the pace for the evening was set from there. There was absolutely no room for error.

On the day of the wedding, while the family made their way to the church, I was again situated in that same souped-up kitchen, making sure that the staff was finishing the final details for the event. The first-course plates were all lined up, waiting to be garnished with components of foie gras and caviar. Cases of chilled champagne were being stacked behind the bar, while a steady stream of waiters filed in and out of the kitchen buzzing about the extravagance of it all: custom Bernardaud plates flown in from France, the infamous $30,000 cake, and enough Cristal (or so we thought) to make a rap star blush. The band had just finished setting up their equipment and was performing a sound check, when I noticed the waitstaff using the fine linen to soak up excess water from the floor. The water was seeping into the kitchen from beneath the door. I figured it was someone hosing down the front entryway, so I ignored it and went back to what I was doing. It wasn't until a little while later, after a hurried waiter had slipped on a suddenly sizable puddle of water and dropped an entire tray of plates, that I began to worry.

When I went to investigate, I discovered that the grounds-keeper had been scrambling around for the last fifteen minutes, trying to divert a massive flood of water from entering the house. A major water line, just outside the gate, had burst for no apparent reason, sending gallons upon gallons of water racing down the driveway and right toward the front door. The guests were scheduled to return to the property in less than an hour and the driveway resembled Niagara Falls.

At least a dozen frantic phone calls were made to the city, demanding that someone come out immediately and fix the problem. Yet despite the fact that you needed hip waders just to cross the driveway, I remained confident that things would turn out fine. After all, the menu was right on target. The trays of hors d'oeuvres were ready to go, and the first-course setup had just begun.

Unconcerned, I stepped outside for a moment to get some air . . . and noticed that the beautiful day that we had started out having had gradually turned to a dim, ugly gray. The sky was heavy with clouds, and the morning blueness had completely faded away. Funny thing, the bride's mother had mentioned earlier that there was "zero" chance of precipitation. According to the multiple weather reports she had checked, we were in store for a perfect weekend of sunshine.

Twenty minutes later, someone did arrive—as promised—and turned off the flow of water. With the driveway rapidly drying out, and the house rescued from the impending flood, we were back on track. A white carpet was rolled out to welcome guests, uniformed valets prepared to park cars, and a lady with a headset and a clipboard screamed, "GUESTS ARE ARRIVING IN FIFTEEN MINUTES, PEOPLE!" As the last of the water in the kitchen was being removed via mops and buckets, the first guests showed up.

And that, of course, is when the storm hit. What had seemed to be just an overcast sky had swiftly transformed into a monstrous thunderstorm, with rain pouring down and pelting the disoriented guests. What was meant to be an indoor-outdoor reception had instantly turned into a *very* cramped cocktail hour. Instead of casually walking the grounds, sipping

champagne, and enjoying the well-planned sunset for the afternoon, guests found themselves jammed between the banquet
tables of the main tent, downing glasses of Cristal—and any
cocktail they could get their hands on. The amount of alcohol
consumed within the first hour of this rainy mess was unim-
aginable. Drunken guests mingled among workers with duct
tape, who scrambled to patch holes in the leaky tent. The lady
with the headset stormed into the kitchen and announced that
everything was on hold until the tent was completely "patched
up." Meanwhile the band, which wasn't scheduled to play until
dinner, took it upon itself to appease the drunken crowd with an
equally disastrous cover of "Louie, Louie." . . .

The bride, the bridesmaids, the groom, and the groomsmen all
remained in the guesthouse, waiting for a break in the weather. It
never came. So two hours and many cover songs later, the
wedding party relented and filed in, huddled under umbrel-
las—all except for the bride, whose grand entrance was thwarted
by a nasty gust of wind and a broken umbrella. As I learned that
day, 200 feet of uncovered walkway in a rainstorm can do a lot
of damage to a delicate white dress and hours of makeup. Ushers
tried diverting the soaked bride to the kitchen, where possible
touch-ups could be arranged before her entrance.

Just as she entered the kitchen, however, her makeup and hair
a riotous mess, the sniffling bride slipped on the wet floor,
landing with a vicious thud.

And then the electricity in the entire house went out.

There we all stood, in silence—until the bride wailed, "Does
anybody care about what's happening here? This is *my day*,
damn it! Somebody help me *up*!"

All I could do was huddle in the corner, nervous that in the
event that the lights did return, the extent of her considerable
anger somehow would be fully directed toward me.

Festive sounds were still coming from the tent, where the by-now very drunk guests didn't seem to mind one bit that the music had stopped or the lights had gone out—had they even noticed? In desperation, the lady with the clipboard ordered the valets to pull the cars around the exterior of the tent and use their headlights to help illuminate the inside. At the same time, candles were being lit and distributed throughout the dining area, while an army of generators chugged along to keep the kitchen up and running.

Finally, it was time for dinner.

Once the lady with the clipboard managed to wrestle the guests into their seats, the show was on. Using gas stoves and Sterno cans to keep things warm, the lovingly prepared meal began—three hours into the reception, served to a roomful of people who could barely hold their forks, let alone find them in the dark.

When the power finally returned, it was in the middle of the main-course service. If it wasn't for the band resuming play, the guests might have actually stayed in their seats to eat it. . . .

As for the $30,000 cake, painstakingly attended by more staff members than the soaking bride, it sat pristine and untouched the entire evening.

Toward the end of the night, I took a moment to walk through the tent, to see if I could help console the bride's parents. The band had just broken into a playful rendition of "Singin' in the Rain" when I finally found the couple, seated quietly, looking strangely calm and intoxicated. They seemed humbled by the fact that Mother Nature had put on such a show.

Later, as the guests were leaving, and the skies began to magically clear, the three of us stood outside, next to the fresh tree stump, staring up as the stars appeared, and I thought, Who would believe this unbelievable story about an unbelievable evening that all started with the utterance of those four cursed words, "Nothing is impossible here"?

An Italian in Paris
GIORGIO LOCATELLI

Giorgio Locatelli, from Lombardy, is considered by many to be the best Italian chef in the UK. Giorgio has been involved with several groundbreaking Italian restaurants in London, most notably Zafferano, where he earned his first Michelin star in 1999. In 2002, Giorgio and his wife, Plaxy, opened their first independent restaurant, Locanda Locatelli, which gained a Michelin star in its first year. Giorgio has a very successful TV career and has co-written a cookbook with restaurateur Tony Allan, called Tony and Giorgio. *Giorgio is currently working on his second book, to be published in 2006.*

I N 1 9 8 9, after four years working at the Savoy in London, I thought it was about time I finally went to Paris. In those days Paris was like a finishing school for chefs. The only reason I'd gone to London instead was because I thought it was a lot hipper than Paris, and also because the Savoy was the place where Escoffier had cooked and developed haute cuisine. Nowadays everyone is cooking Italian, but the big buzzword for a chef coming from Italy at that time was "international"; we had to cook all sorts of food, especially French, and the biggest stage of all was in Paris.

So, after four years, I told the Savoy's head chef, Anton Edelmann, that I was leaving. He was pissed off at first, and didn't want me to leave. But he shared the same passion for food that I had, and he had traveled a lot by the time he was thirty, so he eventually wished me the best, even offering to set me up with a job in Paris. When he was younger, he had worked with the directors of Laurent, a famous old restaurant, and he sent me there. The pay wasn't going to be as good—in London I was a senior sous-chef, earning £400 a week, while at Laurent I was going to be a *commis rotissier* making about a third of that (and half of that would go to rent)—but I took it gladly, since it was important to me that I go to Paris.

I arrived on a Friday, with just my knives and a few chef's jackets. I had a contact there, a girl with a room for rent in the Bastille district, very central and on a direct Métro line to the restaurant. We went out for dinner, and then the next day, while wandering the city on my own, I timed the route from home to work. Twice.

On Monday morning, I was supposed to be at the restaurant at eight; I arrived at ten to seven. I sat in a café on the corner of the Champs Elysées, ordered a café au lait, and looked around me, for the first time realizing where I was. I have to admit I felt quite proud that I'd actually made it to Paris.

The first thing they said when I turned up at Laurent was, "The laundry's over there." We got four jackets and two pairs of trousers a week, so I didn't need the few things I'd brought from London. The restaurant even had a shower.

So I started work. The job of the *commis rotissier*, among other things, is to stay all afternoon when everyone else has gone off on a break, and to cook Laurent's famous pommes soufflées, served with châteaubriand and béarnaise sauce, a dish which has never gone off the menu.

The trick to pommes soufflées is to slice the potatoes exactly the right thickness, then dry them properly, so that when they hit the oil in a big pan, at just the right temperature, they puff up perfectly. You can't let them hit the bottom of the pan, or else they are ruined. Trust me—I made so many of them in the first month that the skin on my arms was bright red.

One afternoon, however, they refused to cook properly. I was supposed to have gone on my break hours before, and these fucking potatoes just would not puff up. I was getting more and more frustrated with them, when the sous chef walked in and, seeing me, said, "Well, what do you expect? You're a spaghetti. And, even worse, you learned to cook with *les rosbifs*!"

Charming.

The irony, though, was that the same guys who called me "spaghetti" would come and ask me questions about the classic Escoffier répertoire. At that time, a lot of French chefs had come from bourgeois restaurants outside Paris and didn't really know how to do the fancy sauces, or which garnishes went with which dishes, whereas the Savoy taught us all of them.

I learned a lot at Laurent, though. The Savoy was a restaurant on a truly grand scale, but Laurent was a much more human size, and it showed me that it was possible, with technique and timing, to do things I would have thought were impossible for a smaller place. The cost control was amazing: the cheese cellar was run like a military operation, with twenty-five different cheeses from twenty-five different farms, and the wine list was superb. Laurent was a model of a restaurant that I could imagine running; it was a fantastic, inspiring business.

Laurent's owner was Sir James Goldsmith. When one of his

daughters was getting married, naturally the reception was held in the restaurant. We had a huge, elegant, multitiered wedding cake delivered. It looked like a traditional British wedding cake, but it was actually much more fragile, with layers of cream, fruit, meringue and liqueur-soaked sponge. Of course somebody managed to drop it when we took it out of the van.

This was a disaster. You can't have the boss's daughter getting married with a bashed-up cake, so we sent for an emergency *patissier* who turned up with his spatula in hand, looking a bit like Donatello. I don't know whether he repaired the cake with anything edible—in fact I know there was a chunk of polystyrene in it by the time he'd finished—but it looked pretty good. In any case, we hid the broken side against an enormous vase of flowers, so we just about got away with it, although I wouldn't have liked to get the slice with the polystyrene.

Though I was eventually promoted to *chef de partie* in the fish section, money was still tight. Sometimes I got to supplement my wages with a bit of outside work, like cooking at Vincennes race course, for the Prix d'Amérique. Cash in hand was a real bonus, and it meant I could afford to go back home to Italy a couple of times a year. After one such trip, I drove my little Fiat Panda all the way back from Italy to Paris, and it was fantastic having a car in Paris. One weekend, I drove to Alain Chappel's restaurant; because he was a consultant chef for Laurent, I got to meet him. He was amazing. I even got to go to the market with him: he would visit every stall and pick up just one bunch of carrots, say, from each of them.

Anyway, I'd had a pretty good year and a half living and working in Paris—although it felt a bit provincial after London, where it was already quite rock-and-roll to be a chef; in Paris I was just a fucking cook—when I decided that I'd broaden my experience and take a job at Tour d'Argent. Also, I was eager to get a big fuck-off name on my CV.

They offered me a job as a *chef de partie* in the *garde-manger*, which caused instant resentment among the French *commis* chefs, who refused to understand how a spaghetti could be a *chef de partie*. I don't think I got called by my real name once in the whole time I worked in Paris. "Rital" was the favorite insult, but I was also called "wop," "spic," "spaghetti," "macaroni," "chink" . . . anything but my name.

The only time I even *saw* my real name was back at Laurent, at Christmas, when we had a vote to see who would do the much-disliked job of playing Father Christmas for the kids' party in the restaurant. I checked the trash afterward, and every piece of paper had my name on it. It was a conspiracy, organized by the sous-chef, who has since become a friend but back then was a bit of a bastard. The only problem, apart from the early start—Father Christmas had to come in early on Saturday—was that I didn't speak much French, so the kids probably got the wrong presents.

At Tour d'Argent, the work was much harder and more pressurized than it had been at Laurent. There were twenty-five of us in the kitchen, and another four or five in the pastry section downstairs. I thought I had made some progress while in Paris, but now I realized that, to the chefs at Tour d'Argent, I was just as much of an outsider as ever.

The head chef—I didn't like him at all—used to ask me questions about Italian cooking. At Laurent, now and again I cooked some Italian food—we had a dish of risotto with scallops and champagne sauce, served with Dover sole, and we used to do a bit of tagliolini, and lasagne for staff dinner—so I said I'd cook him some polenta, which I bought from a little Italian shop in the Jewish Quarter.

I brought it back to the restaurant and showed Chef and the sous-chef all the different ways you can prepare polenta—soft, hard, in diamonds, grilled—but they were unbelievable bastards. They just didn't believe Italians could cook. No matter what I did to the polenta, Chef just crossed his arms and, with a sniff, shook his head. But I refused to give up, and in the following days insisted on making it again, varying the method. The only direction I got from Chef was that he wanted it lighter. So I reduced the amount of grain that I used. "Lighter," he insisted. Then I made it with milk, not water. "Lighter." Then half cream and half milk, with lots of butter whisked in at the end . . . until eventually, one day, he said, "*Ça, c'est un vrai purée de maïs!*" But it never, *ever* went on the menu.

One night, I was told to cook dinner for Claude Terrail, the big boss. I cooked him some brill in olive oil and grilled slices of eggplant with roasted tomatoes and marjoram. When he'd finished his meal, he came into the kitchen—the first time I'd ever seen him in there—and demanded, "Who cooked my dinner?"

I was squirming. I thought he was going to explode.

To my surprise, however, he shouted at all the other chefs, saying that they were feeding him cream and butter every night, that they were trying to kill him, and that from now on I would be cooking his dinner every night. I was rather pleased with myself, but I didn't know then that it would lead indirectly to the greatest humiliation of my life. If Terrail hadn't liked his dinner, Chef wouldn't have done the terrine, and I wouldn't have been in the fridge . . . but I'm jumping ahead of myself.

After the episode with Terrail and his dinner, Chef said that we should do something with these vegetables that the boss had liked so much, so we added to the menu a terrine of thin slices of eggplant, zucchini, and peppers, layered with langoustines and set in a little jelly. A serving consisted of two slices of terrine, with three langoustines in each slice. We kept the terrines in the walk-in pastry fridge downstairs, to keep them really cold and make them easier to slice.

One day, I ran downstairs to get the next terrine, went into the fridge, and saw a chef who seemed to be bending down to look at something on the bottom shelf. I guessed it was one of the junior chefs, and I was just about to kick his ass when he stood up and turned around.

It was Chef, his mustache twitching. He had picked up a couple of button onions that he had found on the floor of the fridge, and he handed them to me. *"Tiens, tiens, petit Italien! Regards-ça, rital!"* So I put the onions in my trouser pocket, without thinking, and I rushed upstairs with the terrine. He was obviously trying to make a point about wastage in the kitchen, but I wasn't really in the mood.

I carried on with the service—we were packed that night, and it went on so late that we were still sending out starters at 11:45 p.m.—and at some point I put my hand in my pocket and felt something wet and horrible. It was the two onions. I whispered "Old bastard!" to myself, and threw them in my trash bin, thinking he would have forgotten about them.

At one o'clock in the morning we had finally finished for the night. We were all changing, somebody was having a shower, when the *plongeur* came down and told us that our presence was required upstairs. I could feel that something was wrong.

We all raced up the stairs, and when we got into the kitchen, everybody was given a plastic garbage bag to cut open and spread out on the floor at his station. By this time I realized what was happening.

I don't know whether Chef had set me up deliberately or not—maybe he thought I was getting a bit too big for my boots—but I knew that I was wrong: it might not seem like a big deal, just a couple of onions, but as a chef, if you are really dedicated, you can't throw food away. It's the same philosophy that my mother and grandmother had, and the same idea that I try to instill in the chefs who work with me now. It had crossed my mind to throw them in somebody else's bin, but I didn't, and anyway, Chef knew who he'd given the onions to.

Anyway, at this point, I was just hoping that the onions had miraculously gotten trapped in an empty can or something.

No such luck. As I turned my bin over onto the plastic sheet, the two onions rolled out onto the floor, and I felt like a very naughty schoolboy. Chef, who was a huge motherfucker, suddenly seemed even huger than normal. He made me feel about two feet tall. He had a big stick in his hand, like a school-master or a sergeant major, so he could search through the stuff you had thrown away, and he stabbed angrily at the two onions.

I didn't say a word. I just stood there while he shouted at me. It seemed like he shouted for hours, getting ever louder and redder in the face.

It was the biggest humiliation I have ever felt in my entire life. Chef clearly got a big kick out of screaming at people: I'm sure that was his motivation, nothing to do with wastage or a philosophy of cooking, but still, I knew that I shouldn't have done it. After this, they told me every fucking day that I wasn't good enough to be a chef, and at that point I almost believed them.

I think it was at exactly that moment that I realized I didn't belong in that world. I left Tour d'Argent a couple of weeks later; I didn't even ask for a certificate. Since that day I have never again applied for a job. I didn't need the fuck-off name on my CV, either. Which, given all the shit I went through in Paris, is a little bit ironic.

I have never, since then, cooked a mousse. I have never cooked *quenelles de brochet* again, or lobster Don Carlo, which was a particularly crap dish of lobster with *sauce gribiche*.

I occasionally hire a French chef at Locanda Locatelli, mainly for the pleasure of firing him, but I have never cooked another pomme soufflé, and I never wear a tall hat. And I still feel just a little bit sick every time I see a button onion.

A Night at the Opera
MICHAEL LOMONACO

A native of Brooklyn, New York, and a passionate proponent of regional American cuisine, Michael Lomonaco earned his culinary degree from New York Technical College, and was the executive chef of '21' and Windows on the World before taking the reins at Guastavino's. Lomonaco is the co-author of The '21' Cookbook *and* Nightly Specials, *and host of the Travel Channel's show* Epicurious. *He previously hosted* Michael's Place *on Food Network. He began his career in such legendary New York restaurants as Maxwell's Plum and Le Cirque.*

IN MANHATTAN, a city full of mythical beings and institutions, '21' has always shimmered and sparkled just a bit more than the rest. First opened as a speakeasy on New Year's Eve in 1930, the restaurant evolved over generations into a fabled landmark, a legend in its own right, as famous as many of the luminaries who dine there.

'21' is the fulfillment of everyone's notion of how an exclusive, clubby New York City restaurant should look and feel.

The wood-paneled rooms and upholstered leather chairs contribute to this effect, as do the hundreds of toys that dangle from the ceiling in the central Bar Room—miniature trucks and other vehicles mostly, gifts from prominent regulars—in sharp contrast to the power brokering that goes on beneath them. Then there are the remnants of the restaurant's speakeasy days, like the wine cellar that can be entered only by inserting a long, wiry rod into the lone proper hole among a hundred indistinguishable ones on its vaultlike door.

Ironically, you couldn't call '21' a hot spot. It doesn't attract young, glamorous movie stars, or even much media attention, though it used to. There is no velvet rope outside. But for generations it has catered to certain select subspecies of New Yorkers awash primarily in old money: political giants, titans of industry, Park Avenue socialites, the media elite, and so on. It has been graced by foreign heads of state, by astronauts, athletes, even by fictional characters (Gordon Gekko takes his young protégé there for lunch in *Wall Street*).

Most notably, every American president since Franklin Delano Roosevelt has dined at '21.' During my tenure there—as sous-chef from 1987 to 1988, and executive chef from 1989 to 1996—I was privileged to cook for Jimmy Carter, Bill Clinton, Ronald Reagan, Richard Nixon, and on one memorable evening, Gerald and Betty Ford *and* George and Barbara Bush. Mrs. Bush was exceptionally charming. "Can I have dessert?" she asked as she turned her empty dish up at me, proudly declaring herself a member of the "Clean Plate Club."

'21' isn't a private club, but many of its regulars dine there so often that they treat it like one. If a new staff member doesn't comport himself properly, or if something is askew, they are apt to wave over a dining room captain and, with a stern frown, let him know, so strong is their sense of propriety and possession.

Patrons also think nothing of making special requests of the dining room or the kitchen. For instance, it is perfectly normal for a customer to say to his waiter, "I feel like some lamb chops. Do you have any lamb in the house?" When the order makes its way to the kitchen, the chef takes a rack of lamb, butchers it into chops, and prepares it however the diner likes.

I kept all kinds of provisions on hand for special requests like that. There was peanut butter and jelly—once famously ordered by Cary Grant long before my time—and pasta, although they weren't featured in any regular menu items. There were even some items we kept stocked for the express purpose of feeding Frank Sinatra, who still swung through town once or twice a year.

Some chefs take umbrage at special requests, but I embraced them. I always thought of that kind of customized cooking as cooking on the edge, flying by the seat of your pants. Plus, I *loved* it when I'd set a dish of chicken hash before a guest, prepared just the way he liked it.

Even a billionaire wasn't above smiling like a little kid when I got it right.

One fall night in 1990, not long after I had returned to '21' as executive chef, Bruce Snyder, the dining room manager, came into the kitchen and told me that he had just received a call from one of our regulars, a prominent Park Avenue socialite who was attending the opera that evening—the premiere of Verdi's *Un Ballo in Maschera* (A Masked Ball) featuring the great Luciano Pavarotti—and wanted us to set a table for herself and about twenty guests.

Since they were coming from the Metropolitan Opera House, just uptown at Lincoln Center, they wouldn't be arriving until about eleven thirty, much later than we would normally accept a reservation, especially for such a large party.

But because she was an important customer, Bruce had agreed. We did whatever we could for our most valued regulars.

Oh, and there was one other reason.

Luciano Pavarotti would be their guest of honor.

At the time of this story, Pavarotti was at the height of his powers, a true living legend. You didn't have to know opera to know Pavarotti, the gigantic, bearded figure who had attained a new level of popular success that July when the Three Tenors—Placido Domingo, Jose Carreras, and Pavarotti himself—debuted as an entity at the World Cup in Rome.

Our customer didn't want a private room, asking instead that a large table be set up in the middle of the Bar Room, the heart of the restaurant. With a standing bar at one side, diners seated on the outskirts of the room, and all those toys hanging from the ceiling, it had the air of festivity and conviviality that she wanted to lend to her little soiree.

When Bruce told me Pavarotti was coming, I was ecstatic. Between working at '21' and at another bastion of celebrity, Le Cirque, I had become accustomed to cooking for the rich and famous on a daily and nightly basis. But there were certain figures who transcended the crowd, even in places like those. Mick Jagger was one, as was the King of Spain, who used to visit Le Cirque at the very tail end of lunch service or late in the evening, when most dinner guests were sipping their digestifs.

Pavarotti was such a figure, one who would siphon the attention of even the most jaded New Yorker. And he was coming to our restaurant for dinner.

It was then, and remains today, my firmly held belief that moments like these are reason enough to live in New York and work at a place like '21.'

*   *   *

The news that such a guest is coming triggers all sorts of extra activity: the front-of-the-house team ordered flowers especially for this table of honor and let a few waiters and busboys know they'd have to stay late. The wine steward made a survey of the cellar and took the liberty of chilling a variety of champagnes, including our house Billecart-Salmon; a rose; and so on.

As for me, I was getting more excited by the minute.

Before I became a chef, I was an actor. If you look real close, you can see me wordlessly menacing Woody Allen in a scene toward the middle of *Broadway Danny Rose*. For a time during my acting years, I made a living as a stage manager, and all of those old instincts kicked in on that night. I wasn't just getting the kitchen ready to produce food; I was getting ready for *our* performance.

The first thing I did was solicit volunteers from the staff, securing a sous-chef, two line cooks, and a pastry cook who were willing to go as late as we had to. I don't think they quite shared my level of enthusiasm—it would have been hard to— but they were game for the challenge.

Next, I checked my inventory, to make sure everything was perfect. I tasted soups and sauces with even more scrutiny than usual, sniffed raw fish and oysters to guarantee utmost fresh- ness, and examined all the vegetables.

I also made a mental note of ingredients that looked especially fresh, like the assorted wild mushrooms, in case I was called on to do a little cooking on the edge—*especially* if I were asked to do it for the great Luciano Pavarotti.

At about ten thirty, as most of the tables started to empty, Bruce orchestrated his team. They pushed a number of tables together in the center of the Bar Room, draped a huge, white tablecloth over them, then laid out the finest glassware and silverware. A procession of busboys appeared with the flower arrangements and proceeded to carefully decorate.

I continued to pace nervously around the kitchen, retasting and stirring soups, reassuring myself by reassuring my crew, and generally shuffling about.

As concerned as I was about Pavarotti coming to '21,' I was equally—if not more—daunted by the prospect of his *not* showing up. After this buildup, the disappointment would be crushing.

Shortly after eleven, the private party began to arrive, in subgroups of two, three, and four. They were fresh from the opera and younger and more vibrant than I expected; most were in their mid- to late forties. They were in full opera dress, designer tuxes for the men and evening gowns and glimmering jewelry for the women. Like so many visitors to '21,' they exuded the casual confidence that comes naturally with power and privilege.

As they entered the Bar Room and began ordering champagne and martinis, and nibbling on the caviar and foie gras hors d'oeuvres we had set out, the room began to buzz. Word had spread among the late-night diners seated at the smaller tables along the perimeter of the room that this was Pavarotti's group, many of whom, it was clear from their conversation, had enjoyed a private audience with him backstage after the performance.

Before too long, the restaurant was pulsating with one shared thought, as vivid as a flashing neon sign: "Pavarotti is coming. Pavarotti is coming."

As I stood outside the kitchen doors, leaning against the wall, I seemed to be the only one bothered by the unmistakable fact that Pavarotti had not arrived with this crowd. Was it possible that he wasn't going to show? Between my personal connection to the performing arts, a fondness for music, *and* an Italian-American background in which the likes of Pavarotti constituted a certain kind of royalty, I was unabashedly excited at the opportunity to cook for him. But this uncertainty . . . it was killing me. I must have looked like a nervous wreck.

Joe, a veteran captain of whom I was enormously fond, stood by me for a moment, witnessing yet another of my sighs.

"Ah, Joe, he's not coming," I said, shaking my head.

"Not to worry, my boy," Joe said. "He'll be here."

As reassuring as Joe could often be, I wasn't convinced. Neither, it seemed, were our guests, who began to cast sideways glances at the door, searching for the great tenor. They were also nursing their drinks and taking smaller nibbles out of the hors d'oeuvres, stalling for time, in order to avoid being seated.

That magical aura was beginning to fade and the air was fast going out of the evening. Soon, I heard the feared question surface throughout the room, "Where is the maestro? Where is Pavarotti?"

At about a quarter past twelve, an air of resignation had settled over the Bar Room. Masking their dejection as best as they could, the party took their seats and ordered dinner.

In the kitchen, my skeleton crew and I were going about our work, preparing oysters, smoked salmon, salads, and other first courses. But we did it silently, with very little enthusiasm.

We were supposed to be cooking for Pavarotti. Now we were just cooking for a bunch of people who only had a table because they said Pavarotti would be there.

In those days, you entered the kitchen at '21' though two swinging doors with huge glass panes set in their centers. You could stand at the salad station and look right though those doors to the restaurant's front door. As I helped prepare food for Pavarotti's crowd, I kept glancing up to see if he had finally arrived.

He didn't, and the first courses were served to the Pavarotti-less gathering.

Human beings are resilient organisms, so it's no wonder that the party, with time to adjust to the situation and replenished by the first bites of their first courses, had regained its rhythm and was again emitting the happy sounds of an opening-night feast.

I made a few perfunctory rounds, checking in on the party and making sure everything was to their liking. I smiled. I shook hands. I laughed at jokes. But I had my own little internal production of *Pagliacci* running in my head, because Pavarotti was still nowhere in sight.

At about twelve twenty-five, I was back in the kitchen. More out of habit than hope, I stole a peek through the looking-glass doors.

But this time, I saw a large, bearded man, dressed in a theatrical manner, floating in as though on a parade float.

I squinted. Could it be?

Another look confirmed that it was unmistakably Luciano Pavarotti, still in his costume from *Un Ballo in Maschera*. Done up as Riccardo, the governor of the opera's town, he was wearing a blue brocade jacket with a billowy white shirt, and a scarf tied extravagantly around his neck. Below the waist, huge, puffy pantaloons stopped at the knee, where they met bright white stockings that flowed into shoes with big brass buckles. The image was topped off by a black wig with a knot in the back.

Larger than life, indeed.

Word trickled ahead of Pavarotti and broke across the Bar Room. "The maestro has arrived. The maestro has arrived."

Waiters, managers, and diners were craning their heads to get a look at the operatic superstar.

Finally, he made it to the party: Pavarotti stood in the entrance to the Bar Room. His dinner companions and the rest of the diners—many of whom had also been to the opera—rose to their feet. "Bravo, maestro. Bravo!" they shouted.

Pavarotti took a huge, sweeping bow and with a broad smile joined the party, seated at the head of the table.

He was remarkably attentive to his companions, accepting their compliments with graciousness and what appeared to be genuine enthusiasm and warmth, feeding off their excitement. But excitement isn't enough to sustain you, especially when you've just come off the stage at the Metropolitan. Gradually his eyes went from the patrons to their plates, until he was focused on nothing but their food.

Watching this from the kitchen, I knew that he must be ravenous. Even in my limited acting career, I learned how the physical and emotional exertion required for a performance could leave you starving. Just imagine how hungry the great Pavarotti must be.

As this thought crystallized in my head, Pavarotti's hunger peaked. He picked up his fork and began spearing the food on other people's plates.

Before too long, it became clear to the others at the table that the way to get Pavarotti's attention was to share your food with him.

"Maestro, try my soup!"

"Signor Pavarotti, try my salad!"

Within minutes, it looked as though some force of nature had upended the table and all of the plates had slid down to Pavarotti's end. He had before him a sampling of just about every dish on the menu.

Quickly, Joe took me by the elbow, escorted me to the table, and introduced me to Pavarotti. "Maestro, this is our chef. Michael Lomonaco."

"Ah, Lomonaco," said Pavarotti, taking my hand. His voice was full of enthusiasm. A *paesano* in the kitchen.

I tried to welcome him in my meager Italian, but he was quite comfortable in English and spared me the trouble.

"I don't want too much," he said. "Just a little bit. Maybe a little smoked salmon." He pinched an inch of space between his thumb and forefinger to demonstrate his modest appetite.

"Very good, maestro."

I began to turn away, but he stopped me by putting up his hand. He glanced disapprovingly at the portion of smoked salmon before the woman next to him. "But more than *that*, please."

I turned again, to go fetch Signor Pavarotti his double portion of salmon, but he grabbed my arm, stopping me.

"And maybe some pasta."

"Pasta, of course," I said, trying to mask my excitement. Cooking pasta for Pavarotti. My family was going to be so proud.

"What kind?"

"You decide."

My mind's eye flashed back to those mushrooms. "We have some beautiful wild mushrooms. And some black truffles."

"*Bravo. Perfecto.* But just a little. I'm really not that hungry."

So, at one thirty in the morning, I went into the kitchen and made Pavarotti's dinner, slicing the finest of our mushrooms—chanterelles and porcini—sautéing them in butter, finishing them with some chicken stock, butter, and cream, and tossing them with freshly cooked fettuccine. I plated the pasta, finished it with a scattering of minced chives, and shaved a generous amount of black truffle over it.

When it was finally served to him, it went fast.

A few minutes later, I stuck my head out of the kitchen. Pavarotti was again being subjected to a barrage of food, this time desserts.

"Maestro, try my fruit soup!"

"Maestro, try my poached pear."

Those who weren't offering him food were posing for pictures with him. If Pavarotti wasn't chewing, he was saying "Cheese," and all this after a three-hour performance.

I recognized this as my chance. Not only would I grant him a break, but I would amaze Pavarotti with a dessert created just for him. I approached the table and asked him what he'd like.

He shook his head: "Not much. I'm not so hungry. Maybe just some *sorbétto*. Do you have *sorbétto*?"

"Yes, of course, we have coconut, raspberry, and"—I delayed the last one for effect, knowing it would appeal to his Italian soul—"and grapefruit-Campari."

"*Ah, bene*," he said. "*Tutto*." Which means *all*.

Then he smiled, and added, "But not too much."

I returned to the kitchen and fixed Pavarotti a beautiful bowl of sorbet, double portions of all three, along with some berries and a sprig of mint. I presented it myself. It wasn't cooking on the edge, but it was a thrill, to be sure.

At about two thirty in the morning, the last morsel of food had been eaten, the last drop of wine drained from the last glass, the last photograph had been taken, and it dawned on the party that the evening had reached its end.

Pavarotti, his host, and the other twenty or so guests stood up en masse and walked through the rooms of '21.'

In their costumes—Pavarotti's extravagant getup and the others' black ties and evening dresses—they looked like the cast of an opera themselves, making a grand exit, never to return, a theatrical mirage that appeared in our dining room all too briefly, then vanished.

My crew took off for the night. The porters and cleanup guys were finally able to begin *their* jobs, which wouldn't be over until sunup. God bless 'em.

I had a long way to go to get home, because in those days my wife, Diane, and I still lived in Brooklyn. But I lingered for a few more minutes, strolling around the kitchen, letting the echoes of the evening die down in my head.

I paused at the door, taking in the room. And then I turned out the lights, closing down *my* theater for the evening, and went home to get some rest before tomorrow's performance in this most unique of all restaurants, this living dream on West Fifty-second Street.

A User's Guide to
Opening a Hamptons Restaurant
PINO LUONGO

A native of Tuscany, Pino Luongo is the unstoppable force behind some of New York City's most influential Italian restaurants, including the groundbreaking Il Cantinori, which he opened in 1983. Other Luongo classics include Coco Pazzo and Centolire. The author of four cookbooks, Luongo was also the subject of a memorable chapter in Anthony Bourdain's Kitchen Confidential. *Some of Luongo's restaurants, like Sapore di Mare, Mad 61, and Le Madri, have faded into history, but still conjure fond memories for those who dined there.*

I GREW UP IN Tuscany, and some of my happiest recollections are of summers at the beach in Porto Ecole and Porto Santo Stefano, where the sun shone brightly all day and my friends and I spent months splashing in the surf, cruising around in our convertibles, and eating by the shore. Music from those long-ago days still echoes in my mind, like Mungo Jerry's "In the Summertime" or those opening piano blasts of the Beatles' "The Long and Winding Road," taking me right back to 1971.

I came to New York City in 1980, and three years later, I opened my first restaurant, Il Cantinori, a menuless trattoria on East Tenth Street where we served different dishes every night based on the market and my mood. It was a sensation and, though I haven't been a part of it for a long time, still does a solid business.

As much as I loved living in New York City (and still do), I had come to miss the ocean. Manhattan is surrounded by water, of course, but we're talking rivers—sluggish, filthy rivers that separate it from New Jersey and the outer boroughs. So in the fall of 1986, I decided to spend some time by the beach, in the fabled Hamptons.

If you don't know, the Hamptons are a weekend playground for the rich and famous, about two hours east of the city, or four hours on a summer Friday when the Long Island Expressway is jammed beyond belief.

The Hamptons are where everyone from Puff Daddy to Steven Spielberg go to relax, be seen, and luxuriate in their palatial homes. They have been fashionable forever; *The Great Gatsby* takes place in the Hamptons, even though F. Scott Fitzgerald made up different names for them.

I never cared one way or another about the scene out there. What I loved was being near the ocean. It just makes me feel good—so good that I didn't even care if it was summer or not; the first time I rented in the Hamptons was in the off season, from Labor Day through Memorial Day, instead of the other way around.

I was newly married and my wife, Jessie, and I took a house that wasn't winterized. It was chilly and drafty and the toilet water froze, but it was near the Napeague Bay, not far from Montauk, so I was happy to be there.

I remember driving around the Hamptons in those dark, winter days and thinking to myself how few restaurants there were in the towns along 27, the Montauk Highway, which connects the dots on the Hamptons map, from Southampton to Bridgehampton to East Hampton and on out to Montauk.

There's so little action, I thought, in the summer this place must be magic.

Inspired by the proximity to water and by a fierce longing for summer, I began to envision a restaurant that would capture all the charm of Porto Ecole and Porto Santo Stefano, a restaurant that could re-create those long-ago days—that sense of summer, salt, sand, tanned skin, and the simple food that brought each day to a perfect close.

I started tapping the steering wheel, singing *"In the summertime, when the sun goes down . . ."*

Later that winter, I was driving along 27, about to round the bend into East Hampton, when I passed what looked like a haunted house. Formerly the home of Charlotte's The Hidden Pond restaurant, and before that the home of a state senator, the property was available and the owners had gone into bankruptcy, explained a sign.

The place was an eyesore: a Tudor-style English house with a dark wooden frame and a sad, gray tint to the stucco. It was in merciless disrepair, with huge nicks in the walls and cracks in the wood.

But I saw potential in it, and I loved that it was situated at the end of one of the splits of Georgica Pond, which flows alongside 27 where Bridgehampton and East Hampton meet. Plus, I fancy myself the Bob Vila of the restaurant industry, able to turn "This Old Restaurant" into something shiny and new.

So it was that in February 1987, I assumed ownership of the space and went to work transforming it into a spot-on replica of a Mediterranean villa, with tile floors, terra-cotta accents, and lots of wide open spaces through which the summer breeze could blow, carrying that precious scent of the sea right through the dining room.

I named my new pet project Sapore di Mare, meaning "taste of the sea," and we opened on May 23, 1987. The restaurant exceeded my wildest hopes: it was an instant success. Friends and customers from the city, many of whom had weekend homes in the Hamptons, showed up in our first days and weeks, and their reaction was a unanimous "wow."

But I'll tell you something: I was banging out the wrong song on my steering wheel the fateful day that I spotted this space. I should've picked "The Long and Winding Road," because that's what it was like operating a restaurant out there. Really long, and really fucking winding.

We had a good run at Sapore di Mare, but we also had our challenges. And many of them were challenges unique to this kind of moneyed, resort community. So, for anyone out there interested in opening a restaurant in the Hamptons, here's my hard-earned advice:

1. Don't Hire Your Own Family

A constant struggle in the early days of Sapore di Mare was that the Hamptons' supply of seasoned hospitality professionals was very poor.

I was blessed with a great chef, an American named Mark Strausman who cooks with the soul of an Italian and later became my chef at Coco Pazzo; and a maître d' named Ariel Lacayo, a sharply dressed, smooth-tongued Latin American who works with me today at Centolire, where people still remember him from those days at the beach.

But we had big problems finding support in the kitchen or the dining room. It quickly became apparent to me that no matter how many ads we ran in the paper, and no matter how many phone calls I made, we were going to have trouble filling all the positions. As for the few employees that we *did* manage to find—locals who had worked in diners and greasy-spoon joints—they could barely handle the pressure. Most of them stopped showing up for work after a few days, never to be heard from again.

I was able to both cook and work the dining room, but you can only do so much at once. So, when we opened, I told Ariel to keep the crowd to a manageable size, even turning away business if necessary. And to make sure that he didn't cave into the pressure of clamoring customers, I asked Jessie, then five months pregnant, to work the door with him.

This was a sound enough plan, but the Hamptons in the summer are populated with everyone who ever set foot in Il Cantinori, or so it seemed. So, as the hour approached eight o'clock each evening, the phone began to ring off the hook. Jessie would dutifully tell all comers that we were fully booked. In most towns, that would have been the end of the discussion.

But not in the Hamptons.

In fact, there was no *discussion*. A typical exchange went like this:

Ring. Ring.

JESSIE: Hello?

CUSTOMER: This is Ms. So-and-So. Do you have a table available at nine p.m.?

JESSIE: No, I'm sorry, we're fully booked.

CUSTOMER: Just tell Pino we're coming over.

JESSIE: But . . .

Click. Dial tone. Sound of Jessie slamming down the phone.

"Tell Pino we're coming over" was the most-uttered phrase in the Hamptons that summer, along with "I'm a friend of Pino's," favored by guests who didn't even bother to call, and instead just showed up, their version of "Open Sesame."

About once a night, poor Jessie would come swinging through the door to the kitchen, which opened right onto the pasta station, where I usually cooked. She would tell me of the latest inhuman treatment she had received, and then sulk back to the dining room.

It breaks a man's heart to see his wife look so sad, especially when she's trying to help him out. But what could I do? I needed somebody I could trust minding the store.

And so it went in those early days, the rousing success marred only by my wife's misery.

One night, I was going about my business at the pasta station when I had that sixth-sense intuition, unique to chefs and restaurateurs, that I had better go check on the dining room. I did: everything was fine. But my radar wasn't totally busted. Sitting *on* the reservation desk was Jessie, staring off into space, shell-shocked.

It was clear that this couldn't continue. All that lay ahead for me was trouble: a series of tense battles on the home front, the evil product of seeds planted in the restaurant. Moments later, as I watched my dear wife withstand an earful of abuse from yet another unannounced group, I decided that I had no choice. I had to get rid of her.

But I couldn't bring myself to fire her.

At the end of the night, I pulled Ariel aside and told him, "Tomorrow morning, the moment you get up, find me a new hostess. Don't go to the beach. Don't come in here. Get on the phone and find me someone and have her here by three thirty,"—an hour before Jessie's scheduled arrival.

The next day, Ariel had a new hostess installed, as directed. When Jessie showed up, she jerked a thumb in the girl's direction and asked Ariel what was going on.

"Pino had to replace you," he said, trying to sound soothing on my behalf. "It was too much stress for you."

"Oh really?"

Jessie came swinging into the kitchen and stared at me with a look so cold that the pasta water stopped boiling: "You know, I really don't care about working here," she screamed. "I was trying to help you out. But *you . . . you . . .* you *coward*. You couldn't tell me yourself?"

"That's right," I said. "I couldn't do it. But what's important is I'd rather keep you as a wife than as an employee."

I guess I was losing my touch as a ladies' man, because she spun around in a rage and stomped out of the kitchen. But she was home that night when I got back from work, and though she didn't admit it right away, she was happier. We have three kids today and a good marriage, and it's all because I did the right thing and replaced her that night, sparing her any more indignities at the hands of my dear Hamptons customers.

2. Don't Hire Your Customers' Family

That first summer, while I was in New York City running Il Cantinori during the week, I would get frantic calls from Mark, the chef, increasingly concerned by our lack of help. Our employment problems continued unabated and we were only getting busier and busier. If I had known what an ongoing headache this would be, I probably never would have opened the restaurant.

I was in a desperate situation, so when two of my regular customers (too ridiculously affluent and influential to name) asked me to give their home-from-college kids—we'll call them Mitch and Missy—summer jobs, I thought, Sure, why not? And I hired them as a busboy and busgirl.

Before we go any further, you have to understand that I come from an Italian family and that we pride ourselves on our work ethic. The idea that some people simply have no pride whatsoever was completely beyond me.

But I got a quick lesson.

The trouble started almost immediately, when Missy showed up for her first day at work in her BMW convertible and parked it in the lot next to the highway. Our innkeeper, a very serious, old Dominican, instructed her to park it out back—the front lot was for customers. "Oh, Chico," she said to him without breaking stride, her blond hair flowing behind her in the summer wind, "I *am* a customer."

Instead of showing up at five minutes to four, like the employees who needed the job, she and Mitch showed up at four thirty, fresh from the beach, unkempt, and smelling of the sea and sand.

"You, boy," I said to the young man. "Do you have a watch?"

"Yes, Mr. Luongo."

"What time are you supposed to be here?"

"Four o'clock."

"And what time is it?"

He looked down at his Rolex. "Four thirty."

"So?"

"I'm sorry, Mr. Luongo. I fell asleep at the beach."

I looked at his unshaven face, his salt-caked hair. "What are you going to do about a shower?"

"Oh, I don't need a shower, Mr. Luongo. I'm just a busboy."

"Just a busboy? Look at these other people who are 'just

busboys,' " I said, gesturing at the well-groomed crew, in freshly cleaned black slacks and white shirts: my proud, hardworking team.

"How many times have you come to my restaurant? Do the busboys look like this?" I pointed at him, to make sure he understood what *this* meant.

"You're right, Mr. Luongo. I'm sorry. It'll never happen again."

Once they got to work, things weren't much better. Missy had an aversion to soiled dishes, an unfortunate trait in a busgirl. When she approached an abandoned table, with its half-eaten pastas, napkins dropped in sauce, and cigarette butts in the wineglasses, she would scrunch up her face and hold her breath. Then, to avoid breaking a nail, she would only pick up one or two dishes at a time, scurry to the kitchen with them, and come back for the next puny load.

On a scale of one to ten, I'd say she was a minus ten.

As if I didn't have enough problems to deal with, every time I left the kitchen, I'd find these kids doing something unbelievable. Like the time I discovered them in the middle of Saturday-night service, passing a cigarette back and forth in the parking lot out behind the kitchen. Or when they took a break that same night to sit at the bar and have a cocktail.

When I saw *that*, I pulled them aside.

"Kids, listen. In Italy, we have an expression that if you look the other way three times, you are stupid. And I'm starting to feel like an idiot."

I presented them with a choice: "I'll give you one more chance. Be here at four o'clock tomorrow. *Or else.*"

Mitch—he's probably a lawyer today—jumped right in. "Yes, Mr. Luongo. That's perfect. I feel like the past few days, we've just been breaking the ice."

"Listen," I said. "We're not breaking the ice. You're breaking my balls. Now get out of here."

The next day, with a fool's optimism, I pushed myself all morning and into the afternoon. I got *my* work done early so I could spend some time with Mitch and Missy when they arrived, show them how I expected them to work, turn them into the kind of proud workers I respected.

I had been a busboy in my life. I had done everything you could do in a restaurant, and that's part of why I resented them so much. I didn't care who their parents were; the fact that they thought they could disrespect my beautiful Sapore di Mare, the place I had built with my own sweat and hard work—that was the most offensive thing of all.

You already know what happened next. They didn't show up at four o'clock. They didn't even show up by four fifteen. When they finally did show up, at four thirty, I was sitting in the balcony overlooking the dining room. I watched them prance in through the front door, even though Chico—hardworking, proud Chico—told them not to every day. As always, they were fresh from the beach, with messy hair and that salty smell.

I don't know how much you know about the restaurant industry in New York, but if you read the papers here in the 1980s, then you might have heard I had a temper in those days. I'm not going to deny it. I had a massive temper. And this was the kind of thing that set it off.

"You two," I said as I stood up and charged down the stairs. They looked terrified, like they were about to be gored by a bull.

"You know what? That's it. You better get out of here. In fact, you better get out of here right now. Actually, you know what, GET THE FUCK OUT OF HERE. NOW!"

They didn't move.

"NOW!"

"But, Mr. Luongo," Mitch said. "What about our tips from last night?"

"*Tips?*" I actually laughed. "You want your tips? I'll give you a tip: you go home and tell your fathers that you are *fired*. You incompetent, spoiled, rich brats." They stood there for a second, in shock.

Mitch jerked his head in the direction of the bar, suggesting to Missy that they have a drink before leaving.

"Now!" I bellowed. "Get the fuck out of here, you little brats. Out, out, out," and I chased them right out the door.

Both Mitch's and Missy's fathers called me, outraged, vowing that they'd never come back to Sapore di Mare again.

But they did. They had to. They were friends of Pino's.

3. Teach Your Employees English

It's pretty common to have restaurant employees who don't speak English. It's so common that there's a pamphlet-sized book sold in certain industry supply shops called *Kitchen Spanish*. But if you ever open a restaurant in the Hamptons, teach your employees English. Or you might find yourself without a staff.

One summer day when I was working in the city as usual, Mark called me from Sapore and told me the following story:

It was a quiet weekday, and in the Hamptons, it gets so quiet that you can stand along the highway and hear the wind blow through the trees. All of a sudden, out of nowhere, five black sedans screeched into the Sapore di Mare parking lot and surrounded the building.

A group of federal agents marched into the place and began interrogating everybody on the staff. They didn't check for proof of citizenship or ask to see green cards. Any employees who didn't speak English were simply corralled and taken away in the cars, off to who-knows-where.

"Thank God I can still manage a Brooklyn accent or they might have taken *me*," Mark said.

I hung up the phone and looked around the kitchen. My crew was finishing their prep for that night's dinner. The *mise en place* containers—the little stainless-steel vessels in which prepared ingredients are held along the line—were full and, having been there since the early morning, the crew was winding down and thinking about going home for the day.

"Guys, listen up." I told them what had happened at Sapore, and that I needed them to go out to my car. I was going to drive them to the Hamptons, they would work a shift out there, and I'd have them back by morning.

"Pino, no, please no," they begged.

But I had no choice. We had to be ready for dinner at the beach. So we piled into the car, drove out to the Hamptons, and I assigned each of them to a station. They were real troupers, prepping and then cooking all night, only to pile back into my car at eleven forty-five that night for the return trip to Manhattan.

The next day, I got my Sapore staff back. They weren't happy, and neither was I. I suppose I could've sued the government, but I had other priorities, like replenishing my ever-dwindling reservoir of employees, a task that had become even harder that morning with the new prerequisite that they speak English.

4. All Rules Are Open to Interpretation

One of my favorite images from Sapore di Mare was Ralph Lauren.

Not the brand. The man.

Within a few months of Sapore's opening, the clientele began taking the summertime theme to extremes. They'd show up looking as though they had just come from the beach, which I'm sure many of them had. There were wearing shorts, sandals, even bathing suits.

Many of our customers understood the spirit of Sapore, and would arrive in casual but elegant attire. The bathing-suiters, however, were rapidly becoming the majority.

So we made a new rule: no shorts. Just like at the Vatican.

And then one night, Ralph Lauren, driving home with his wife and a few friends, decided to drop in for dinner. The friends met our dress code, but Ralph was wearing shorts.

Ralph Lauren in shorts doesn't look like most people in shorts. I didn't see him when he came in, but I'm sure he was as fashionable as ever.

Nonetheless, Ariel didn't want to make any exceptions. We didn't keep any pants in the cloakroom the way some restaurants keep jackets. So my quick-thinking maître d' ran into the kitchen and emerged with a pair of black-and-white checkered chef pants, presenting them to Ralph Lauren.

Ralph, gentleman that he is, disappeared good-naturedly into the men's room and emerged in his new outfit.

By the time I heard what had happened and caught up with Ralph, I was mortified. But Ralph is a sport. He said it was no big deal and that he was happy to comply.

And, you know what? He looked good. He looked so good that I'm surprised chef pants didn't become the next big fashion craze out there.

Even in the Hamptons, I guess, absurdity has its limitations.

5. Most Mistakes Can Be Corrected

Okay, after all this bad news, let me share a story with a happy ending.

Saturday afternoon at Sapore was the eye of the storm between Friday night and Saturday night. It was also a time when many of our celebrity customers came in for lunch, to enjoy the restaurant's patio away from the eyes of the masses.

One Saturday afternoon, we were hosting Billy Joel and Christie Brinkley, along with their little daughter Alexis, and another couple that have also since gone their separate ways, Alec Baldwin and Kim Basinger.

I was busy in the kitchen, getting ready for the evening service. The only management presence in the dining room was the current occupant of our revolving-door position of receptionist-hostess.

At about three o'clock, I began thinking about the dinner hour and went into the dining room to see if Ariel had shown up yet. There he was, the picture of Hamptons style, in a white linen suit with brown leather slip-on shoes.

With a list of that night's reservations in hand, we walked the floor together, determining who we'd seat where, a very political exercise at a hot spot like Sapore. We also personally greeted Alec and Kim and Billy and Christie, all of whom were regulars, and—I must say—absolutely charming.

As we made the rounds, I noticed, out of the corner of my eye, pedaling up to the entrance on a bicycle, a woman in her midsixties, or so I'd have guessed. It was tough to tell: she was wearing a straw hat and sunglasses so it was hard to see her face.

But something about her seemed familiar.

We couldn't hear the exchange that followed, but from the

gestures—the woman spoke, the reservationist shook her head from side to side, the woman shrugged happily, hopped on her bike and left—we could tell that she had been denied a reservation.

My sixth sense was speaking to me, telling me that something wasn't right. I sent Ariel over to see what happened. He returned and informed me that she was looking for a table for four for eight o'clock.

"And?" I asked.

"The girl told her that we were fully—"

I realized who it was: "Jesus Christ, Ariel, that was Jacqueline Kennedy Onassis."

He considered that for a moment.

"Oh, my God, Pino! You're right!"

I pointed to the highway: "Go after her!"

Ariel's jaw dropped, but he didn't move.

"We cannot allow this to happen. Go!"

"Pino, she's gone down the highway."

"So go chase her down the fucking highway! This cannot happen. Not here!"

With a shrug, Ariel began walking toward the road.

"You're not going to get her if you walk. Run!"

Ariel began running in his immaculate white linen suit, slipping his jacket off as he started. Our driveway was covered with gravel, so he couldn't really pick up any speed until he got to the highway.

I went out to the edge of my property and looked down the sloping highway. I could see the former First Lady about half a mile down the road, stopped at an intersection, straddling her bike, and behind her, coming up fast, my own Latin Gatsby, running down the road after her to gallantly offer her a table.

She was about to start pedaling again, but he called out to her and she stopped and turned around. They spoke. She nodded and he waved good-bye.

Ariel returned to our parking lot, drenched in sweat. He reported his success. She had accepted the reservation and his apology.

I was so happy. I had always admired Jackie O. Not just her style, but also her strength after her husband was assassinated and all those stories about how she had raised her children, Caroline and John, Jr., to be humble and polite. She clearly lived those values herself. I mean, here she was in the Hamptons, where *everyone* wants you to know who they are, and she didn't even divulge her identity to get a table at a restaurant.

I had to compliment Ariel on his triumph: "I'm proud of you, Ariel. You did what the best maître d' in the Hamptons should do, and you should feel good about it."

He nodded, still catching his breath and fanning himself off. "Thanks, Pino."

I looked him up and down. Sweat was literally dripping off his suit.

"Now, go take a shower," I said. "You stink!"

I'm telling you, our work is *never* done.

Our Big Brake
MARY SUE MILLIKEN
AND SUSAN FENIGER

Mary Sue Milliken and Susan Feniger first came together at City Cafe in Los Angeles in 1981, and have been business partners for more than two decades. Today, they own the popular Border Grill restaurants in Santa Monica and Las Vegas at Mandalay Bay, and Ciudad restaurant in Downtown L.A. They have authored five cookbooks, taped 396 episodes of their television programs Too Hot Tamales *and* Tamales World Tour *on Food Network, and host the show* In the KFI Kitchen with Mary Sue and Susan *on KFI 640AM Los Angeles. Milliken and Feniger also created the Border Girls brand of fresh prepared foods for Whole Foods Markets, and a line of pepper mills manufactured by Vic Firth.*

S o, it was 1983 and the two of us were running our little City Cafe, near the corner of Melrose and Martel in Los Angeles. It was a small place we had opened two years earlier, about 900 square feet, with ten tables and eleven seats at the bar; the entire staff consisted of the two of us, with a dishwasher who doubled as a busboy and a waitress who dabbled in heroin addiction when she wasn't on duty.

Ah, those were the days.

In terms of our industry's culture, this was an era ago, because there was no such thing as a celebrity chef. Sure, there were television cooking teachers like the great Julia Child, but no fellow whisks had risen from the restaurant world to national prominence. To put things in perspective, Wolfgang Puck had just recently opened Spago, and not long before that, Alice Waters had launched Chez Panisse.

Because there was no such thing as a celebrity chef, it wasn't as common as it is today for folks who do what we do to participate in big-ticket charity events where for a couple hundred bucks you can sit down to four courses prepared by four different chefs, or maybe stroll around tasting signature dishes from up to fifty chefs at little food stations.

The idea was starting to catch on, however, and people like Wolfgang were at the forefront of the movement. We hadn't been a part of this new trend, so we were flattered when we were finally invited to participate in a benefit: the organizers for a prominent national food and wine group called and asked us to "do a course" for a dinner set to take place in the ballroom of the Biltmore Hotel, an art deco relic of Old Hollywood that was past its prime but still maintained a faint air of glamour and did a steady business in its ballroom, which was to be the site of this event.

Today, prepping and packing for a benefit are as innate to a chef as sharpening a knife or caramelizing onions. Young cooks learn this art at their first jobs and know what kind of containers to buy, the perfect-sized cooler, and how to seal everything so it travels without spilling so much as a drop. But we had never packed up our food for anything, much less cooked for 250 people, the number expected at the dinner.

We were charged with preparing the first course, and we settled on one of our most popular appetizers at the time, Seared Eggplant with Tomato *Concassé* and Hollandaise *Glacage*. We figured this to be a transport-friendly selection because we could sear the eggplant slices at City and bring along some buckets full of *concassé* (coarsely chopped, cooked tomatoes and herbs) and hollandaise. When we got to the Biltmore, all we'd have to do is lay out the eggplant on sheet pans, top them with *concassé* , whip some cream and fold it with the Parmesan into the warm hollandaise, nap it on, and flash it under the broiler. Easy.

The first course was to be served at seven fifteen. Not wanting the hollandaise to sit around getting stiff, we planned a most efficient itinerary: we'd load up the car at five thirty, arrive by six thirty, and be ready promptly at seven fifteen.

And our vehicle to greatness? Suze's rickety old red Datsun station wagon, a car so decrepit, so run down, so patched with authentic Toledo rust and punctuated with dents, that it was a wonder California renewed its registration every few years. The car was truly disgusting, not only on the outside, but also on the inside, with frayed fabric underfoot, tears in the seat upholstery, and debris in every available receptacle. Susan never had time to clean it, and we both drove Honda scooters to and from work. The only time we were in that old jalopy was to get to and from the fish market and various other purveyors. The interior emitted an unfortunate aroma that was the by-product of the coming together of fish juice, herb scraps, and whatever else had dripped, fallen, or grown on the carpet.

But it was a reliable vehicle, and we had a great fondness for its character. We even loaned it to one of our best customers to move some plants. She decided to return it with a full tank, and while pumping the gas a thief grabbed her keys, punched her in the jaw, and made off with that trusty old Datsun. The police found the car and returned it later that day—I guess the thief couldn't take the smell. This made the car somehow even more loveable to us.

So there we were on a typically balmy Thursday afternoon in Los Angeles. We had the seared eggplant slices packed up in a couple of empty orange crates (hey, they came free with the produce), with paper towels between the layers, and we loaded the crates in the way back along with a couple of buckets of tomato *concassé* and grated Parmesan. The backseats had long since refused to fold down so we set the buckets of warm, silky hollandaise on the seats directly behind us. The buckets—originally holding dish soap—were covered with plastic wrap, and held in place by packing tape. But to be safe, we supported them with sundry other items, like bowls of utensils, rolled-up aprons, and so on. We would have strapped them in with seat belts, but those were long gone.

We were still shouting last-minute instructions to the skeleton crew who would be manning the stove as we got into the car and slammed the doors shut. As usual, Mary Sue—known for her speed behind the wheel—drove, even though it wasn't her car. We pulled away from the curb . . .

. . . and immediately had to stop.

Because we were in uncharted territory.

Rush hour.

We had heard of rush hour. And we knew that rush hour in Los Angeles was supposed to be among the more onerous on the planet. But rush hour is when chefs are just getting ready for the body of their workday to commence, so we are safely ensconced in our places of business. We suppose we had *seen* rush hour before, maybe through the windows of the restaurant. But rush hour cannot be fully appreciated until you are in a car, caught in the snarl, and have someplace to be.

Rush hour sucks. And to this day we do everything possible not to drive in L.A. between 3 and 7 p.m.

In search of less clogged roadways, we gradually snaked our way down to Sixth Street, bumping along the sloping, potholed streets of Los Angeles, the crates of eggplant bouncing up and down and the hollandaise lapping up against the sides of the bucket. Taking Sixth, we began our exodus east to Grand Avenue. With the time ticking away, Mary Sue began driving more aggressively, weaving in and out of the right-hand lane to pass the slower drivers, or those who simply didn't have to be at the Biltmore Hotel to serve a first course to 250 foodies in less than an hour.

So there we were, running our little automotive slalom course though the streets of Los Angeles, when all of a sudden some jerk runs a stop sign on an adjacent street, screeching out right in front of us.

Mary Sue slammed on the brakes and we came to an abrupt, lurching stop that threw us into the dash and caused the boxes of eggplant to smack against the seat backs, and the buckets of hollandaise to fall over on their sides. The liquid sloshed forcefully enough against the plastic wrap to dislodge it. We both instinctively threw an arm back from the front seat but not before we heard the unmistakable *splash* of 10 gallons of hot buttery emulsion being deposited in the disgusting, fish-scented foot wells behind us.

Some of the sauce seeped through the space between our seat backs and seats, catching us on the rear, and as the warm hollandaise soaked through to our butts, we looked at each other in horror: "Oh. My. God."

Susan peered over the headrest into the foot wells. "You're not going to believe this," she said, reaching down and grabbing one of the buckets, verifying that there was, in fact, just about 3 inches of sauce remaining. "You're really not going to believe this."

We pulled over to the curb, got out, and shifted into crisis mode. Quickly, we ran through the possible options: Go back to our place and remake the hollandaise? Well, that would have been a fine idea but not for two chefs who set off on their little adventure with a mere fifteen-minute contingency. Ask the hotel chef to help us out? Surely he'd have eggs, but did he keep gallons of extra clarified butter just laying around? Doubtful. More than likely he used that fake canned stuff, anyway.

We should add that this was in the prehistoric days before cell phones were prevalent, so we couldn't call out for reinforcements, or even get answers to our questions from the hotel's chef.

Maybe we could stretch the paltry amount of surviving hollandaise by adding even more cheese and cream to it? No, probably not a good idea: the yolks wouldn't set up when flashed under the broiler, and with too much cheese the sauce would certainly break and turn our elegant appetizer into a greasy mess.

"What are we going to do?"

There was only one answer. The moment that followed was akin to the one in desert-island tales, when the poor shipwrecked souls decide they have to turn to cannibalism, or perish. We looked down into the pools of hollandaise sitting in those foot wells, those disgusting, fish-juice-stained foot wells, and, without a word, we nodded to each other, solemnly acknowledging what must be done. Then we each took a bucket, got down on our knees, and with cupped hands began bailing the hollandaise from the car floor back into the buckets. Glancing up at each other we knew that we had both come to the same unspoken decision—that as long as we didn't actually touch the unspeakable floor of Lake Hollandaise, dislodging its bacteriological horrors, we could live with ourselves.

We have to add here that we'd *never* do such a thing today—heck, we'd never find ourselves in this predicament today—but twenty-plus years ago, for two gals who were just starting out, the moment was as hilarious as it was horrific, and it wasn't long before the two of us were shuddering with laughter at our predicament, thanks in part to the questions we'd ask each other:

Mary Sue: "You *never* let Stella (her dog) in the car, right Suze?"

Susan: "Is that black pepper . . . or dirt?"

Mary Sue: "You promise you won't tell anyone?"

As the amount in the buckets began to finally exceed the amount left slopping in the car, we gave each other status reports:

"How's it goin', Milliken?"

"Pretty good."

"How much do you have?"

"About a gallon and a half. But if I go much deeper I might hit carpet."

Hit carpet. Tee hee. We started laughing again at the very thought of the godforsaken floor.

And so it went.

We got the buckets as full as they were going to get, secured them extra well, and hopped back in the car. The rest of the journey was spent recalling Mary Sue's mom's strong convictions about food that had touched the floor being GOOD for you because ingesting a few foreign particles helped your body build it's immunities and people who were too germ-a-phobic had weak systems as a result.

"Right, Milliken, we're doing these diners a favor they won't even know about! Whatever you need to tell yourself is fine—but let's figure out how we're gonna explain our butter butts."

"I don't know about you, but I'm gonna wear two aprons, front and back, and say it's a fashion statement."

When we arrived at the hotel at the corner of Fifth Street and Grand Avenue, it was just minutes before seven o'clock. An assistant manager was waiting for us at the entrance and when he sighted us, his brow relaxed and he picked up the house phone to call for reinforcements; within seconds, we were greeted by an army of cooks who descended on the car like vultures, flying all the food back to the kitchen.

We joined them and oversaw the assembly-line production. Before anyone could get a good look at the hollandaise, Susan cranked a ton of black pepper into each bucket to help camouflage any "extras" we might have picked up accidentally. We didn't dare make eye contact with each other, or we would have burst out laughing again.

At exactly seven fifteen, we served the dish. It was a big hit. We watched from the kitchen door as the diners, 250 of Los Angeles' most savvy food lovers, dug into the eggplant with gusto. Some of them even soaked up the last remnants of hollandaise with their dinner rolls.

After dessert, the chefs were introduced to the gathering and asked to talk about their dishes.

When we got up, Susan took the microphone and proceeded to tell everyone how honored we were to be there, at our first benefit event, and described our dish by its new name: "Seared Eggplant with Tomato *Concassé* and *Black Pepper* Hollandaise."

Like they say, necessity is the mother of invention.

A Chef in the Family
SARA MOULTON

A lifetime food enthusiast, Sara Moulton graduated from the University of Michigan in 1974, and from the Culinary Institute of America in 1977. She worked in restaurants for several years, including a postgraduate stage with a master chef in Chartres, France. In the early 1980s, Moulton worked at La Tulipe in New York and cofounded the New York Women's Culinary Alliance. In 1983, she worked as an instructor at Peter Kump's New York Cooking School, then took a job in the test kitchen at Gourmet magazine, which led to her becoming the magazine's executive chef, a position she holds to this day. In 1997, she became an on-air food correspondent for Good Morning America. Moulton has hosted two Food Network shows, Cooking Live and Sara's Secrets. Her first cookbook, Sara Moulton Cooks at Home, was published in 2002.

PUT SOMEONE IN a uniform and you confer upon her a sense of authority. Put her in a uniform *and* throw a little knowledge her way, and that person becomes downright unbearable. For proof of this axiom, you need look no further than your average, first-or second-year culinary student.

Chef-instructors warn kitchen aspirants against getting a big head. "Just because you have a degree, doesn't make you a chef," they tell you on the last day of school, their stern message lent an air of finality by their French and German accents. Culinary school instructors are fond of reminding their beaming graduates that "commencement" means "beginning" and that when they leave the hallowed halls of Academy X, their education is only just starting. Translation: "Get over yourselves, because you don't know nothin' yet."

None of that makes the slightest dent in the humongous egos of most culinary students. As far as they're concerned, they know it all. If you don't believe me, just ask one: she'll tell you herself.

I know this because I worked in restaurants for seven years and I had a chance to interview young cooks for jobs, many of the applicants right out of cooking school. To a person, they had an attitude, ready to tell their co-workers and bosses what they didn't know, and to share their own dish ideas with executive chefs who had been cooking professionally since before the young cooks were born.

Truth be told, I also know this because I myself was once guilty of this behavior, back in the mid-1970s, when I was a student at the Culinary Institute of America in Hyde Park, New York, the finest cooking school in the country by my, and most industry folks', estimation.

In the fall of 1976, I was in my second year at the Culinary Institute, which in their two-year program was my senior year. I was feeling very confident. I had attended an excellent private high school in New York City, graduated from the University of Michigan, and at twenty-three was older than many of the other students, who were right out of high school. Consequently, I was a better studier than most attendees, who were primarily interested in guzzling beer, and—let's be honest—getting laid as often as possible.

As my head swelled with knowledge, I became more and more insufferable, driving all who loved me screaming out of the kitchen. For instance, my then-boyfriend (and now-husband), Bill, was an accomplished home cook. When I was in college, I'd go over to his apartment and he'd be cooking calf's liver, or braising a brisket, or making a textbook-perfect omelet.

Bill hadn't been to cooking school—he had learned a lot from his mother, also a very good cook, and through his own self-discipline—and I was the beneficiary of his gifts, a very well-fed girlfriend, indeed.

After I started cooking school, though, I became such a backseat chef that Bill eventually stopped cooking. And who can blame him? Does anybody enjoy cooking a meal while the person for whom you're preparing it is standing there telling you: "You haven't heated the pan enough," or "You didn't pound that chicken breast thinly enough," or "You should have added more acid to that vinaigrette"?

By my second year, I was a force to be reckoned with, a culinary goddess of the highest order, capable of spreading knowledge and good taste wherever I went.

None moved more quickly out of my path than my own family. That fall, when Thanksgiving weekend rolled around, I climbed into my trusty yellow Volkswagen and made the three-plus-hour drive to my sister Anne's home in Providence, Rhode Island, where she lived in a brownstone with her husband, John.

Anne and I always had a healthy sibling rivalry. In many ways, I was the Snow White to her Rose Red. Two and a half years older than I was, dark haired and pretty, Anne always had some piece of good news when we were growing up, or a handsome new boyfriend to show off. And there I was, little sis, trying to steal attention and affection with smart-alecky comments, or flirting with her new beau. I have to admit, I was a pretty obnoxious younger sister.

Though we loved the heck out of each other, in those days the echoes of our childhood squabbles still reverberated when we got together, even in her grown-up home. Not surprisingly, that Thanksgiving I showed up ready to demonstrate to my family how skillfully we did things at the CIA—that's insider speak, I smugly informed them, for Culinary Institute of America. No sooner had I arrived than I had donned my chef's coat and white apron and gracelessly taken over the kitchen.

Anne's home was airy and open; the kitchen flowed right into the living room, where my family was drinking wine and catching up, some seated on the couch, some on the floor lounging on big throw pillows. I was situated only a few yards away, but they paid me no mind, uninterested in my fanatical, self-satisfied plans.

I really went to town that day. Even though my mother made a wonderful gravy, I decided to set them straight with mine, starting of course with a homemade stock that I prepared right there.

I made stuffing as well, and of course a turkey. I had never cooked a turkey before—most chefs probably don't "do turkey"—but I faked it, acting as though it, too, were something about which I had been professionally schooled.

With the stock made and the turkey roasting, it was time to turn my attention to mashed potatoes. Oh, I'm sorry. Did I say "mashed potatoes?" I meant to say "potato puree," the real name by which any serious gourmet would refer to them. How much I had grown at the CIA!

I took out my russet potatoes, and felt them in the palm of my hand, one at a time. Ah, I had chosen well. They each weighed almost exactly the same and were of similar length and circumference. Why is this important? you ask. Why, so they'll cook at the same rate, of course. If you'd been to cooking school, you'd know that, too.

After boiling the potatoes in their skins, I peeled them and transferred them to a dry pan and heated them over low heat, stirring to help evaporate any lingering moisture.

I had my milk warmed—*just* enough—on a low burner, and the butter set out at room temperature, cut into little cubes to facilitate its melting into the puree.

Then it was time to run the potatoes though a food mill. I rummaged through the cupboards, searching for one. But I couldn't find a mill, or even a ricer.

Out of options, I plugged in the food processor, dropped in the potatoes, and started the motor. Within seconds, the potatoes turned to glue as the starch rapidly overdeveloped. It was so thick and pasty that the machine actually stopped running.

"Oh, darn," I muttered.

Upon hearing this, Anne sprang up off of the couch with a wicked look in her eye.

Everything is fixable. That's my philosophy. Unless it's burnt, in which case you either lie and say it's smoked, or order out for pizza. But I learned that day that overprocessed potatoes cannot be saved.

I tried, though. As Anne approached, dancing into the kitchen with an excited step, I furiously attempted to cover the mistake, adding hot milk and butter to the jammed processor. But it had no effect. The potatoes, and the machine itself, were ruined.

Anne didn't mind. A broken food processor was a small price to pay for sweet revenge on her know-it-all little sister, the girl who used to flirt with her dates, and cackle at her every misfortune.

"Well, lookie, lookie here," she said with a big grin as she peered over my shoulder into the processor's bowl. "The master chef who can't even make mashed potatoes. Wonder what they'd say about that at the ol' C.I.A."

Christmas had come early for Anne that year. I had inadvertently given her a gift that she enjoys to this day, a choice moment to call on whenever she feels the need to exact her revenge for all those moments of her youth that were spoiled by her little sister.

Thirty years later, Anne and I are closer than we ever have been. I love her to death, and vice versa. But she'll never love me too much to remind me, with a twinkle in her eye, of the day my culinary vanity came crashing down to earth in her airy Rhode Island brownstone.

For the Birds
TAMARA MURPHY

Tamara Murphy worked in a number of New York City restaurants before moving to Seattle in 1988. She worked at Dominique's, then became executive chef at Campagne, near the Pike Place Market, where she was nominated for the James Beard Foundation's Rising Star Chef of the Year Award. While at Campagne, Murphy was named one of the Best New Chefs in the United States by Food and Wine Magazine. *In 1993, she became executive chef of Café Campagne, a sister restaurant to Campagne, and in 1995, she was named Best Chef/Pacific Northwest and Hawaii by the James Beard Foundation. In 1999, she partnered with Bryan Hill, the former general manager and wine director of Campagne, to open Brasa, which has been honored by both* Food and Wine *and* Gourmet *magazines as one of Seattle's top tables.*

I T HAPPENED AT my very first job in Seattle.
I had lived in New York City and had worked for some very fine establishments, the dream of most young cooks. But

wouldn't you know it, I was on my way to fame and fortune in the Big Apple when I was struck by the travel itch, a condition that's been known to inflict many of us in this transient profession.

I was young enough to act on such whimsical notions, so I packed my bags and off I went with a friend. Taking to the southern region, we ate and drank our way through the states of Bliss and Oblivion, and in time, landed here in Seattle, as far away from New York as you can get without crossing an ocean. It was September, and despite the picture painted by popular opinion, it *never* rained in Seattle that month. I thought it was the most beautiful place I had ever seen: it was sunny all day, stayed light out until almost ten o'clock at night, and then turned perfectly cool and breezy. Life was sophisticated but laid back—people actually hung out on their stoops and drank locally brewed microbeers with their neighbors, just like in the movies.

And the food! The Pike Place Market alone was a revelation, where farmers set out their fantastically enormous fruits and vegetables for sale, and the fish guys tossed monkfish around like baseballs. It wasn't long before my inner chef was reawakened: I envisioned salmon jumping right into my sauté pan. I had to stay.

You'd think—at least I thought—that a young cook with New York chops would have no problem landing a job in Seattle. But you'd be wrong. It proved enormously difficult to find employment of the culinary sort in my adopted home. Turns out that a New York résumé was not in my favor—not at all. My least favorite quip was, "Honey, get some experience here in Seattle and then we'll chat."

Chat? I was from New York, where cooks don't chat. They growl, sweat, and curse their way through the evening service, and often through life in general. But I'm adaptable. I have to be: adaptability is the key to being a great cook—which is kind of the moral of this story, but we'll get to that in a minute . . .

Eventually, mercifully, I was hired by a Frenchman who was an incredible chef and a terrible businessman. This combination is pretty common, owing, I guess, to right-brain/left-brain dynamics. He was also a brilliant teacher. My cooks have heard this story a hundred times, so if they pick this up, they'll skip right over this part. But they should read it, because it keeps me from screaming my head off trying to drill this kind of performance into them, and I don't think they can hear it enough.

When I started that job, I was at the bottom. It was a small restaurant with about forty-five seats, and there were only three cooks plus my chef. As the new kid, I was low person on the totem pole and, trust me, the lowest of three is *way* low. I had to sweep and mop the kitchen at the end of the night, which was extremely humbling. I was from New York, after all, where cooks didn't clean; the guys who didn't speak English—those of "don't ask, don't tell" immigration status—did that.

Despite my lackey role, the chef liked me. Empowered by the sense of belonging, I asked him one day to teach me how to make his pâté. "When you clean my floors properly, I will teach you," he said.

"Please explain," I softly asked him, carefully probing so as not to set him off; French chefs tend to explode like a cheese soufflé baked at too high a temperature if you push them.

"Every day the crumbs and grease continue to build in the corners of my kitchen floor," he said, pointing to the crusty corners of the room. "If you make my pâté every day with the same diligence that you clean my floors, my pâté will look the same!" He curled up his face in distaste at the thought. "So, when you learn that a perfectly clean floor, which requires *no skill at all*, is your most important job, only then will I begin to show you the art of charcuterie!"

How much lower than *that* can you get?

Okay, big surprise: I took his words to heart, gave him the immaculate floors he needed to function, performed the rest of my tasks with renewed vigor, and three months later I was his sous-chef.

I was well into my tenure in this position when a party of ten reserved two weeks in advance for dinner at the restaurant. (This is tremendously early by Seattle standards, the equivalent of calling a year ahead in New York or San Francisco.) The guest of honor adored pheasant, so the party requested a pheasant dish. Since we didn't have one on the menu, I ordered the birds special, just for them.

My chef had a previous engagement on the evening in question, and would not be on the line. But this was no problem. I had proven myself by then, and he was completely comfortable with me handling the birds, the special table, and the rest of the night's affairs. We had been through a lot in a short time, and in addition to getting my work done, I had learned to inspire my successors on the bottom rung to sweep and mop the floors as though their lives depended on it: the floors were spotless.

The day of the pheasant dinner, I spent a good part of the afternoon carefully prepping the birds and the accompaniments I had selected. I was going to roast the pheasants, then debone them, marinate them in a mixture of balsamic, grapefruit, cloves, and garlic, and finish them on the grill.

The reservation was for seven o'clock. At five o'clock, I rubbed the two-pound pheasants with olive oil, tossed them with herbs, and placed them in the oven, planning to roast them for twenty minutes. But soon the evening's dinner service began, and it was busier than usual. We were quickly slammed and I forgot about the pheasants. When I opened the door of the pheasant's oven at six forty-five, dark smoke billowed out. As I hurriedly fanned it away, I saw that these were not just over-cooked birds; they were as black and shriveled as carbon paper!

The moment that I was taking this in, a waiter entered the kitchen and announced the arrival of the party of ten, including the pheasant-loving guest of honor. I believe I have never felt my stomach drop and churn as it did just then. I know that all the color ran from my face, and I was sure I was about to faint. There was no other restaurant nearby that was going to have pheasant. No pun intended, but my goose was cooked.

The only bird I had remotely close to a pheasant was a chicken. I grabbed four of them, removed the breasts, leaving the wings partially intact so they resembled pheasants, and threw those babies in the deep fryer. My two cooks looked at me like I was nuts, but this was a trick I had picked up from an old-school line cook in New York City. Once, when I had forgotten to fire a lamb rack that was supposed to be cooked well done, he took one and threw it in the fryer where it cooked in less than eight minutes, saving me the wrath of the very cranky chef.

After a few minutes, I took the breasts out of the fryer, slapped the marinade on them, tossed them on the grill, then plated them with apricots and foie gras. I sent the mock pheasant out to the table, where it was promptly declared the plumpest and most delicious pheasant they had ever tasted. Personally, I think the foie gras acted as a decoy. I mean, who would serve foie gras with chicken?

Please don't misunderstand my intentions. I wasn't trying to pull a fast one, or get away with something. It was all for the happiness of my guests. They enjoyed their pheasant, even if it was really chicken, and I know my chef would have been proud—if only he knew.

Chef's Table
CINDY PAWLCYN

After receiving her bachelor's in restaurant management, and studying at Le Cordon Bleu and La Varenne in Paris, Cindy Pawlcyn moved to California in 1980 to work at MacArthur Park. She became opening chef at Meadowood, worked under Bruce LeFavour at Rose and LeFavour, and opened her own restaurant, Mustards Grill, in 1983. Since then, Pawlcyn has been involved in conceptualizing and opening more than a dozen restaurants, including Rio Grill, Fog City Diner, Bix, Roti, Buckeye Roadhouse, and Tra Vigne. She currently operates Mustards Grill and her Cindy's Backstreet Kitchen, in St. Helena. Pawlcyn is an inductee of Who's Who of Cooking in America, has been nominated for the James Beard Foundation award for Best Chef/California twice, and her Mustards Grill Napa Valley Cookbook *won a James Beard Award.*

THERE ARE LOTS of ways to keep tabs on what's going on in your own restaurant. You can install hidden cameras. You can walk around like a prison guard. You can hire a company that dispatches anonymous reviewers who send you a written report detailing everything you and your team got right, and wrong.

Me? I like to take a seat in the dining room and eat a meal in each of my restaurants at least once a week. Sure, the staff recognizes me, but even so, there's nothing like seeing things from the customer's point of view to get a sense of how you're doing, what's working, and what isn't.

I don't dine alone in my restaurants—sometimes my mom will join me, or one of my stepkids. In many ways, it's like going out to dinner anywhere else: I dress incognito, in my civvies, engage in typical lunch or dinner conversation, and always manage to enjoy myself.

But it's never quite the same when the chef is in the dining room—it's not the same for my customers, it's not the same for the waiters, and it's not the same for the guys in the kitchen.

First of all, it's often apparent to the other customers that I have some relationship to the restaurant, because the waiters and managers talk to me like I was one of their own. *Real* observant guests might notice that I often order without the aid of a menu, and don't receive a check.

There's another way I sometimes get found out: when I see something wrong—water glasses that aren't being refilled, dishes that aren't plated correctly, or any other egregious mistake—I can't sit still.

Sometimes this passes without incident: if there's a manager nearby, I'll wave him or her over and whisper the situation, then let things get resolved without any further involvement, although I won't take my eyes off the problem until it's been fixed—admittedly not the most flattering way to treat my dining companion.

But if there's no manager within sight, then I'll take matters into my own hands. And that's when things can get messy.

My regular companions know when this is about to happen. They recognize the way I start to fidget, growing more and more anxious. "Don't get upset," they say, but it's hopeless advice; I'm already boiling over and leaping into action.

Like the time I spotted a couple, out for dinner on their anniversary, presented with their meal. Even from my distant vantage point across the dining room I could tell that the liver one of them had been served was cooked to death. It happens—the guys in the kitchen fall behind in their work, then leave something on the heat for too long while they're trying to catch up.

I excused myself from my table, marched up to the couple, and asked what was wrong.

"Our food is overcooked," the man said, hesitantly, because I looked like just another customer, and he wasn't sure why I was so concerned.

I took their plates and headed straight into the kitchen to remedy the situation. I didn't identify myself. I never do; I want to get the problem resolved as quickly as possible, and introductions just eat up time. But I probably should.

"Wow," people like that couple have been heard to say, "I've never had a fellow customer do *that* for me."

But I'm not always the masked stranger riding into town and anonymously saving imperiled entrees. Some of my most memorable chef-dining moments have involved customers who know me, like Robin Lail, daughter of the family that for years owned Inglenook wine, and who now runs her own Lail Vineyards in Napa Valley. Recently, she and her husband, Jon, were having dinner at my newer restaurant, Cindy's Backstreet Kitchen in St. Helena.

I've known Robin for years—she's a very active community

member—and if I were in my whites, I would have dropped by the table to visit. She's a charming and elegant woman and I always enjoy speaking with her. But as I was doing the observation thing, I stayed put.

Until the Tabasco sauce arrived.

Robin comes in for dinner all the time and often orders Chicken Pollo Loco, a spicy, marinated chicken cooked under a weight to expose as much skin as possible to the heat of the oven, crisping it beautifully. Chicken Pollo Loco is made red hot by a variety of chili peppers, but as hot as it is, Robin always shakes a little Tabasco sauce over it, probably more for the vinegar than the spice.

On this particular night, when she asked for the sauce, the waiter dutifully retrieved it for her. No problem, right? Well, it wouldn't have been, except for one tiny but very significant detail: the waiter took the Tabasco sauce from the kitchen rather than the waiter station.

A lot of the guys in my kitchen remove the spigot-stopper from Tabasco bottles to facilitate pouring large quantities onto their french fries. So when Robin delicately inverted the bottle above her chicken, about a quarter cup of sauce, instead of a few drops, gushed out. Her face immediately crumpled, like a little kid who just dropped her ice cream cone on the sidewalk.

I guess Robin and Jon were trying to make it in time for a movie at the little theater next door, because she didn't say anything; she just took a knife and fork and began eating the Tabasco-soaked chicken as her husband looked on incredulously.

That's when I intervened, swooping in to steal her dish, then returning with a fresh one in record time.

The entire transaction took place without a word, except her whispered "Thank you" when I deposited a Tabasco-free Chicken Pollo Loco before her.

Then there was the time when my presence caused one of my best staff members to call it an early night.

This was at Mustards, and one of my favorite waiters was looking after my table for a celebration dinner. We treated ourselves to a bottle of champagne. When our glasses got low, she refilled them . . . with sparkling water, diluting the champagne in the glass enough that they all had to be dumped out.

I was so fond of this waiter that I laughed off the mistake. And were this any other table, she simply would have treated us to a new bottle and moved on.

But she was mortified. So much so that she left for the night, too embarrassed to return and serve us any more.

She needn't have been, she's a total pro and—I believe—one of the finest waiters in the universe.

But that's the kind of thing that can happen when, for better or for worse, the chef is in the house.

Our First Friday
NEIL PERRY

Neil Perry opened Sydney's Rockpool restaurant in 1989 with his business partner and cousin Trish Richards. Through his Rockpool Consulting, he heads a team of consultants to Qantas Airways and created a range of Neil Perry Fresh food products in conjunction with Woolworth's Supermarkets. He is the author of Rockpool *and* Simply Asian, *and is working on a third book and four classical/recipe CDs. He is also a television presenter on* The LifeStyle Channel. *Before Rockpool, Perry worked at Sails restaurant at McMahons Point and in Rose Bay, then became head chef at Barrenjoey Restaurant in Palm Beach and Perry's in Paddington. In October 1986, he opened the Blue Water Grill at Bondi Beach. Rockpool won the* Sydney Morning Herald Good Food Guide's *Restaurant of the Year 2004 award and is a perennial member of the Top 50 restaurants in the world ranking by UK magazine* Restaurant.

Opening a new restaurant is a stressful business. It doesn't matter how many times you've done it, how much you plan, or how many experts you surround yourself with, there will always be surprises waiting around every corner.

Some surprises aren't really surprises, because you learn to expect them: it's likely that one cook or another will quit at a highly inconvenient time, often the week of your launch; some piece of kitchen equipment will give you trouble, either because it doesn't function properly or because it's an unfamiliar model and there's a struggle to master it; and your opening day will be rescheduled at least three times.

But there are certain surprises you simply can't anticipate, no matter how active and boundless your imagination. The debut week of my restaurant Rockpool, sixteen years ago in Sydney, was proof positive of this statement. In addition to the intensity of construction, dining room design, menu planning, hiring, and training, once we opened, we were faced with the daily drama of getting the place up and running for lunch, then shutting down, going through a whole new round of prep, and reopening for dinner.

For kitchen professionals, doing lunch and dinner is like cramming two workdays into one calendar day. It was very hectic and difficult, an extreme test of physical and mental stamina, for both me and my crew of twelve cooks, all of whom worked both shifts back to back. If you were there in the morning, you were there when the restaurant closed after midnight.

A nice break in the day—the eye of the storm, so to speak—was our nightly staff dinner, served about thirty minutes before the first customers arrived each evening.

Some restaurants are pretty cheap when it comes to their staff meal; they feed their employees the lowliest of ingredients and expect them to shovel it down in seconds, then get right back to work. But at Rockpool, our staff meals were done in the proper spirit, a gesture of thanks for everyone's hard work and a chance for the men to have some shared downtime in the midst of a grueling schedule.

On our first Friday night, we were going to have lamb chops for staff dinner. One of the guys was barbecuing the chops on our indoor grill, and as the char-tinged smoke wafted through the kitchen, our hunger pangs spiked. We had been around food all day, but this was to be *our* food, and it was at this moment that our professional indifference to all the delicious temptations before us finally gave way. We paced around with ravenous, impatient grins on our faces, tortured by the tantalizing smell of the chops, eager to dig in to a richly deserved feast.

I was deep in this heightened, near-excruciating state of anticipation when all of a sudden I felt a spray of icy water in my face, a forceful, unending blast shocking in its temperature, its magnitude—its very existence. Where on earth was it coming from?

Shaking my head, trying in vain to avoid the rush, I looked around to see that all of the guys were being hosed down as well. Water was catching them right in the face. Some were ducking or cowering to protect themselves, others were defiantly squinting into the gush to determine its source.

I was stunned. We all were. What in the world was happening? Had a pipe burst in the ceiling? *Were* there even pipes in the ceiling?

Finally, I realized what had happened: lamb chops are fatty things, and the fat dripping into the flames of the barbecue had caused some pretty big flare-ups. Those flare-ups, in turn, had set off the sprinkler system. It was only at that moment that I noticed there was a fire alarm going off as well.

I don't know if you've ever experienced the deluge created by an industrial sprinkler system, but it is unforgettable. It dumps what feels like thirty thousand liters of water per second, and it covers a pretty fair whack of territory, dispersing it in all directions.

The effect was like being on a leaky submarine, with water pouring down on us without end. And the water got *everywhere*. It soaked our clothes, it collected on the counters and ruined all the *place* (short for *mise en place*—the prepared ingredients at each station), it pooled up on the floor, it flowed under the doors. It was absolute chaos, and there was nothing we could do but watch.

Soon enough, the alarm was drowned out by the sound of approaching sirens. The fire brigade raced onto the scene with three trucks, and a small army of men rushed through the door, ready to put out any blaze in its path. More hoses—just what we needed.

Once the situation became clear, the firemen turned off the alarm and the sprinklers and returned peace and quiet to our soggy kitchen. We explained about the lamb chops and they kindly laughed it off; I think they must respond to food-triggered alarms all the time.

It was their captain who told me what our problem was: sprinkler systems are set to go off when heat-sensitive tubing inside turns a certain color. Most restaurants have tubing with a relatively high resistance, but our contractor had made a mistake and used the conventional type. It was a miracle, really, that the alarm hadn't gone off on our first night.

With the sprinklers switched off and the fire trucks headed back to the station, we turned our attention to trying to salvage our evening. Our first guests would be showing up in any minute . . .

We spent the next twenty minutes just getting the water out—mopping up the counters with kitchen towels, pushing the water from the floor out the back door with brooms and mops, and throwing away the *place* that was destroyed.

Then we ran off to the lockers to change into whatever extra clothes we had so we could be as dry as possible that night. One thing none of us had were extra shoes, so it was a very squeaky couple of hours in the kitchen.

Yet somehow we made it through the evening. We had to take a few items off the menu—for example, the deep-fryer was full of water and we couldn't get it to turn on, so any fried preparations were removed. Other dishes were prepared as you would prepare them at home—completely made to order, with the cook doing all the chopping and slicing he normally would have completed before staff meal.

Amazingly, even though we have an open kitchen at Rockpool, the customers had no idea that anything disastrous had happened, which is a real tribute to my opening team.

After service that night, I took the men out for about four hundred beers. We probably consumed as much liquid as had poured down on us earlier in the evening, and we had earned every precious drop.

Alibi
MICHEL RICHARD

A pioneer in French/California cuisine, Michel Richard's first kitchen job was as an apprentice in a patisserie in Champagne, France, a job he followed by moving to Paris to work in Gaston Lenotre's esteemed pastry shop. In 1975, he moved to Santa Fe, then, in 1977, to Los Angeles, where he opened his own Michel Richard. In 1987, he launched Citrus, and in 1988, was inducted into the James Beard Foundation's Who's Who in American Food and Beverage. A year later, he opened Citronelle, and went on to open Bistro M in San Francisco, and Citronelle in Baltimore and Philadelphia. In 1994, he opened Citronelle in the Latham Hotel Georgetown in Washington, D.C. In 1998, he moved to Washington, D.C., to cook full time at Michel Richard Citronelle. Richard is the author of Home Cooking with a French Accent, *published in 1993. He was a nominee for the James Beard Foundation's Chef of the Year Award for 1996.*

I N THE 1980s, I owned a pastry shop at the corner of Third Street and Robertson Boulevard in Beverly Hills. We catered to a very affluent, stylish, often famous clientele, and to make them happy, I worked day and night, and was always trying to catch up.

One day, a woman came in and hired us to cater a wedding for two hundred people. Now, this was a quarter-century ago, and I cannot remember who the woman was, whether she was the bride, or the mother of the bride, or a bridesmaid, or a friend. I don't even remember what she looked like.

I do remember, however, that she wanted the cake to be *spectacular*. In addition to it being big enough to serve two hundred people, she insisted that the cake have two doves on top, instead of little bride and groom figurines. And not just any doves: blown-sugar doves. In those days, I was fond of blowing sugar, done the same way you blow glass—by heating a quantity of it to the melting point, inserting a long thin straw into the center, and very carefully blowing, turning, and ma-nipulating the melted sugar with various tools to create the desired shape, then letting it cool and harden.

The wedding was held on a scorching-hot Saturday after-noon, the kind of painfully bright and blistering day you have only in Southern California or the desert, where the sun merci-lessly beats down on you.

I sent my staff ahead to the home where the wedding was taking place and loaded up with all of the food—except for the cake. In those days, I had to do all special preparations myself—first, because my name was on the shop; and second, because there weren't any young cooks around in L.A. who could manage it. Today, sure. But then? No way. And I was so busy that I never had time to train anyone anyway.

Carefully, I assembled the layers of the cake and decorated it with frosting, making it as special as I could, piping tiny white flourishes that were all the same size and perfectly spaced. Even though I was worried about arriving at the reception too late, I took my time. It was heaven to be quietly decorating a cake in the privacy of my own shop.

Then I made the beautiful little doves, heating the sugar and blowing the shapes out of the blob. They were lovely, like big Christmas tree ornaments, and I delicately perched them atop the cake. Voilà!

Finished, I packed the cake up in a big, shiny white box, placed it in the backseat of my car, and started driving to the wedding. Running late, as I always was in those days, I drove fast, scooting around the less-trafficked backstreets. Hey, I was late for a wedding, what cop would give me a hard time?

As I was heading into the heart of Beverly Hills, I took a sharp turn, and heard the cake slide across the backseat—followed by a cracking sound, similar to shattering glass. One of the doves must have broken.

That's too bad, I thought. But at least I had another dove. Like with kidneys, I figured that I could survive with just one.

A little while later, I arrived at the beautiful estate, pulling into the enormous cul-de-sac out front. I couldn't see any of the wedding party, because they were all out back. It was just me and my cake in the customer's driveway.

No sooner did I step out of the car than I was greeted by the wedding director, an officious, highly organized woman in business attire with a clipboard clasped under her arm.

"*Bonjour*, Chef Richard," she said, welcoming me in my native language.

"Good afternoon," I replied, trying to appear calm and not give her the slightest idea that there was a problem.

"I have the cake," I continued, forcing a big smile, and pointing at the box in the backseat.

"Of course. We have a place for it." She directed me to the two-car garage where she said I would find a subzero refrigerator in which I could store the cake until the proper time.

You drive everywhere in L.A., even the shortest distances, so I got back in the car and drove it to the far end of the driveway, pulling up in front of the garage. I hopped out of the car again, opened the big stainless-steel refrigerator door to make sure it was empty, and picked up the cake box, lifting it carefully with both arms and being sure to keep it level.

I walked up to the refrigerator and tried to slide the cake inside. Wouldn't you know it—it didn't fit. But it *almost* fit. So I pushed as hard as I could, forcing it, little by little, into the refrigerator, the box crumpling faintly at the sides.

No sooner did I squeeze the cake into the refrigerator than the shelf collapsed under the tremendous weight, and both the shelf and the cake crashed to the bottom of the refrigerator. I heard the distinctive tinkle of breaking glass again—the second dove had been destroyed. With a sigh, I lifted the lid of the box. There they were, crystalline shards piled up on top of the cake.

Even worse, the cake itself was hurt this time. Thanks to the impact of the landing, the frosting was dripping off the sides as though it were melting.

I had no idea how I was going to save the cake, or explain the poor broken doves, but I had other priorities at that moment, like checking on my staff. Since the door to the refrigerator couldn't be shut, I closed it as far as I could and secured it by dragging over a big, heavy box from the side of the garage and pressing it up against the door.

Quickly, I circled the house, following the sounds of music and distant conversation until I found myself in an enormous backyard with a swimming pool. The beautiful guests were all standing around in their elegant sports coats and dresses, sipping champagne, and eating hors d'oeuvres. They seemed very happy and impressed with the food and my staff, laughing and enjoying a beautiful afternoon.

But as I stood there staring at the pleased reception, all I could think about were those sugar shards. How could I possibly fix them?

Shaking my head with frustration, I left the party and walked back out front, across the driveway, and to the garage.

As I approached the door, I heard the clicking of my footsteps on the driveway mixed in with other footsteps.

I spun around and saw that the owner of the house had two big dogs, Dobermans, who were following me out to the garage.

Normally, I might have been scared to have two Dobermans so close to me. But not this time, because my prayers had been answered. I knew how to get out of my predicament!

"Come here, doggies. Come here," I said.

The dogs glanced at each other, then decided to follow me to the garage. I raced over to the refrigerator, shoved the box away, swung the door open, and lifted the lid of the cake box.

"Bon appétit!" I said.

As soon as the dogs got a scent of the food, they quickened their pace, dashing right for the cake and attacking it, snorting with joy. I pushed their faces into the cake, encouraging them to eat faster. As they came up for air, shards of sugar clung to the frosting that surrounded their mouths like clown makeup.

I ran off calling for the wedding coordinator, who had just come out of the house and was approaching the garage.

"Madame! Madame! The dogs eat my beautiful wedding cake," I cried, sounding terribly upset. This was Hollywood, after all, and I was giving an Oscar-worthy performance.

"What?" she yelled, and we hurried over to the garage together. There were the dogs, munching away.

Horrified, the wedding coordinator chased the animals away, screaming at them. Then she turned to me. "Chef Richard," she said imploringly. "I'm so sorry. So sorry. Can you fix it?"

"Well," I said, trying to appear pensive.

"Please . . ."

"Okay. I know what to do," I said.

"Oh, thank you!" she said and gave me a big hug.

I drove to a nearby store, where I purchased strawberries, whipping cream, and fresh mint. When I got back to the house, I dressed what was left of the cake with whipped cream, then topped it with the berries and mint. By the time I was done with it, it looked like a giant strawberry shortcake.

The coordinator and the happy couple thanked me for being so clever and saving the day. "You are such a quick thinker," the bride said when we were introduced.

She had no idea how right she was.

You Really Ought to
Think About Becoming a Waiter
ERIC RIPERT

In 1995, as executive chef of Le Bernardin, Eric Ripert became one of an elite group of chefs to earn four stars from the New York Times. *Prior to arriving at Le Bernardin, he studied at the culinary institute in Perpignan and worked at some of the world's finest restaurants, including Paris's La Tour D'Argent and Jamin and also Jean-Louis at the Watergate Hotel in Washington, D.C. He is the author of two cookbooks,* Le Bernardin Cookbook *and* A Return to Cooking.

M OST AMERICAN CHEFS I know never considered becoming a waiter, not even for a second. But there comes a moment in every French cooking student's life when he has to make a crucial decision: "Am I going to become a chef or am I going to become a waiter?"

They have to make this decision because French culinary schools insist that you spend time learning to be a front-of-the-house professional as well as a cook. For this reason, many of my classmates not only considered becoming waiters, they actually did.

I never wanted to be a waiter. I had always had a passion for eating and cooking, so had dreamed of becoming a chef since I was a little kid. But I almost became a waiter anyway. In fact, if it weren't for the day that my mother came to lunch at our school's restaurant, I might be a waiter right now.

When I was fifteen years old, I enrolled in the culinary institute in Perpignan, a town of about one hundred thousand people in the South of France. Perpignan was the closest serious cooking school to my home of Andorra, a co-principality on the southern slope of the Pyrenees mountains between France and Spain, approximately three and a half hours away by car. The school had a three-year program for younger kids and a more intensive, two-year program for guys like me. It also offered courses in hairdressing and nursing, so it wasn't a bad place for a fifteen-year-old boy to find himself for two years.

Though situated in an ancient town, the school was contemporary in every way, with modern, meticulously maintained buildings, state-of-the-art classrooms and kitchen equipment, and a handsome little restaurant where we were able to practice our trade on real customers.

The school had an interesting history: many of the instructors had previously cooked or served aboard the legendary French luxury liner *Le France*. Once the pride of the nation, *Le France* had been so grossly mismanaged that the government-owned ship was permanently docked. Its last port of call was Perpignan, and many of the chefs, cooks, and waiters stayed in town, becoming instructors at the school.

All of my teachers were very knowledgeable and very strict, after a 1950s-era model of discipline, discipline, discipline. They treated us like cadets in a military academy, like the crew of their own landlocked ship: you didn't question their authority, *ever*. If you did, or if you screwed up badly enough, you might find a sauté pan hurled at you. Adding to this military air was the classic uniform that the three hundred to four hundred culinary students all dressed in: crisp white apron and jacket, a tall white toque (cylindrical paper hat), and a white neckerchief. A kitchen team is called a *brigade*, and that's what we looked like: an army of cooks.

As with any French culinary school, we devoted just as much time to learning about the dining room as we did to learning about the culinary arts. We spent two days per week serving customers in the school's student-operated restaurant, two days in the kitchen, and one day in the classroom studying the fundamentals of cuisine, as well as management, accounting, and other related topics.

Although it never interested me, being a waiter was appealing to many of my classmates, even those who initially wanted to be chefs. The kitchen was a tough place and it required great patience. Just like a piano student needs to learn notes before he can play scales, and then songs, a culinary student starts with the basics. And the basics can be pretty tedious. The first thing I remember learning to do was clean the stove, and I wasn't even the one who had dirtied it.

In the dining room, however, you got to the heart of the work right away. And you didn't just wait on tables; you also learned how to debone ducks and chickens, fillet fish, and perform such flamboyant acts as flambéing, so if you still had a desire to cook, you got to do a little of that, too.

More important, there were only a certain number of spots in each program, so while the schoolmasters would try to accommodate your wish, it was simply a mathematical fact that some students were going to end up in the dining room.

There was an additional factor, too, one which might be difficult for contemporary diners to fully comprehend: in many countries, waiting tables is a way for out-of-work actors or unskilled laborers to pay the rent. But in France, it's a proud profession with a noble history. Accordingly, the dining room instructors were just as passionate about their work as the chef-instructors were about theirs. So becoming a waiter began to look very appealing to some of the guys, especially when they found themselves ducking a flying sauté pan.

No single person inspired more people to become waiters at the Perpignan culinary institute than the tough-but-fair manager-instructor of the school's restaurant, Monsieur Moccan. M. Moccan was like a Dickens character: well into his forties, he was a chubby, slightly hunchbacked, bespectacled figure who strode through the dining room greeting customers with one voice and using another, stronger, firmer voice to correct any mistakes in his path.

M. Moccan thought I was the best waiter in my class, and he took every opportunity to tell me so. He tried to push me, more than anyone, out to the front of the house for the rest of my life.

But I never changed my answer: I wanted to work in the kitchen.

Toward the end of my first year of school, a decision had to be made about what the focus of my second year, and consequently my career, would be. Of course, my mind was made up, but I was only sixteen, and they wanted me in the dining room, so it was decided that my mother and stepfather would make the drive from Andorra, have lunch in our restaurant, and meet with the administrators to discuss my future.

To make the day as special as possible, and afford me an opportunity to impress my family, M. Moccan appointed me sommelier for the afternoon. The thought was that with nothing to do put pour wine and shuttle cocktails from the bar to the tables, an accomplished waiter like me would have an easy time of it and put a big smile on Mom's face.

I donned the regulation waiter's uniform (white jacket with epaulets, bow tie, black pants, black socks, and leather shoes), and began the shift uneventfully, walking the midsized room, surveying the hundred or so seats, just as comfortable as I always was.

As the lunch service progressed and the dining room filled to capacity, a *real* military man came into our little academy: a colonel from the French army, about sixty years old, rather skinny, in uniform, with his wife and a civilian couple. I took their cocktail orders, got the drinks from the bartender, and returned with one of our round, rimmed drinks trays balanced on my open palm. Before I could get one glass on the table, something happened that had never happened before: I lost control of the tray, turning all four drinks over on the colonel and soaking his beautiful starched uniform.

To his credit, the colonel didn't lose his composure. He wasn't happy, but he was a true gentleman about my mistake and he sat there patiently while I patted his back dry.

M. Moccan hurried over to the scene of the disaster and pulled me aside, supportive as ever. "Don't get stressed out. The guy's going to be okay. He's knows it's the restaurant of the school." But he was also just as firm as he always was. "Go fill up your tray again, come back, and serve them," he instructed. "You have to finish the job."

So I got the drinks again and came back as fast as I could. It turns out I came back too fast because they hadn't had a chance to clean the floor. As I approached the colonel's wife, I slipped on the ice cubes from the first disaster and upended the tray on her. I expected her to start screaming, but I think they were all in shock at this point. Nobody said a word to me as I did my best to clean the table and help her dry herself off.

Once again, M. Moccan began whispering in my ear, telling me to go back to the bar and finish the job. I remember thinking that I hadn't even started it yet.

When I returned to the bar, the bartender looked at me as though he had just found out I had six weeks to live—his eyes conveyed pity, sadness, and discomfort. With a sigh, he replenished my tray once again and I gingerly made my way back to my little table of horrors. En route, I noticed that a quarter-inch of water had collected in the well of the tray. Convinced that lightning couldn't possibly strike three times, and unwilling to lose any more time before successfully serving the table their drinks, I resolved simply to be careful and leave the water where it was. I delivered three of the drinks without incident, then turned to the colonel. He nodded slightly to me. I nodded in return. And as I reached for his drink, the tray tipped, spilling the water right in his face.

That was it. The colonel shot up out of his chair and began screaming, "That's enough! Get this guy out of here!"

I flinched, taking a few nervous backward steps. But he wasn't yelling at me. He was yelling at M. Moccan, who was suddenly nowhere to be found—until I spotted him through the little window in the kitchen door, laughing uncontrollably, unable to compose himself and return to the dining room.

"As for *you* . . ." the colonel shouted at me. And I stood there while he dressed me down in full view of the customers, who watched in awe, and my mother, slowly turning green, struggled to understand why the school so desperately wanted her son to become a waiter.

I never did get to spend time at my mother's table that day, and I'm sure I didn't impress her, especially with where I ended up next: demoted to dishwasher. But at least I had found my way back to the kitchen, and I never came out again.

You're in the Army Now
ALAIN SAILHAC

Alain Sailhac began his career in France in the 1950s, cooking at the Hôtel Claridge and Hôtel Normandie. He worked in kitchens all over the world before moving to New York City and becoming executive chef of Le Cygne, where he earned the first four-star rating ever awarded by the New York Times. *He went on to become the executive chef at Le Cirque, which also earned four stars. Among his many honors is being named Chef of the Year by the Master Chefs of France in 1997. He currently serves as executive vice president and senior dean of studies of the French Culinary Institute in New York City.*

IN 1956, I was called upon to serve my mandatory time in the French army. Because I was a cook with experience in Paris restaurants, I was appointed chef de cuisine of a base that abutted the "Zone Interdict," the dangerous no-man's-land on the border of Tunisia and Algeria, which was fighting for its independence.

The base was an odd collection of barracks, tents, and houses that had been abandoned by their fearful occupants. I was in charge of two kitchens and a staff of about twenty cooks. The food in the army wasn't very exciting. For breakfast, we served coffee and bread. Then we served lunch and dinner in the mess hall, a big tent with long wooden tables and folding wooden chairs.

As chef de cuisine, I was also in charge of cooking special meals for visiting generals and preparing daily rations for the men—essentially anything having to do with food was my responsibility. The rations were a nighttime job; I'd spend hours packing up little boxes with the designated provisions, including two cigarettes per soldier. It was one of the reasons that I developed a schedule shared only by the camp lookouts: I'd work at night, killing the downtime by playing poker with the other insomniacs, and sleep during the day.

There were several kitchen challenges unique to a military base. For one thing, the number of soldiers stationed there changed all the time; one day you might be cooking for a thousand guys, the next for fifty, so meal preparation involved plenty of improvisation and last-minute adjustments.

For dinner, we made stew a lot because it was the smart thing to do with the tough pieces of meat we were supplied by the military; and if you had extra, you could serve it again a day or two later. Occasionally, we'd get a good leg or shank of some animal and we'd roast it, but even then it sometimes came out chewy. There's only so much you can do with poor ingredients.

But sometimes we got lucky. Our base was very secluded; you couldn't set foot outside its perimeter because we were under constant bombardment by the enemy. Two rings of barbed-wire fences surrounded the compound, with just enough room between them to walk around the circumference of the encampment.

Sentries were on the lookout at all times, training rifles on the rugged terrain. Their orders were to shoot anything that moved, *on sight*, because if the enemy was within range, that meant we were within *their* range, and there wasn't a second to spare.

So, they'd see something move, and they'd shoot it dead. More often than not it wasn't an enemy soldier, but rather a wild cow, donkey, pig, or some other animal that had stumbled into view. When that happened, they would sneak out into the no-man's-land outside the camp and quickly drag the carcass back, delivering it to my kitchen door. I'd come up with something to do with it, and run it as a special.

Even with these occasional treats, however, the men were still apt to complain about the lack of meat. And who could blame them? They were risking their lives; they deserved a good meal.

So one day, I decided to take matters into my own hands. I grabbed my rifle, went out to the edge of the base, and began walking along inside the barbed-wire corridor, my eyes trained on the craggy land just beyond my reach.

Before too long, I spotted a wild steer grazing on a meager patch of grass. With enthusiastic thoughts of the meal I would soon prepare, I raised my rifle, took aim, and squeezed the trigger.

But I missed—the shot ricocheted off a nearby rock.

The steer spun its head around in my direction and, with a snort, it started charging at me. I got off another shot, but only nicked him in the side, making him even angrier. He picked up steam, running so hard that I was sure he was going to burst right though the fence and trample me to death.

I was frozen in my tracks, unable to turn and run.

My heart racing, I got down on one knee. With slippery, shaky hands, I aimed my rifle, steadying its butt on my shoulder. This time, I was patient. Waiting. Waiting.

Finally, I pulled the trigger.

Boom! I hit the steer right in the head, dropping him instantly. I sank to the ground, looking up to the heavens in relief.

I was saddened and upset. Sure, I had been butchering animals for years, but I had never killed anything larger than a chicken. And I certainly never found myself fighting for my life against an animal bound for the kitchen.

It's funny, I suppose, that this was the most intense life-and-death moment I experienced in the army, but it didn't seem so at the time. The men were happy to have beef for dinner that night, but this horrible incident haunted me for days.

Accidents happen in the army. They happen with machinery. They happen with coordinates and directions. And they happen with food.

Every day, at four in the morning, I made coffee, 200 liters of it, in a big, stainless-steel vat. Then I sweetened it with about 12 pounds of sugar.

As the chef, and the only person in the mess hall at that hour, I got to have the first cup of the day. So one morning, as usual, I made the coffee, added the sugar, poured myself a cup, and took a sip.

I spit it right out.

It was the most disgusting coffee I had ever tasted. I looked at the cup, then at the vat, in search of some kind of explanation. But it looked fine. Had I imagined it? I *was* pretty tired. Curious, I tasted it again—and immediately spit it out again.

I wasn't imagining anything. And then it hit me, what must have happened. I had put 12 pounds of something in the coffee, alright, but it wasn't sugar.

It was salt.

In the army, you can't just make another 200-liter vat of

coffee, because you don't have extra provisions like that. So to try to cover up my mistake, I added 12 pounds of sugar to the vat.

I poured myself a cup and tasted it.

Somehow, it was even worse.

What was I going to do? Soldiers need their coffee. They *love* their coffee. But what could I possibly do? Baffled, I decided to say nothing, just wait and see. Maybe nobody would notice.

Within minutes, the first soldiers began coming in for breakfast. A group of four men each took a hunk of bread and fixed themselves a cup of coffee, then sat at a table.

All four took a sip.

And all four spit it out.

One of the men waved me over.

"What'd you put in this coffee?" he growled at me.

"Why, nothing. What's wrong?"

"It's disgusting."

"Maybe there's something wrong with the coffee. I'll go check," I said, and left, hoping that maybe they would leave before noticing that I never came back.

But already more soldiers were on the way. It was a busy week at the base and about four hundred men had slept there the night before.

I watched from the kitchen as soldier after soldier went through the same routine: pouring a coffee, sitting, tasting it, spitting it out, and then looking around for a chef to scream at.

Soon enough, four hundred people had spit out their coffee and a big, angry mob was beginning to form.

Finally, I emerged from the kitchen, admitted my mistake, and made my apologies to the troops. They laughed and shook it off.

But not the base commandant. He was so upset with me that he sentenced me to one week in the brig.

Hearing of this, my captain upped the punishment to two weeks.

The brig wasn't really a prison. It was just a small, stand-alone room with a locked door. There was no actual cell and no other prisoners with me. While I was there, I slept a lot, and talked though the window to the guard who paced back and forth outside with a rifle resting on his shoulder. Three times a day, he'd let me out and we'd go for a walk.

It ended up being a nice little break. I was almost disappointed when they let me out of the brig after just one week.

Each soldier is supposed to serve twelve to eighteen months in the army, but because we were at war, I ended up staying in the army for twenty-eight months. They say that time in the military builds character, and mine certainly did: I never shot another living thing and I never put salt in the coffee again.

The Big Chill
MARCUS SAMUELSSON

The youngest chef ever to receive three stars from the New York Times, *and winner of the James Beard Foundation Award for Rising Star Chef in 1999 and Best Chef/New York City in 2003, Marcus Samuelsson was born in Ethiopia, raised in Sweden, and trained all over the world, before making Swedish food hip at Restaurant Aquavit in Midtown Manhattan. He is also an author of cookbooks in both Sweden and the United States.*

T HE GLORIFICATION OF celebrity chefs has created the impression that my colleagues, and the cooks who work for us, spend our lives clowning around in the kitchen, then head off into the night, gallivanting around town and partying until dawn.

Sure, there are moments like that for any chef or cook, but generally speaking, our work is more serious and taxing than most people realize. This is especially true of ambitious culinary students and novice cooks who lead disciplined, cruelly solitary existences that can be aptly compared to those of Olympic trainees or long-distance runners. They might blow off steam together after work, but for the most part, their goal demands stamina of the mind and body and a single-minded devotion to their work. Without that sense of purpose, it's likely that they'll crack under the pressure, retreating from the industry or letting it destroy them.

I've seen guys crack in all kinds of ways. I once saw a cook so fatigued and distracted that he stuck his hand in a meat grinder and didn't get it out until four fingers were gone. I've seen good cooks driven to acts of self-destruction, going broke or turning to heroin. It's always the same: the pressure slowly builds, sometimes over several years, until they simply can't take it anymore. They say "fuck it" and do something drastic and stupid.

Kitchen professionals are prone to breakdowns because nobody cares about their problems. At the end of the day, you're all alone. When you fuck up, nobody wants to know the reason; they just want to chew you out and leave you to pick up the pieces.

There have been many moments in my career when I, myself, was this close to throwing in the towel. Like when I worked for a cruise line and the *entremetier* (cook in charge of vegetable preparations), after months of smooth sailing, suddenly "went down"—a phrase we used to describe when someone fell victim to seasickness. Normally we'd have called the corporate headquarters and had a replacement cook flown in to meet us at our next port of call. But we were too far out to sea to orchestrate a switch. Like any true pro, the *entremetier* tried his best to hang in there, working himself so hard that he vomited, repeatedly, into a garbage can right at his station. Finally we kicked him out, and in a gesture of camaraderie, attempted to cover for him by divvying up his dishes, one to the meat station, one to the fish station, and so on.

That didn't work. It's just too much to monitor the doneness of fifteen pieces of fish *and* sauté, say, some brussels sprouts to order—so even though the *entremetier* tried his best, and the rest of us were doing one-and-a-half jobs each, all that mattered was whether or not the kitchen unit was getting the job done, and we weren't. Everybody, and I mean *everybody*, came into the kitchen to chew us out, including the captain of the ship itself.

You know that old expression, "It's not whether you win or lose; it's how you play the game." That line was definitely *not* coined by a chef. Because for a chef, it's *only* about whether or not you pull through. If you fail, nobody cares how hard you tried.

My loneliest, most discouraging professional moment came in the winter of 1988 when—thanks to the placement department of my culinary school—I was hired as a *commis* (lowest cook on the totem pole; a cog in the culinary machine) at La Terrasse, the fine dining room of the Victoria-Jungfrau hotel in Interlaken, Switzerland, an insanely ritzy hotel that catered to a mix of superwealthy Americans, Europeans, and Arabs, many of whom stayed for months at a time.

The kitchens of Victoria-Jungfrau in general, and La Terrasse in particular, had a reputation more or less comparable to that of the Navy Seals boot camp. The assumption was that they would break you and you would quit or be fired, and go crawling back to wherever you had come from. Turnover was so brisk that new students arrived every day, from places as far away as India and Japan. The upside was that those who survived were the best of the best, exactly the people you'd want to work with and learn from. And if you yourself could make it through all the hardships, then you'd be a better man, and a better cook.

Everybody had their own reasons for subjecting themselves to the rigors of this kitchen. I was there because I was eager to leave Sweden and cook at a three-star Michelin restaurant in France. But I was only eighteen and didn't feel ready yet, and thought that a turn in a place like La Terrasse would prepare me.

The setting was like something out of an opulent dream: a resort, more than a century old, set against the spectacular Jungfrau Mountain, where guests alternated between spa treatments, scenic hikes, and gourmet meals.

Days were long in the restaurant's huge kitchen. You worked all morning—me, at the *garde manger*, or salads and cold appetizers, station—preparing and serving lunch, and also doing advance prep for dinner. The not-so-secret personal goal of each cook was to get your dinner prep done before lunch, so that when the last lunch order was out, you could take a few hours off, either catching a nap in your little dormitory-sized room in the staff residence out back, or maybe sneaking in some skiing before returning for dinner service.

From the day I arrived, I led a very solitary existence at Victoria-Jungfrau. First of all, I don't think they had ever seen a black man in the kitchen before me. They sure as hell didn't expect one to show up when they hired a guy named Marcus Samuelsson from Sweden. But what can I tell you? I was born in Ethiopia, orphaned at a young age, and raised by a Swedish family. Anyway, it's my real name.

Then there was the language barrier. The chefs in that kitchen spoke German and French, a little English, and maybe a little Italian. I spoke none of those languages. This wasn't just a social handicap. Every morning, there was a kitchen meeting in which the executive chef, a real ogre in his sixties, reviewed the day's menu in German. I didn't understand him, and the printed menu, written in French, was of no use to me either. So I was dependent on my direct supervisor (the *chef de partie*, the person in charge of a station such as meat or fish, whom I refer to as "*my* chef") and colleagues to help me make sense of my work for the day after we left the meeting.

I had scarcely been there two weeks when New Year's Eve rolled along. As it is for any restaurant, New Year's Eve was one of the biggest nights of the year for La Terrasse, both for the diners, and for the staff, who planned to work hard all day, then reward themselves by partying until dawn.

My chef and I were charged with making one dish that night: smoked salmon served with a thin sliver of avocado terrine. To make the terrine, you prepared a béchamel (a white sauce of flour, butter, and milk), then folded in an avocado puree. The mixture was poured into a mold and a gelatinous liquid was poured over it. It was then refrigerated so the gelatin would set up and suspend the beautiful puree.

My chef took the salmon for himself, assigned me the terrine, and we got to work in our little corner of the kitchen. He retrieved a whole salmon from the butcher and began making the preparations for smoking it, removing any lingering pin bones from the animal's flesh with a pair of kitchen tweezers.

Eagerly, I went to get some gelatin from the supply room, but discovered that all they had was the powdered variety.

Having only used sheet gelatin, I turned the package over to read the instructions. On the back of the box there were what I'm sure were very helpful tips, written in not one but three languages: German, French, and Italian. This was about the time when I realized that this wasn't going to be my day.

Rather than asking for help—which I'm not sure I could have done anyway, since I didn't speak anyone's language—I decided, with all the confidence and lack of foresight of an eighteen-year-old, to wing it. I bloomed what felt like the right amount of gelatin, prepared the terrine, set it in on a steel utility rack in the walk-in refrigerator, and left for the afternoon.

This was one of those times when you know you've made a mistake and spend several hours delaying the admission of it, even to yourself. I spent the afternoon in my room, trying to catch a nap, but I couldn't sleep. As I tossed and turned, I couldn't get the image of that green glop out of my mind, and I grew more and more anxious as the afternoon wore on.

When I returned to the kitchen at around four o'clock, I hesitantly went to check on the terrine, fearing the worst. Which was just what I found. Not only had the terrine failed to set, but it was disgusting, with a green slush in the center of the mold, and an algaelike attempt at coagulation along the edges.

This was the second moment when I could have reasonably raised my hand, admitted my mistake, and salvaged the day. It would have been very simple: we would have let the failed version melt, then added the proper amount of gelatin, and refrigerated it.

Instead, I decided to pop the terrine in the freezer and *force* it to set up.

Now, in most kitchens, the chef will make his rounds before service, checking on sauces and other preparations at the stations at which they are prepared. But at La Terrasse, a kitchen steeped in tradition and formality, we did it a little differently: each cook presented his dish to the chef, showing it to him, then slicing off a taste for his approval.

As the presentation hour approached, I retrieved the mold from the freezer. It now resembled a partially defrosted, frozen avocado soup, slushy around the edges with a little *granité* island of avocado in the middle. Even the smell of it was bad. It was like I had accidentally come up with *real* mold, the kind of thing you find in a filthy motel bathtub.

Slowly, shivering with the dread of what was to come, I approached the executive chef, who was giving off his customary glower.

"Chef," I mumbled, raising up the slimy green creation.

The chef took one look at the terrine and unleashed a fury at me the likes of which I had never heard, before or since. Miraculously, the verbal beating my chef received for not detecting and solving the problem was even worse. It was a tongue lashing so severe that this grown man was reduced to tears and, unable to recover from the shame, he left for the night.

As a consequence, the executive chef stepped in to cover for him. So this man who had just been telling me to go back where I came from—in a foreign language that, for the first time, I understood perfectly—proceeded to lord over me all night. He ordered me around imperiously, giving me a sneer so sharp I could have cut my finger on it. It was a terrible night. We didn't even try to save the terrine. Instead, the chef instructed me to take a spoon to any solid portions I could find and make little avocado quenelles. The next few hours were a blur of tears and quenelles, a cruel memory set against the echo of the veteran German chefs snickering in the background.

I expected to be screamed at one last time after service had finished, but at the end of the night, the chef just left me without another word. He went off to a corner of the dining room and quietly savored a glass of champagne. I wondered how he could enjoy anything after a day in which he had had to publicly savage two of his workers. But now, years later, I understand: the incident was just one event in one day of a chef's life. He had dealt with it and, because he had come up with the quenelle solution, the guests were happy and he was able to move on without a second thought.

When the rest of the crew went out that night to party in the town and usher in the New Year, I staggered back to my room, alone. I felt like the lowest of the low, and didn't want to see anyone.

But here's the thing: that was the night that I could have said "screw it" and quit. It would have been easy to leave. In fact, it would have been the easiest, most appealing thing in the world. I had left a lot back home, including a girl I loved and a group of teenage friends who were hanging out and having fun in the last days of that time of life when you really have no responsibilities to anyone but yourself.

But I wanted to be a chef. I wanted it more than anything. So I swore to stick it out, to work seven days a week, to get harassed in languages I didn't speak, to do whatever it took to make it.

Over the next two weeks the chef put us on the graveyard shift, a vicious, soul-crushing schedule meant to break us. There were no days off. There was nothing but work, shouting, and more work. I saw lots of other cooks come and go during those two weeks, unwilling to endure it, but I held on. I had made my decision, and there was no going back. I still had a long way to go before I made it, but I knew that, at last, I was on my way to becoming one of those hardened veterans who had come through Victoria-Jungfrau.

Ultimately, I learned German to near-fluency and, against all odds, stayed for two years at La Terrasse, becoming a *chef de partie*. I learned everything that I would need to carry me on to those French kitchens I had set my sights on, and in time, to New York City.

But as much as I grew in those two years, the most valuable lesson was the one that took place while I was absorbing that harsh German punishment on New Year's Eve 1989. That was the moment when I resolved to never give anyone reason to speak to me like that again. It's a strange, backward-seeming motivation for such a noble profession—taking inspiration from the desire not to screw up—but like I've said, cooking is at heart a lonely business, and you do whatever it takes to get through the day.

Neverland
BILL TELEPAN

A native of New Jersey, Bill Telepan attended the Culinary Institute of America, then worked in a number of the best restaurants in New York City, including Gotham Bar and Grill, where he was sous-chef for several years, Daniel, and Le Bernardin. He also spent six months working under the great Alain Chapel at his restaurant in Mionnay, France. He was executive chef of Ansonia on New York's Upper West Side and of JUdson Grill in midtown Manhattan, where he received three stars from the New York Times. *He is set to open a new restaurant, Telepan, in fall 2005. Telepan is also the author of* Inspired by Ingredients: Market Menus and Family Favorites from a Three-Star Chef.

A BIG REASON I love being a chef is all the stuff that goes with it—the unusual working hours, the palling around with other chefs and cooks, the horsing around in the kitchen.

Don't get me wrong. I love food, and I take the food itself very seriously. But being a chef means that, on some level, you don't have to grow up. You may have perfectly normal adult relationships outside the four walls of your workplace, but when you don your apron and step into your arena every day, it's like entering a professional Neverland.

This is, I believe, a distinctly American phenomenon. You certainly don't find it in European kitchens, a lesson I learned early in my career when I went to work in France.

In 1990, I was a twenty-three-year-old cook, and I was doing great. I had been to the Culinary Institute of America and I was working in a well-regarded restaurant in New York City, paying my dues as a line cook. I loved my work and felt that I was on my way to wherever I wanted to go.

But something was missing. I had never been to France. And the more I got to know about the best American chefs, the more I realized that they had all worked in France at some point in their careers. They talked about those days with awe and romance. Clearly, something magical happened over there that took their understanding of food and their craft to a new level.

So, one day, I decided to take the leap, move temporarily to France, and spend some time working in a three-star Michelin restaurant.

I've always been self-reliant, maybe to a fault. Rather than asking for help from one of the chefs I knew, I made the securing of a job overseas into my own personal pet project. I wrote a letter in English, had it translated by a woman I knew who spoke French, and then had it double-checked by the teacher of my weekly French class. I then handwrote thirty copies of the letter, addressing them to the nineteen three-star Michelin chefs at the time, and eleven highly regarded two-star chefs.

The responses were not encouraging. In fact, twenty never bothered to respond at all. Five said I'd have to pay them for the privilege of working in their kitchen (fat chance). Four said no.

The single favorable reply came from Alain Chapel, a three-star master chef, who said I could work for him at his eponymous restaurant, but that he wouldn't pay me and that I'd have to stay for two years.

I made the necessary arrangements and set off to France, arriving by train in Mionnay, about twelve miles north of Lyon. As I stepped onto the platform, I looked every bit the brash American cook, with my leather jacket, T-shirt, and pack of smokes.

I turned up at Chapel's restaurant in the middle of the afternoon, and what I saw when I opened the door floored me: it was the day before the restaurant was to reopen for the New Year and Chapel himself was actually dining with the staff; they were all sitting in the dining room, in their starched kitchen whites, having lunch and sipping wine.

I had never seen anything so civilized in my entire life.

Chapel noticed me standing there and before I could introduce myself, he asked me to leave, telling me to come back tomorrow, "when the work begins."

I was embarrassed and scared, and I tore out of there.

I was also uninformed. What time *was* the right time? I came back the next day at eight o'clock, but it turned out I was an hour late. Fortunately, Chapel hadn't arrived yet, and determined not to be sent away twice, I dove in and started helping out. Nobody questioned my presence—or offered me any direction. I didn't really know what to do, so I tried to look busy, my confusion only enhanced by the setting, which was overwhelmingly elegant: there were fresh flowers on all the tables, silver trays at the waiter stations, and in the kitchen the equipment was flawlessly maintained, from the unmarred copper pots and pans to the Le Creuset casseroles.

It didn't matter that I had spent three years in one of the best restaurants in the United States—I felt like a total ignoramus.

Among the eighteen cooks, there were two Japanese guys, a pair of young Belgians, and the rest were French. But no matter their nationality, *none* of them wanted anything to do with the dumb Yank who had shown up in the middle of lunch the day before and then come late again that morning. They probably thought I'd be gone for good by the end of the day.

Soon enough, Chapel drove up with his little truck, bringing fruits, vegetables, and livestock from the market, as he did several times each week. These market runs are legendary to anyone who has ever worked for Chapel, and for an American like me, it was an epiphany to see this chef's profound connection to local farmers.

I joined the other guys, helping to unload the truck, trying to blend in and look like I knew what the hell I was doing.

Finally, Maurice, the chef de cuisine—a refreshingly soft-spoken guy for a French chef—introduced himself and assigned me to the fish station, called *poissonnier*.

I didn't really enjoy my first month at Chapel. I might have been part of the fish team, but I never touched a single fish. Instead I would make tomato *concassé* (coarsely chopped tomatoes), pick herbs from the restaurant's garden, and act as a runner, retrieving stuff from the walk-in refrigerator.

I got to know the walk-in very well, and I must say that there were things about it that fascinated me. I was used to big, stainless-steel refrigerators back home. This one was a small box, about 10 feet long and 5 feet wide, and it was made even smaller by the wooden shelves that lined its walls, reducing the area in which you could move to a slender 2½-foot aisle. The shelves popped in and out of little holes that made it easy to remove them for cleaning—a charming and old-fashioned touch.

I was also fascinated by how well organized and immaculate the walk-in was kept. Stocks weren't stored in big white buckets like they were in U.S. kitchens, but in stainless-steel canisters. The fruits and vegetables, some of them still in their crates from the market and caked with dirt, were plumper and more vibrant than any I had seen. In the back were the fish and meat, arranged neatly enough for a photo shoot.

But as much as I respected the treasures of the walk-in, I wasn't satisfied with the work I was doing. I had been a line cook back home and here I was relegated to basic prep work.

One of the reasons I was so underutilized was that often, especially during lunch, there were more employees than guests. It wasn't unusual to do just four covers for lunch, or sometimes none at all. There'd be more than a dozen cooks in the kitchen and not one person in the dining room.

An additional reason for permanent residency on the bench was a cook on the fish station whom I'll call Sushi Guy. He was from Japan, and had been referred to Chapel by a well-regarded sushi master. At first I found him impressive and intimidating— he had beautiful sushi knives and did all the butchering. But in time I came to almost hate him. Though he never said a word to me, his message was clear: I'll take care of the fish, New Guy, you deal with the petty stuff. And he was usually so proficient that he didn't need any assistance. But one day he was hopelessly backed up, so I got my knives and my cutting board and set up next to him, preparing to give him a hand. He turned toward me, muttered something in Japanese, and pushed me away—literally shoved me backward with the palms of his hands.

I tried to explain that I was trying to help, but he wouldn't have any of it. He just gave me an intense stare, made marginally frightening by the knife in his hand.

I was so offended that I wished we were back home so I could wait for him out back after work and have a good, old-fashioned street fight with him. But we didn't do that kind of thing in Mionnay.

Things got better, though, thanks largely to a big-hearted guy named Bernard. An accomplished cook at just twenty-five years of age, Bernard was French but spoke English and wanted to practice his English on me. Our station's *saucier*, he would let me help him, teaching me all kinds of classic sauces. Best of all, he instructed using English—until Chapel caught us. "No, no, no," he scolded Bernard. "English is the language of politics. French is the language of cuisine."

So Bernard and I spoke French from then on. By that time we were friends anyway. His acceptance was like a stamp of approval. One by one, the others started to befriend me. First among the converts were the other fish guys, Anton and Ernest. Then came the two Belgians, Carl and Xavier, big, strapping guys who worked the meat station, along with a seven-year veteran of Chapel's kitchen named Freddy. Carl and Xavier were as goofy as they were huge—well over 6 feet tall—and they loved to make fun of the lone American.

"You stupid American," they would say, shaking their heads in mock contempt. And I'd answer back, "If it wasn't for us Americans, you'd be speaking German!" Then Carl and Xavier would crack up, laughing their big, meaty chuckles. It was a routine we did at least once a day.

Eventually I got on well with everyone in the kitchen, including the pastry guys—though I can't remember their names anymore—and the *other* Japanese guy, Mitzu, a great cook with an infectious grin and a great sense of humor. I loved singing to Mitzu; my favorite song was a faux Irish number that

I serenaded him with every day: "*His name was Mitzu, oh Mitzu, O'Reilly.*"

So, once the ice was broken, things were great for me at Chapel. I loved waking up in the morning and coming to work, then going out with the guys after the dinner shift. I even saw my enemy, Sushi Guy, humbled. One night after service I was going out to a *moules-frites* joint with the Belgians and Sushi Guy forced himself on us, tagging along without an invitation. We got crazy-drunk, and Sushi Guy spent the entire night out of control, fighting off bouts of nausea and being unbelievably loud and undignified—bursting out in laughter one moment, and looking like he might pass out, or throw up, the next.

In the morning, when we got to work, Sushi Guy sheepishly tried to apologize to us and explain himself. Big mistake. We really didn't care; if anything, his night of debauchery had humanized him. But in apologizing, he firmly established himself as King Geek of the Universe and his clout in the kitchen plummeted. Even in a French kitchen, it's possible to be too square.

By the third month, I was as at home at Alain Chapel as I ever was in New York or New Jersey. Maybe *too* much at home . . .

One day, things in the kitchen were particularly laid back. It was one of our dead days for lunch, and all morning Anton, Ernest, and I were picking on the Belgians.

"Hey, shut up, you stupid American."

"You know if it wasn't for us stupid Americans, you'd all be speaking German right now."

"Ha ha ha ha ha."

Like that.

This had been going on for hours when I went into the walk-in to get some fish. Carl and Xavier were in there and as soon as they saw me, they started up with the whole stupid-American routine again.

I was so at ease by this point that I had totally reverted back to my childhood self—which wasn't really that far in the past anyway.

I stepped up to Xavier, pulled his arm toward me in a wresting maneuver, spinning him around and getting him in a headlock from behind. As he struggled, we both twisted around, grazing one of the shelves. Its contents bounced violently, then settled.

At some point during my struggle with Xavier, Anton and Ernest had wandered into the walk-in; the next thing I knew, Carl and Ernest were going at it. They weren't punching each other—there was barely enough room in there to throw a decent haymaker—no, they had grabbed each other by the shoulders and were grappling for control. Finally, Carl—the 6-foot Belgian—managed to gain some momentum and thrust Ernest into the back of the walk-in. The shelves there—built for easy removal—broke away, like in an action movie where staircases and windows explode on contact. I remember thinking, like a little kid, how cool that was, and I let Xavier push me into the shelf behind me so I could be like a superhero myself. Sure enough, as I connected, the shelves in my path gave way: rectangular plastic containers of perfectly chopped shallots, carrots, and celery came crashing down to the ground, spilling their contents all over the place.

Carl spun around to witness Anton coming up behind him, ready to avenge the downing of Ernest.

"Yaaaaaah!"

But Carl was already in full flow. He caught the charging Anton like he was a ballerina and flung him aside. *Those* shelves crashed next and buckets of stock—clear vegetable, blond chicken, dark veal—fell to the ground, bursting open on contact, and splashing all over the ground.

It was an all-out food fight—the Fish Guys versus the Meat Guys—but instead of throwing food at each other, we were throwing each other at the food.

Through all of this, Xavier and I were still struggling for dominance, spinning around and around, and each time we grazed a shelf, something else would be knocked over. Finally, I twisted him too hard and we lost our balance; we crashed into an overturned crate of herbs, collapsing on the floor.

"The Fish Guys win!" I shouted. "We still have one guy standing."

"No fair, you stupid American, there's three of you and only two of us."

We could've probably argued all day, but suddenly Carl's face froze. Anton and I turned around to see what he was looking at.

Maurice, the chef de cuisine, Chapel's lieutenant, was standing in the doorway of the walk-in, shaking his head sadly from side to side.

"Chapel's going to be here tonight," Maurice said, all business. "We have a lot of reservations. So you better get going and clean this up."

Then he left. It was as merciful a response as I can imagine.

None of us took our lunch break that day. While the other cooks left to enjoy their afternoon break, we stayed to clean up the walk-in, wiping down the walls and mopping the floor. And we busted our butts all afternoon to catch up, making quickie stocks and slicing fruits and vegetables so fast that it's a miracle one of us didn't lose a finger.

As well as we did, we were still a little behind: a few things were unready for service that night. So when Chapel showed up,

Maurice was forced to tell him what had happened. The master was very cold to us that night—it was a quiet, harsh evening in the kitchen.

I left Chapel after six months, when my money ran out and I needed to get back home to some paying work. I stayed in touch with many of the other cooks, and for a long time. We wrote to each other for years, before we moved on to other friendships, to families, to—dare I say it?—our adult lives.

I still hear about them once in a while. A few years ago, a couple I know returned from the Riviera and were telling me about the restaurants. There was one they hadn't made it to, a little place in Provence run by a hot young Japanese chef they had heard about named Mitzu.

"I know him!" I said, then started singing: "*His name was Mitzu, oh Mitzu, O'Reilly.*"

I broke off, lost in a memory of that kitchen, those guys, and our daily taunting and torments, our little playpen in the back of a three-star Michelin restaurant.

When I came to, my friends were looking at me like I was nuts.

"Sorry," I said to them. "You were saying?"

Friends and Family
LAURENT TOURONDEL

*Laurent Tourondel honed his craft in the world's great cities—
Paris, London, Moscow, and New York—working for such
masters as the Troisgros family and Joel Robuchon. While
serving as executive chef at Caesars Palace in Las Vegas, he
was named one of* Food & Wine Magazine's *Ten Best New
Chefs in 1998. His next stop was Cello in New York City, where
he was awarded three stars by the* New York Times *in 1999, the
same year* New York Magazine *named him one of ninety-nine
people to watch. In 2004, he opened BLT Steak, Bistro Laurent
Tourondel, and followed it in 2005 with BLT Fish. His first
cookbook,* Go Fish, *was published in 2004.*

T HERE'S AN ANAGRAM used in just about every kitchen
in the English-speaking world: VIP. It stands—as it does
outside of the kitchen—for "very important person."

There are a number of reasons you might designate a customer VIP. He or she might be an affluent regular who comes in
often and spends a considerable amount on wine. He or she

might be a celebrity who is accustomed to special treatment. Or he or she might be a fellow chef whom you admire.

You do what you can for VIP customers, wanting them to feel well taken care of. You might give them one of the better tables in the house, or maybe send them a little something extra, like a midcourse or some desserts. If they order foie gras, you might have the waiter bring out a glass of Sauternes, the sweet dessert wine, as an accompaniment. That kind of thing.

The craziest gesture I ever made for a VIP customer was to open a new restaurant on a day when I should have stayed in bed. But, of course, you don't know such things until it's too late.

As I tell this story, I've just opened BLT Fish, the second of three restaurants bearing my new brand, Bistro Laurent Tourondel. The first was BLT Steak, which opened in March 2004 in midtown Manhattan and was an instant success.

Did I say "instant success"?

Better make that "*almost* instant success." Because our first night was an evening I'd like to forget.

At the beginning of 2004, I hadn't cooked professionally in a year and a half. The owner of my last restaurant, a three-star jewel box called Cello on the Upper East Side, had closed it unceremoniously—while I was away in Venezuela, no less—and I had spent the past eighteen months recovering from the shock, distracting myself by writing a cookbook, traveling, and meeting with a number of restaurateurs, investors, and potential partners who wanted to brainstorm concepts for my next place.

Though I was spending a lot of time in other cities and countries, there was never any doubt that I'd stay in New York. I love being a New York City chef, and I wasn't planning to go anywhere.

The result of this lengthy period of professional blind-dating was that I ended up "married" to Jimmy Haber, a tall, slender, perpetually youthful-looking New Yorker who owned two spaces that he periodically transformed into new restaurants. One was in Chelsea; the other in Midtown.

Jimmy and I decided to open BLT Steak, in the Midtown location, which was to mark my return to the New York spotlight.

More casual than Cello, with a focus on beef, sides, and sauces, BLT Steak was a concept that seemed right in line with the times, including an à la carte menu—one of the big trends of the early 2000s—that invited each diner to create his or her own meal, drawing from lists of cuts of beef, a few fish, sides, and sauces.

At a time when most kitchens are geared to completing entire dishes—a protein, a starch, and a vegetable plated together— this approach would be new to my team of five cooks. As a result, one of the biggest question marks was how well my team, most of whom had just met that week, would coordinate themselves. I had a few young veterans, like Mark Forgione, son of the great American chef Larry Forgione, whom I had hired as my meat man, the guy on the grill. But two of my cooks were new to the big leagues, trying their hand on the hot line for the first time, having only worked *garde manger* (salads and cold appetizers) before.

The early signs, however, were positive. We had done well with the restaurant equivalent of dress rehearsals: two "friends and family" nights in which VIP guests, personal friends, and relatives of the owners come in for a free meal in exchange for acting as our guinea pigs, letting us work out any kinks in our system on their time.

Those evenings had gone off without a hitch. The friends and family members had loved the space—you entered past a small lounge, shadowed a long bar, and emerged into an intimate dining room, with plush seats and lacquered wooden tables. On the back wall was a bulletin board on which we posted the menu, the wine list, and nightly specials. And the staff had been crisp and attentive from the start, consummate professionals who did a good job of shepherding customers through our potentially confusing menu.

Our first "official" night was to be a Saturday. Jimmy and I decided to soft-pedal the opening, delaying the announcement to the media so we could start slowly, get comfortable, and pick things up at our own pace. This kind of debut is known in the industry as a "soft opening" and another good reason for it is to fly under the radar of the food critics, so they don't show up on your first or second day, when you're still getting your bearings.

But when I walked into the restaurant on Saturday morning and checked the computer's reservation system, I saw that we were expecting an even quieter evening than I would have liked. In fact, there were just two parties on the books.

I spoke to Jimmy about this.

"Should we close for the night and open on Monday?" he offered.

Unfortunately we couldn't wait until Monday, I explained, because one of the customers was a *super*-VIP from my old Cello days, an honest-to-goodness princess from a faraway country I'd rather not name, who was a loyal longtime customer.

"Okay, then," Jimmy said, considering his options. "I'll invite a few friends."

What the hell, I thought. We'll open as planned, our VIP will come in as expected, and we'll have one more friends and family night in the bag. A real win-win situation.

Or so I thought.

*   *   *

Our first few hours that night were silent, as you'd expect of a restaurant on East Fifty-seventh Street that nobody knew was open on a winter Saturday. I was standing around the kitchen with my team of five cooks, just hanging out and talking.

This isn't such a bad night, I remember thinking. We're all getting a chance to know one another.

Not that we weren't ready to cook: our ingredients were prepped, our ovens were fired up, and we were eager to spring into action. There just weren't any customers.

After a few hours of this, at about eight o'clock, Kelly, a normally unshakable manager, came running into the kitchen. She was uncharacteristically pale, and short of breath. Beads of sweat broke out on her forehead before our eyes. As she fanned herself with her hand, she told us that *eighty-five* people had just walked in the door and were ordering drinks at the bar.

The friends and family had arrived.

I thought back to my conversation with Jimmy. Should I have mentioned that his guests should be spread out over four or five hours? I guess I thought it was obvious.

It's true what they say: *never* assume anything.

Kelly was followed almost immediately by Keith, my dining room manager, who arrived with a detailed description of the scene: although many of the guests had tables reserved in their names, they didn't want to sit yet, preferring to wait for Jimmy to arrive, and then toast his new venture, wishing him well. The result was that the restaurant had turned into one big cocktail party with the eighty-five guests mingling uproariously, with no idea of how much anxiety was being produced in the kitchen.

When Jimmy finally showed up, he made the rounds, cordially greeting his guests. Keith suggested that perhaps they should get *a few* people seated and let the ordering commence, in an attempt to pace things.

Jimmy walked around, tapping guests on the shoulder and ushering them into the dining room. When they saw the trend, others followed, and before long the entire eighty-five had made their way in to dinner.

But they didn't take their seats.

Instead, they continued to socialize and table-hop and say hi to Jimmy and so on. Tables reserved for four were pulling up chairs and becoming tables for eight.

This would have been fine at a banquet function—a Bar Mitzvah, say, or a wedding—where you're served a salad, a choice of salmon or steak, and a predetermined dessert. But in a restaurant like BLT Steak, with about fifty menu items, it was a recipe for disaster.

In the kitchen, my team and I were waiting, bracing ourselves for the coming storm. All of our eyes were on the little machine that spit out tickets as orders were punched into a computer by the waitstaff in the dining room.

Finally, the computer spit out one ticket.

I grabbed it and began calling out the first order ever at BLT Steak.

"Okay," I said, with a smile, not having done this in more than a year. "Let me have two rib eye–"

Before I could get the words out of my mouth, the machine printed another ticket.

And another.

And another.

Andanotherandanotherandanotherandanotherandanother . . .

A hot New York restaurant, packed to the gills with customers, on its busiest Saturday night of the year, will still find a way to stagger the orders. The most tickets you'd ever see in a flurry would be about ten.

In the space of two minutes, we had received *thirty-five.*

My team and I knew then and there that we were dead. The only question was how long we had to live.

Trying to put on my best face, I continued calling out that first order and one by one the guys got to work. The more seasoned cooks, like Mark, got going with grim determination, the younger ones with visible anxiety, their hands shaking, their eyes wide with fear. They had lost that swagger most kitchen guys have, that confidence that governs all actions, from the squirting of oil into a hot pan to the last sprinkling of salt on a dish as it goes up in the window for pickup.

Keith tipped us off that Jimmy himself was seated at a table of thirteen people. We had our eye out for his ticket and somehow managed to pull it out of the throng. He and his guests had ordered pretty much what you'd expect—an assortment of steaks including four rib eyes, some fish, and a selection of sides. We got his order out, slightly relieved, and went on to the rest.

But not two minutes later, Jimmy's four rib eyes came back, along with the two fish. He and his guests felt that these dishes were undercooked. Just what we needed—a mistake on the owner's table. We dropped everything, redid those orders, then went back to work hacking away at the others.

By now, we had all eighty-five tickets in the kitchen. Because of the unique structure of the menu, one table's order could be 80 percent complete and still not go out. For example, if a table had ordered four steaks, creamed spinach, potatoes, and mushrooms, everything but the mushrooms could be ready and the other components would have to wait.

Every time a waiter came into the kitchen, we'd have to take a survey of each station. So, if he came in and said "Is Table Twenty-two ready?" we'd go around the room:

Meat guy: "Yes!"

Fish guy: "Yes!"

Veg guy: "No."

One single "no" on a table became an overall veto, meaning that the food for that table would have to stay in the kitchen for the time being. So, the waiter would try a different table: "How about Table Thirty-seven?"

Meat guy: "Yes."

Fish guy: "No!"

It didn't matter what the veg guy said, because the fish guy had already thrown a wrench into things.

The result? Each station was hopelessly backed up with finished plates. Mark had a rack filled with sheet pans, the entire tower loaded with plates of cooked steak.

I had never seen so many people working so hard and *getting nothing done*. It was like cooking in quicksand.

I'm normally a pretty forceful presence in the kitchen. "Come on!" I'll shout, "We have to get this done!" Or something like that. For emphasis, I'll maybe slam down a sheet pan.

But at a certain point that evening, I realized that I couldn't push these guys any harder. There was no point. I just rested my hand against the rack and tried to smile it off.

Eventually, I refocused and came to the realization that the only way to bring this evening to a close was to concentrate on one table at a time. With so much food ready, it occurred to me to start bargaining with each table to get them their dinner. So, if a waiter came in looking for the food for Table Eighteen, I would say, "I don't have their hanger steak, but I do have their fish and their sides. If they'll take a rib eye, they can have their dinner."

The waiter would think this over, nod, and say, "Okay. I can sell that. Lemme have it." Then we'd load him up, wish him well, and push him back out into the increasingly hostile dining room.

It took more than three hours, but eventually everything made its way out of the kitchen.

And, in time, our guests began getting up and leaving for the night. I'm told that many of them left shaking their heads, amazed that we were open for business. They looked concerned, I'm told, for their friend Jimmy and his new venture.

And the princess, our raison d'être for coming to work that day? She canceled her reservation. Thank God. I can only imagine what she would have thought if she *had* shown up.

But, you know, I hadn't been in a kitchen for over a year and a half. It was one of my worst nights ever, but I got through it. The guests were all friends and relatives of the owner, so they didn't hold it against us. Within days, we had hit our stride, and I'm sure they've all been back since and had a great time.

The important thing was that my new restaurant was open and though it wasn't a pleasant evening, I had a funny story to tell. And that, too, is part of being a New York City chef.

It was good to be back.

The Trojan Cookie
TOM VALENTI

Widely credited with saving New York's Upper West Side from culinary oblivion with his restaurants Ouest and 'Cesca, Tom Valenti first became known to diners for his hearty, rustic food at Alison on Dominick Street, then at Cascabel and Butterfield 81. He was also the original sous-chef at Gotham Bar and Grill, and had his first taste of fame at Chelsea Central. He is the author of two cookbooks, Welcome to My Kitchen *and* Tom Valenti's Soups, Stews, and One-Pot Meals.

I F Y O U ' V E L I V E D in New York City for two decades or more, dine out with some regularity, and have been to the Red Cat restaurant in Chelsea, you might have experienced a faint sense of déjà vu thanks to the location, the configuration, and the generous view of Tenth Avenue through the floor-to-ceiling window that fronts the place. That's because the Red Cat occupies the same space that used to host Chelsea Central, a once über-popular American bistro that had a great run in the not-as-long-ago-as-they-seem 1980s.

Chelsea Central was the downtown offshoot of Cafe Central, itself a huge success on the Upper West Side in the late seventies and early eighties. Chelsea Central was one of those only-in–New York joints that exuded an effortless cool borne of its off-the-beaten-path location; a pack of celebrity co-owners including Treat Williams (back when he was the star of *Hair* and *Prince of the City*), Peter Weller (back before he became Robocop), and Bruce McGill (who played D-Day in *Animal House*), a staff comprising bartenders the likes of a young, then-unknown Bruce Willis and a waitress named Patti Scialfa, who went on to become part of the E Street Band, and Mrs. Bruce Springsteen—and exactly the kind of clientele you'd expect a place with those elements to attract.

Chelsea Central is remembered for a lot of things. Before its neighborhood had been reborn as a haven for art galleries, the restaurant succeeded in an unlikely location on the western fringe of a no-man's-land that wasn't quite downtown and wasn't quite Midtown. It was a lively spot where people spent lots of late nights at the smoky bar—back when there was such a thing in Manhattan.

It's also remembered as a launching pad for chefs and sous chefs who went on to fame and fortune, such as Rick Moonen, who eventually became the chef of Oceana and then his own rm; Gerry Hayden, who became Charlie Palmer's chef de cuisine at Aureole before opening his own Amuse; and Don Pintabona, who became the too-often unsung hero of the kitchen at the Robert DeNiro–Drew Nieporent partnership Tribeca Grill.

Chelsea Central is remembered for all of those things. But I remember it for something else. I remember it for the cookies.

I was appointed chef of Chelsea Central in 1987, taking the baton from Rick Moonen, the gregarious, universally beloved workhorse who had left to helm the Water Club, a new venture by the River Cafe's Buzzy O'Keefe.

This was to be my first shot at a visible chef's position, and I was fortunate in the extreme to inherit a kitchen crew that included Pintabona and Hayden, great guys and big talents who were cooling their heels, killing time, and taking a paycheck while they waited for Aureole—which would soon become one of the best restaurants in town—to open. Because we had all known one another for some time, I was able to get the respect that I hopefully deserved from them without having to turn cartwheels, which I've never been very good at, either figuratively or literally.

But my good fortune in the kitchen was quickly threatened by a rapidly growing problem with the waitstaff. As the chef, I supposedly reigned supreme at Chelsea Central, but the waiters were huge fans of Rick's; sorry to see him go, they had apparently made a group decision that they didn't have to listen to the new boss.

Now, I'm an easygoing guy; I don't need my ego stroked. But when there's work to be done, and I'm the poor soul charged with making it happen, then I expect to be listened to, simple as that. If I give an order, or set a policy, it should be followed— and anyone within earshot ought to respond with something more or less akin to "Yes, Chef, whatever you say, it'll be my pleasure."

The waitstaff had a considerably different point of view, to say the least. Before too long, we had our own little turf war at the restaurant, between the New Chef and the Front of the House Gang. It was a largely insidious conflict: rather than outright confrontation, the surly staff made their feelings known with harrumphs, eye rolls, and sighs.

I was especially vexed by one particular fellow, an older, slim guy with a shaved head who harrumphed with more gusto, sighed more loudly, and eye-rolled more dramatically than any of them, and who made it his mission to let me know, without any words, that they had a way of working with Rick, and that was how they were going to work with me.

One reason this situation became so frustrating was that dealing with the staff was very much like dealing with bratty children: they were masters at defying me in such subtle, seemingly minor ways that it was difficult to prove that they had done something wrong—much less to do anything about correcting it.

But there was one tangible sign of their insubordination, and it became the focal point of our ongoing standoff. Rather than serving plated desserts from the kitchen, the restaurant availed itself of an Old World dessert trolley that was parked in the dining room, between the swinging kitchen doors and the coffee station. The cart was populated with the full complement of classic sweets: chocolate layer cake, cheesecake, cookies, fruit tarts, and so on.

Here is what would happen: let's say the night's service was over and of twelve slices of cheesecake, five had been served. The Front of the House Gang, under the pretense that the surviving slices wouldn't be up-to-snuff the next day, would divvy up the remaining seven pieces and greedily shovel them down while holed up in the waiter's station. Or if perchance during service, a piece of fruit tart broke on its way from the mold to the plate . . . well, we can't expect our customers to eat *that*, now can we? We'd better eat it ourselves.

This gluttonous approach to decision-making continued on a daily basis. The worst of it was the cookie plate, from which the waitstaff—in their standard-issue uniforms of the day: slacks, white shirts, and black vests—happily snacked all night long, starting right after the family meal (industry-speak for "staff dinner") and continuing until the end of the evening . . . unless of course we ran out, which happened on more than one occasion. It was a bigger problem than it might sound because cookies, like anything else for sale in a restaurant, cost money and time and their disappearance had an adverse effect on my kitchen's bottom line.

Over and over, I insisted that they leave the cookie plate alone, which is a hard thing for a self-respecting man to do on a daily basis. (You try sounding tough when you're talking about cookies.) But not only wouldn't they listen, they would flaunt their defiance, swinging into the kitchen with big, pleased grins on their faces, still chewing or swallowing a cookie.

They were grinning because, when push came to shove, I couldn't do a damn thing about it. Firing one of them would seem petty and . . . well, what other recourse was there?

And so it went. Every single morning I woke up, got dressed, and went to work, only to face the same ridiculous little mutiny as the day before, still at a loss for what to do.

Then one afternoon, on my way to the men's room, I spotted the answer to my prayers. Passing the espresso machine, I noticed a portafilter on the counter, filled with a compacted patty of spent espresso grounds, forged by the water pressure into a miniature chocolate-y disk.

A disk resembling a cookie.

Hmmmm.

Instantly, a wicked little plan was hatched. For the next hour I banged out espressos, carefully turning the tightly packed, well-formed spent grounds into my cupped hand. I covered a plate with a doily, arranged the patties atop it, and proceeded to turn it into the most beautiful cookie plate Chelsea Central had ever seen, piping some whipped cream on top of each "cookie" and finishing with—a private joke for my own added amusement—a chocolate-covered espresso bean.

The key to this plan was that the cookies were bite sized, so even if the enemies noticed a textural oddness, they'd have popped them into their mouths before taking time to investigate further.

I set out the cookies on the dessert trolley and waited.

Hours later, after the staff had come in, enjoyed their family meal, and needed something sweet, I waited still. Waited until my favorite waiter, my black-vested nemesis, came pushing through the kitchen doors, choking and gagging, recovering just enough to give me the look that I'd been waiting for all along, the one that said, "Yes, Chef, whatever you say, it'll be my pleasure."

Believe it or not, that moment became a very positive turning point for the two of us, and for my relationship with the entire Front of the House Gang. They couldn't help but laugh, seeing my caper not as an act of revenge, but as a well-timed, well-executed practical joke, maybe the kind of thing they'd pull on one another, and we got along famously after that. From then on, it was smooth sailing at Chelsea Central, a place whose customers, kitchen, *and staff* I remember with great fondness to this day.

Shit Happens
NORMAN VAN AKEN

Norman Van Aken founded a visionary way of cooking called New World Cuisine, giving new meaning to an entire region of the Americas. Presenting an approach that embodies the essence of this country and its dynamic ethnic mix, Van Aken melds the exotic ingredients and rich cultural heritages of Latin America, the Caribbean, the southern United States, and even touches of Asia. Serving as the catalyst for a new culinary paradigm, Van Aken has earned a place as one of America's greatest chefs. He is the only Floridian to have ever won entrance into the James Beard Foundation Who's Who. In addition to being an award-winning chef, Van Aken is highly regarded as a culinary educator, television celebrity, and cookbook author. He shares his passion for cooking by teaching classes at Norman's as well as culinary schools across the country. He is the author of four cookbooks: Feast of Sunlight, The Great Exotic Fruit Book, Norman's New World Cuisine, *and* New World Kitchen.

I T W A S 1 9 7 8 and I was finally a sous-chef. I still worked a line position but I was moving up—albeit in a world of absolute chaos. I was at the Pier House in Old Town, Key West. Key West at that time was not the well-adjusted, rehabbed, corporately correct, child-safe, real estate gold mine it has become. Nonetheless, we loved the raffish pirate illegal town that it was. We ran to it like children run to an ice cream truck, like hobos run to freight cars . . . it was idyllic, illicit madness.

On this particular morning, however, I woke up in agony, struggling to open my throbbing eyes. It was immediately clear that the day ahead was not likely to go smoothly. Not surprising, really, considering that yesterday had been the annual "Tequila Races" (before the city put an end to them in the early eighties.) The "race" took place right at the Pier House, an event so well attended that the throng of contestants spilled out of the Chart Room bar and onto the deck by the pool. It started with a shot of tequila; afterward, each contestant had to jump into the pool and down a second shot just as they got out. Two shots. No big deal. . . . But then you ran to the edge of the small beach and received a third shot. You swam a short distance to the raft . . . another shot. You got into a small Hobie Cat–type sailboat and sailed out about a mile to a buoy, where you were handed your next shot. Then you sailed back to the raft, anchored, and—that's right—drank another shot . . . Back to the pool for another shot . . . and finally, back to the bar for the last shot. The person with the shortest time to do all of that won. Beautiful. Even if you didn't race, you got caught up in the spectacular insanity; there was no avoiding it.

But the *next* day . . . I pressed an ice bag to my head and lapped at my Café Cubano like one of Hemingway's dazed polydactyl cats. I was not savoring the idea of going to work. As any kitchen rat knows, a hangover is not a reason to call in. You work in pain or, if unavoidable, still drunk.

After a while, I managed to stagger out the door and climb onto my moped. Of course it was drizzling. The city was gloomy and quiet. While cradling my second café I hit a pothole. The moped bucked and hot coffee splashed against my lap, burning through my pants. I cursed and flung the little foam cup away. A moment later, I lurched into the driveway at the very end of Duval Street, where some unfortunate soul was busily rooting through the Dumpster to see what might be salvaged. He threw a hamburger box viciously aside. I hustled past without a word.

Lunch was just starting to pick up in the main dining room. Terry was waiting tables, as he had been doing since the resort opened. He was attending a family from some place like Madison, Wisconsin. Mom, Pop, Buddy, and Sis—they were all putty in his flowing hands. Terry had an incredible way with children, and what could make parents happier than their children actually enjoying the time trapped in a restaurant with Mom and Dad, happily eating food they'd never heard of? Apparently, Terry had won trophies for swimming back in his native Michigan, a reliable icebreaker when waiting on tables like this one. Soon they'd be ordering more food than they could possibly consume.

Meanwhile, things were getting noisy at the pot sink. Trixie was late again. Ah, Trixie, how shall I describe "her"? Think of Janis Joplin as *a man* . . . wearing Buddy Holly glasses that were perpetually fogged up, even in bright sunlight. But "she" worked hard, even if "she" was out all night workin' harder. (I saw Trixie arrive in a limo on more than one morning.) So without old Ms. "T," that meant brother Clyde was tossin' two loads and he was *not* happy about it. His boom box was approaching a volume he'd never get away with if we didn't need him crankin' on the dirty pots, pans, *and* dishes. I could hear Clyde's favorite song, the Commodores' "Brick House" from across the dining room. Hell, I could *feel* the bass line.

> *She's a brick . . . house*
> *Mighty might just lettin' it all hang out*

Clyde did a 360, swatted his dishrag at a pot rack, and sang along.

> *She's a brick . . . house*
> *The lady's stacked*

Clyde winked knowingly

> *and that's a fact,*
> *ain't holding nothing back.*

My hot-line buddy Danny waved me over. He wanted me to join him in the "Rosie Trick." There was a young lady who worked in what were the shortest cut-off blue jeans imaginable. And, oh yes, she had the figure to cover the bet and cash the check—and then some. She was amazingly good-natured and seemed oblivious to our petty mischief. Danny yelled over to the dish room, "Hey, Rosie! We need a stack of plates!" Rosie gently pushed her large-framed aviator-style glasses with the back of her hand, guided her long brown hair behind one ear, and picked up an armload of plates. She strolled over with only the sound of her rubber flip-flops gently slapping the bottoms of her feet to behind the hot line where I worked the grill and Danny sauté. She set the plates on the edge of the stove. As usual, Danny and I both pretended that we were *far* too busy to come away from our tasks to be of help to her. She reached up to put the plates away, arching her back as she situated them high on the rack, four or five plates at a time . . . and on each occasion having to stretch her body *ever* higher over the oven. Eventually, unable to resist, Danny pretended to drop something and sank to his knees to take in the view, relishing it with all the pleasure of a prisoner receiving a cake on Christmas morning.

> *She's a brick . . . house*
> *She's the one, the only one,*
> *who's built like a amazon*

Some of the waiters had two names. One was their "straight name" and one was their "gay name." I came from a very small town in the Midwest, so a lot of this was both new and oddly okay with me. One of the older waiters would tease me at least once a week by saying, "One night with me, baby, and you will throw rocks at your old lady!" But he was like an uncle to all of us, one we loved and watched over. He'd had some seizures and if the owners found out, they might have 86'd him. Makes the *touristas* jumpy, they'd reason.

"Tammy" was reading the *Key West Citizen*. He was standing near the pantry when I heard him shriek. This was not the type of shriek you cry out when you're fearful, as if a car were suddenly swerving out of control and into your lane. No, this was the shriek of a game show contestant who had just won the *BIG MONEY PRIZE SO COME ON DOWN!!* A team of waitstaff rushed Tammy. "*What? What? What?*" they demanded. Trembling with excitement, Tammy pointed to the paper, where it announced that the Philippine fleet would be docking one of their ships at Key West for the entire weekend.

Estimates of more than five hundred sailors on shore leave! Tammy looked up, an angelic glow wreathing his fine-featured face, and beamed, "I just *adore* seafood!" He clutched the paper to his thrust chest and marched out the door to see who else he could share this joyous news with.

> *She knows she got everything*
> *a woman needs to get a man, yeah.*

I glanced at Clyde, still blasting his music. His vibe was beginning to get to me. I think I saw him toss a bottle of Miller High Life, *just emptied*, in the trash. He looked at me like he was "just working man, just working . . ."

> *How can she lose with what she use*
> *36–24–36, what a winning hand!*

At the time, we didn't have an "in house" pastry chef. Nino the Butcher would make the Zuppa Anglaise cake, the pantry girls would make the Key lime pie base, and so on. I took on the task of making the meringue for those Key lime pies and topping them with a towering stack of the sugary goo, then glazing them in a blast-furnace-hot oven. It was just after I set the batch of six pies in the oven that Danny signaled me over. I beat a path over there and caught another installment of the Rosie Act in all its refinement. Danny and I high-fived each other. That's when I heard Betty the Breakfast Cook laughing wickedly. I looked at her with a dumb "*Whaaa?*" expression. She pointed to the oven with her 16-ounce Busch beer can and cackled, "You fucked up the pies, Ace." The glory of Rosie's perfect bottom faded instantly as I raced back across the kitchen and flung open the doors on the rickety Blodgett. It is a bit of a miracle to see

pies literally *on fire* . . . on fucking *fuego! Dios Mio!* Six
cylindrical spires of flame danced in the maw of that oven.
The heat spanked my face hard. I pulled the sheet pan out,
trying to keep away from the Key lime infernos, whipped
around, and dropped the pan on Nino's butcher block. I yanked
a long spatula out of the knife rack and quickly slashed off the
smoldering meringue tops in an effort to salvage the bottom of
the pies and the graham cracker crusts. The tops hissed like
burning ships sinking in the water as they met whatever was in
the garbage can at that moment. Beef blood? Fish heads? I swore
at the dilemma unfolding in front of me. "Shit, fuck, dammit to
fucking hell!" It was eerie how it almost seemed to be occurring
in slow motion. Some faces looked on in horror and some of the
crew were slapping their knees, doubled over laughing. You
could count on it with this team.

> *She knows she's built and knows how to please*
> *Sure enough to knock a man to his knees*
> *Shake it down, shake it down now*

That's when I snapped. I ran over to Clyde's noisemaker and
yanked the cord out of the wall. "That's it, Clyde! No more
fucking Commodores today!!" I'd never had the balls to face
him down before that day. But Clyde knew what crazy looked
like, and he was starin' at a face full of it at that moment.

By now Terry was nearly finished serving lunch to our young
family from the Midwest. He had managed to get Mom and Pop
to order an extra round of daiquiris and he felt confident about
a sizeable tip. He decided to reward himself. The main waiter
station was situated so that the waiters could watch the guests
arriving or leaving from behind a chest-high wall. As the family
happily strolled out, the two kids hoisted on to their parent's

backs as if they were about to have a "chicken fight," they could see Terry bent over, apparently doing some waiter task. Since they'd forged such a wonderful bond, the family called out, "Bye Terry!" Terry suddenly snapped up, startled by the proximity of their voices—and by the stimulants now hitting his brain. Back then it was not uncommon for the waiters to have a little cocaine stash. The managers were either oblivious or doing their own elsewhere.

Normally the family wouldn't have been any wiser, with the plate hidden well out of view. But when Terry bobbed up to jovially wave them "bye-bye," he'd come up with the plastic straw still stuck up his nose. The family wrestled with this grotesque image of their lovable waiter buddy, momentarily trying to make sense of it, and then fled down the hallway and off into the little streets of Key West. Terry was confused as to why they had reacted with horror, until he bent down again, and the little mirror showed him what they'd just seen. He yanked out the straw, composed himself, thought for a moment—and then did "just one more tiny bump since I'm here," plus a "freeze" for good measure, before shimmying back to his tables.

Rosie had a brother who worked with us, too. He liked to think of himself as an American Indian. He had long black hair and a tattoo of Geronimo on his beefy right shoulder, always visible since he wore a vest with no shirt. George helped keep the kitchen clean and did some light prep. That night he was cleaning poached chickens, breaking them down for chicken salad. He had two hotel pans full of meat when he was asked by one of the chefs to take some boxes to the Dumpster. Now, George was one of the sweetest guys on the face of the planet; he immediately stopped what he was doing and gathered up the boxes. When he came back to his chicken work a bit later, though, he looked shaken. I asked him what was wrong. He shook his head and answered, "Fucked up, man." "What's fucked up, George?" I prodded. "I went out to dump those boxes, man, and this poor guy is rootin' through our trash. Man, I saw him this morning too, the same guy . . . And so I went back in and got him a little bit of that chicken I've been pluckin' and he looks at me and says, 'No thanks! I'm a vegetarian!' All huffy with me, man! Freaky, man . . ." Yes, indeed, George. You could say that. Freaky. Wacky. Key Westy even.

I finally got out of work around 10 p.m. I needed drinks. *Plural.* You could always count on the Full Moon Saloon back then. At that hour it was just beginning to happen. Danny and I sat down at the horseshoe-shaped bar and started to unwind.

Buddy D. was bartending. He introduced me to a singer/songwriter who was down from his home state of Alabama, the same place Jimmy Buffett was from. His name was Keith, a nice guy, got a real kick out of the food and restaurant rap Danny and I were filling him in on. He invited the two of us to go over to Buffett's place and see what was going on. They'd been working on a song for most of the afternoon and maybe we could listen in. No *problemo,* my new friend. Buffett's. Sure. Let's go give Jimmy a hand. Why not?

Another guy was at the house when we got there, an excellent bartender as well as one of the island's most heralded cocksmen. Tom was a mellow Vietnam vet who I could never imagine being at war with anything other than a stubborn zipper. By now Jimmy had most of the lyrics down and most of the melody, too. But the opener was where he was still seeking the Muse. It was a song about the odd twists and turns of life. Jimmy and Keith made up nonsense words or just hummed to fill in the gap and then moved on to the part they were happy with. That's when I fell out of Jimmy Buffett's window. First Jimmy, then Tom, and then Keith came hot-footing it around to the water side of the house. Danny stayed put and continued to drink. Tom lifted me up and clapped me on the back to get my lungs to open. Then he reached delicately into my shirt pocket and plucked out my moped key. With motorized transport safely out of the way for the evening, we climbed back up the wooden stairs and Tom fixed fresh drinks. Jimmy picked up his battered Martin and found the notes from before. Words came now and he sang them with a golden smile, "*Shit happens.*"

The Michelin Man
GEOFFREY ZAKARIAN

Geoffrey Zakarian is the executive chef and co-owner of Town
Restaurant *in New York City, a recipient of three stars from the*
New York Times, *and has worked in many of Manhattan's most
celebrated restaurants including stints as chef de cuisine at Le
Cirque, executive chef at the '21' Club, chef partner of Restaurant 44 at the Royalton Hotel, and executive chef of Patroon
Restaurant, where he also received three stars from the* New
York Times. *Before becoming a chef in his own right, Zakarian
trained under some of Europe's finest kitchen masters. His first
book,* Town and Country, *debuts fall 2005.*

T HERE I WAS in a Monaco casino, at the roulette table,
sipping my vodka martini and calmly playing another
round. I was on assignment, trying to stop that pain-in-the-
ass Blofeld from taking over the world's oil supply. But even a
secret agent deserves a night off, to clear the head, refresh the
body.

After about an hour of coolly piling up a stack of five-hundred-dollar chips, *she* came in—the sultry, Eastern European brunette whom I had encountered just that morning on the slopes of Switzerland, right before getting into a ski chase that left twenty henchmen dead and a small chalet in ruins.

Our eyes locked and she took a seat beside me at the table. "We must stop meeting like this, Mr. . . ." She trailed off. I never had given her my name.

"Bond, James—"

Wait, no, that's not what happened.

But that's the way I sometimes thought of myself at the time. It was 1981, and I was a twenty-year-old James Bond enthusiast, discovering Europe for the first time—discovering its ancient architecture, darkly mysterious women, and the food that would change the course of my professional life.

So, this isn't a James Bond tale. Rather, it's the tale of Zakarian, Geoff Zakarian, and how I earned, then lost, my License to Eat.

When we join our hero, I was in college. Though I would eventually become a chef, I wasn't preparing for a career in the kitchen. I don't know where I was headed, really, but for better or worse I was enrolled in Worcester State College in my home state of Massachusetts, where I was majoring in Urban Studies.

I had a fierce desire to blow town, blow the whole country actually, and visit Europe. With the aid of a dedicated professor, I obtained a GMAT loan to finance my trip at the amazingly low interest rate of just 2 percent. While there, I was to research and write a paper on the effect of gambling society—and the influx of wealthy travelers delivered by the advent of rail transportation—on Monaco.

At least that was the plan. But I had never been to Europe. I had never even been out of the country. And no sooner had I arrived in France than I fell in love with everything about it—the style, the relaxed way of life, and especially the food.

I immediately gave up the research project and resolved, instead, to spend a year traveling around Europe, devoting most of my attention to France. All of the country's charms, it seemed to me, were inextricably intertwined, so I decided to use food as the organizing principle of my journey, selecting my destinations based on whether or not the cities and towns had a restaurant that boasted at least one Michelin star.

For the next seven or eight months, I made my way around from town to town. Six days a week I lived on a diet of couscous, which was dirt cheap, especially when purchased in bulk, with an occasional piece of cheese thrown in when I could swing it.

On the seventh day, usually a Friday, I would eat in a restaurant of some renown, preferably a three-star Michelin restaurant.

Dinner Day was a big event for me, the moment to which my entire week built. I would don my one suit, a custom-made blue-gray houndstooth from the shop of the legendary Massachusetts fashion god Alan Bilzerian. To fill it out, I wore a white dress shirt with English spread collar and a handmade, seven-fold blue-gray tie.

I was essentially a poor student—I lived on unalloyed grains all week and slept in dingy little hotels—but when I stepped out on that night, I looked like a million bucks.

And I felt like my hero, James Bond, dapperly lighting out in a European town in search of . . . well, in my case, in search of a good meal. But if I *were* to happen upon a criminal mastermind trying to execute a nefarious plot, I would have absolutely taken him down, and done so with style.

The first three-star restaurant I went to was Vivarois, owned by Claude Peyrot, and his wife, who ran the front of the house.

They epitomized the perfect hosts: elegant, sophisticated, and charming to all who graced their dining room. And yet, it quickly became apparent to me that I was being treated with more generosity than any of the other guests. In broken English, they made certain that I was pleased with everything, pampering me like royalty, even sending extra courses.

Was it the suit? I wondered. It *was* a magnificent piece of sartorial craftsmanship. But did it have mystical powers, wooing all who came into contact with its wearer to heap food and hospitality upon him?

Maybe it did, because this royal treatment continued long after I left Vivarois. Without exception, no matter where I dined, I was the recipient of an embarrassing amount of attention. And strangely, the more stars the restaurant possessed, the more fawning the owner and chef were: even at such three-star bastions of cuisine as Paul Bocuse, Taillevent, and Troisgros— places that probably turned away more customers than they deigned to serve.

Before I went to Europe, I had heard a lot of talk about how nasty the French were. But I found them to be the nicest people on Earth.

One day, about two-thirds into my year abroad, I arrived in La Rochelle, a small coastal town north of Bordeaux.

Having run out of cash, I stopped in a beautiful little bank, an outpost of Crédit Lyonnais, and slid my passport under the teller's window, along with a five-hundred-dollar traveler's check.

"*Francs, s'il vous plait,*" I said to the stoic woman on the other side of the glass. Moments later, without a word, the teller slid back a wad of money.

I've seen people count their money at bank windows, and I suppose I understand the reasons for doing so. But I've never done it. I figure the teller has a lot more at stake than I do—like his or her job—so I trust they've done it right.

A few days later, I donned my suit, hit the town, and enjoyed another glorious meal. After I paid the bill, my wallet had more heft than it usually did at that moment in the week, when it often seemed so empty it could blow away.

Curious, I counted my money—and realized that I had the equivalent of fifteen hundred dollars more than I should have. I checked the bank receipt and discovered that the teller had made an error, reading my traveler's check in pounds rather than dollars, a huge mistake in my favor.

Cool! I thought, and the next day, fearful of being tracked down by the bank, or the local constable, I took off for Paris, eager to disappear into the anonymity a big city affords visitors.

After Paris, I went to Monaco. I had devised a plan to parlay my good fortune into a *real* fortune. So I put on my Bilzerian suit and hit the casino. In honor of my hero, James Bond, I chose the roulette table.

Though I had never gambled before, I won a whopping fifteen *thousand* dollars that night, an amount that would still delight me today, but at the time, when I was a twenty-year-old college student living on couscous, it was almost incomprehensible.

With my winnings I extended the scope and ambition of my culinary mission, zeroing in on the three-star restaurants, sometimes hitting two in one week. Of the twenty-one three-star restaurants around at the time, I ate at eighteen of them.

When my time and finances eventually dwindled, I began making plans for my return to the States. There was only one way to properly bring my international life of mystery to a close: I went to Air France with a bulging wad of cash in my pocket and purchased a ticket on the Concorde.

A few days later, bedecked once again in my magic suit, I boarded the plane at Roissy Charles de Gaulle Airport, toasted the country of France, and headed back home to the small town of Worcester, Massachusetts, racing at more than fourteen hundred miles per hour.

Back in the States, I went on about my life, setting in motion my plans to begin a life in the kitchen. Coming home from school one afternoon, I collected my mail and while shuffling through the pile, I noticed a certified letter from Crédit Lyonnais, a formal-looking envelope postmarked from La Rochelle.

Inside was a letter from a bank executive explaining that they had made a mistake in my favor, and politely but firmly requesting their money back. Tucked in behind the letter was a photocopy of my passport (I guess they photocopy them, though I didn't see it happen), a close-up of my signature, and a number of security camera snapshots of me receiving the money from the teller. My entire dossier, so to speak.

These would be worthy adversaries, indeed.

I decided to meet the problem head on. I wrote them a letter explaining that I was just a student, and suggested that I pay them one hundred dollars per month. They agreed, and let me make the payments interest free, an even better deal than my student loan.

Incidentally, twenty-four years later, I discovered why it was that I had been so well treated in Europe's finest restaurants. In 2005, Edmund Michelin visited Manhattan to host a party announcing that the *Guide* was at long last coming to New York. During his remarks, he jokingly indicated that single diners here were about to find themselves the recipients of extraspecial attention, because, as everyone knew, most of their reviewers were young men who traveled alone.

So it wasn't the suit, after all.

But that's okay. Because it was one hell of a year.

The End of Innocence
JAMIE OLIVER

Jamie Oliver, widely known as the Naked Chef, is one of the UK's best-loved culinary personalities. He has written six best-selling cookbooks, which have been published worldwide and translated into twenty-three languages. Before striking out on his own, Jamie worked at London's Neal Street Restaurant and the River Café. In November 2002, he opened the restaurant Fifteen, also in London, to train disadvantaged youths in the kitchen arts. Two more Fifteen restaurants have since opened in Amsterdam and Cornwall. In 2000, Jamie married his childhood sweetheart, Jools. They have two daughters.

"FRY, YOU BASTARD."

These three words were the first I remember hearing from a restaurant kitchen, and they made such an impression on me. They shaped my view of the mostly abnormal people attracted to the strange, punishing, and freewheeling world of professional cooking!

At the time my family lived in a flat over my parents' pub in a 450-year-old building. I was six years old when the words travelled up from the kitchen through the paper-thin floors into our living room.

"Fry, you bastard."

I could tell from the strange intonation—a sort of half-conscious mumbling—that they were coming from a tall boy—let's call him Gerry—who worked in the place and who I saw coming and going nearly every day of my young life.

But, though I knew whose voice I was hearing, I had no idea what he was referring to.

I was also puzzled by the strange little buzzing sound, short but unmistakably electric, that followed the words.

What is that? I wondered each time he spoke, my curiosity growing almost unbearable.

Again, it came: "Fry, you bastard." Followed by that zippy little buzz.

I couldn't take it any more. I had to know what Gerry was up to.

I ran down the stairs into the pub. As it was very early in the morning, there was nobody around. On tiptoes, I made my way to the kitchen, pushed open the doors, and looked inside.

There was Gerry, standing at a work station, busy peeling and marinading a load of prawns. But he was obviously getting a bit bored and every so often, instead of adding a newly peeled prawn to the bowl of marinade, he'd hold it up and say to it, "Fry, you bastard," then flick it across the room into the fly killer—one of those caged, electrified neon bars that zaps insects dead on contact.

As the shellfish hit the glowing tube, it made the buzzing sound I'd been hearing all morning. On the floor was a pile of blackened prawns. I learnt something that day that I would come to fully appreciate as I began *my* life in this profession:

that you get some real characters in a professional kitchen! My education in the kitchen began early. By the age of seven I was working in the pub, and the other guys taught me all about the practical jokes that were to become part and parcel of my life in the kitchen. Like the night we took poor Gerry's leather jacket, soaked it in water, hung it in the freezer, then returned it to the coat rack, so that when he went to put it on at the end of the evening, after working hard for more than twelve hours and ready to go home, it was rock hard and as cold as ice.

I learnt to dish out practical jokes, and I learnt to take them as well. Because I was quite small, I often found myself locked in the freezer or tossed into the fish sink with all the stinking bits. Nice!

Before long, I took this as a fact of life. And I'll tell you a secret: I *loved* it. Almost as much as the food itself, I loved the guys who played these jokes on me and made me feel part of their team.

I've never been disappointed. No matter where I've worked, there's always been lots of fun, harmless teasing and practical jokes.

When I started college in London, I did some work experience in a hotel. *Everyone* in that kitchen was stark raving mad, from the ex-military head chef to the line cook who came to work decked out as a teddy boy in platform shoes, a long blue felt jacket, and a huge belt buckle. He blasted music from the portable radio at his station and performed *every* task, even peeling little vegetables, with an enormous chef's knife. Now, *that*'s rock and roll!

This is where I learnt that pranks didn't have to be confined to the kitchen. Havoc could be caused by preying on the waiting staff who, let's face it, were more civilised, and therefore easier pickings for the likes of us kitchen blokes than we were for each other.

There was a female manager in that hotel restaurant who was

the constant target of the teddy boy. Every afternoon at about the same time, she'd come into the kitchen to borrow the wine-cellar key from him. One day, in preparation for this ritual, he warmed two kidneys on a steel hotel plate. When he heard her coming down the stairs at the usual time, he got me to drop the kidneys into his trouser pocket.

He then hoisted up two prep trays loaded with food and turned round just as the manager made it to the foot of the stairs.

"May I have the key, please," she said.

"Of course," he replied, indicating that she should get the key from his pocket.

She stuck her hand in and made a horrified face, clearly thinking that he had a hole in his pocket and that instead of the key she had got herself a handful of warm bollocks! Thankfully she saw the funny side of it after she'd got over the shock.

Now, you might think this is unacceptable behaviour, and you're right, of course. But it was harmless, and we'd all be great friends afterwards.

Lest you think it's all fun and games, there are times when these schoolboy pranks are employed for a very good reason.

I have a pet peeve. I can't stand it when people nick food from my station. So when other chefs take this liberty, I always get my revenge!

Like the Aussie who worked with me in an Italian restaurant. I was the pastry chef and he was always grabbing my biscuits as he passed by, or taking a spoon out of his pocket and dipping it, repeatedly, into my sauces and ice creams.

This really annoyed me.

Well, the kitchen had a box of seriously hot Sicilian bell peppers that were fruity and delicious, but also quite lethal in large quantities. I helped myself to some and puréed them so they looked like a berry sauce. I layered this into a glass with some ice cream and asked the Aussie if he'd like to try our new "Tuscan parfait."

"I'd love to!" he exclaimed and grabbed a large spoon.

He scooped up a huge mouthful of the topping and crammed it into his mouth. Beads of sweat instantly appeared on his forehead as he swallowed some. He managed to spit out about half the stuff, then looked at me with red eyes. "You bastard," he shouted at me. "I lived in Asia for years and I can take that spicy . . ." As the chilli took hold, he trailed off and began gasping for air, leaning on the counter of my station.

All the other chefs stopped working and came over to watch.

A minute or two went by and then he collapsed on the floor and began shaking. His face was numb and he literally could not stand back up.

I spent the evening performing his kitchen duties *and* mine, all the while nursing him back to health by making him gargle milk and helping him to pull strips of skin out of his mouth. He was fine by the end of the night and I apologised, because I truly never meant to hurt him. But I wasn't really all that sorry. I guess we both learnt a lesson—and he never nicked any of my food again.

Over the years I have come to realise that not everyone appreciates the fun and games of the kitchen, though . . . And the thing I enjoy doing the most—moonies—are often the *least* appreciated by those who don't share the chefs' sense of humour.

Like the waitress at the River Café who was studying photography. In our very trusting environment at the restaurant, nobody locked his or her locker.

Big mistake.

One day, while this waitress was on the service floor, we took her camera and snapped sixteen photos of the lot of us doing moonies—real rugby-player-after-game stuff. Needless to say, when she took the film to her very proper, very professional lab, the technicians were amused, but she was not.

But the person I offended the most was a Portuguese clean-up man who I'll call Arturo. He was a nervous sort, not unlike Manuel, the character from the TV show *Fawlty Towers*. My mentor, Gennaro, and I were working together at this restaurant— he was the pasta man and I was the pastry chef. And while we loved to cook, nothing made us happier than making Arturo jump.

Gennaro used to do this by dropping a stack of steel trays when Arturo's back was turned. They would clatter really loudly and Arturo would leap in the air, his nerves completely on edge.

My approach was a bit more crude. At the end of the night, Arturo had to pull all the industrial refrigerators out from the wall in order to mop behind them. The units formed little corridors where I loved to taunt him. I'd stand at the end of a refrigerator-corridor, drop my trousers, bend over, slap my backside, and yell, "Hey, Arturo, kiss my arse."

Arturo would try to kick me as I took off, running and laughing.

One day, he was mopping up and Gennaro said, "Go on, give him a moonie."

As ever, I couldn't resist. I turned round and dropped my trousers. "Hey, Arturo, kiss my arse," I said, slapping my bare bottom.

This time, he was ready. Rather than trying to kick me, he managed to smack me with the wet mop . . . right where it hurts . . . And, believe me, it hurt like hell! I learnt my lesson and never pulled a moonie ever again. Lots of other stuff, yes, but never another moonie!

Acknowledgments

First and foremost, we thank the chefs, for your time, stories, and honesty. Obviously, without you, there'd be no book.

Thank you to Karen Rinaldi, for judiciously entertaining all possibilities; Panio Gianopoulos, for your smart editing, quick turnarounds, and good advice at every step of the way; Eleanor Jackson, David Forrer, and Alexis Hurley, for your excellent cheer and relentless dedication to getting it all right; and, for your invaluable assistance and support, Lindsay Autry, Phillip Baltz, Jennifer Baum, Dan Bignold, Thomas Blythe, Bob Bookman, Tony Bourdain, Juli at El Bulli, John Carlin, Rachael Carron, Samantha Clark, Mel Davis, Catherine Drayton, Scott Feldman, Rea Francis, Richard Green, Dan Halpern, Irene Hamburger, Gabrielle Hamilton, Susan Kamil, Chantal Keller, Sean Knight, Bill Knott, Pam Krauss, Lizzie Kremer, Shelley Lance, Mark Lawless, Carol Macarthur, Ellen Malloy, Gary Morris, Stephen Morrison, Aline Oshima, Anna Elena Pedron, Amy Pennington, Liz Ravage, Leah Ross, Felicity Rubinstein, Chiki Sarkar, Lori Silverbush, Belinda Smith, Lee Tulloch, Zoe

Waldie, Christa Weaving, Araminta Whitley, Kimberly Yorio, and Laura Yorke.

—K.W. and A.F.

Personal thanks to my mother, who encouraged me to try everything; my father, who finds the bright side of every catastrophe; Harry Ptak, for always being there to help; Andrew Friedman, for making this collaboration such a pleasure; my colleagues at Inkwell, for their abundance of faith; and Mhelicia Sarmiento, for helping to get my family to the table every night.

—K.W.

My heartfelt thanks to Kimberly Witherspoon, for coming up with a great idea and inviting me along on the adventure. This was a terrific partnership and a lot of fun. And to Colin Dickerman, for remembering me from way back when; David Black, for your constant counsel and friendship; Caitlin Friedman, for making life easy and miraculously fun, even during the home stretch; and Declan and Taylor: you two couldn't have picked a better time to start sleeping through the night.

—A.F.